Generative AI Cybersecurity

Redefining Threat Defense in the Current Era

Table of Contents

Generative AI in Cybersecurity

Abstract

In the ever-evolving landscape of cyber threats, **Generative AI in Cybersecurity: Redefining Threat Defense in the Current Era** explores the transformative potential of generative artificial intelligence in securing the digital frontier. This groundbreaking book delves into how generative AI technologies, such as Generative Adversarial Networks (GANs) and transformers, are revolutionizing the way organizations detect, prevent, and mitigate cyber threats. It provides a comprehensive roadmap to understanding the role of generative AI in modern cybersecurity operations, addressing its applications, challenges, and prospects.

The book begins by examining the foundational principles of generative AI and its revolutionary impact on proactive threat detection, automated incident response, and vulnerability management. From combating advanced persistent threats (APTs) to securing complex environments like cloud, IoT, and edge networks, this book illustrates how generative AI is reshaping traditional security frameworks into adaptive, predictive, and highly automated defense systems.

Exploring the darker side of generative AI, the book highlights its misuse by adversaries for creating sophisticated deepfakes, AI-generated malware, and advanced social engineering campaigns. It balances this discussion with ethical considerations, offering a nuanced perspective on how to mitigate these risks without stifling innovation. Real-world case studies and industry examples are woven throughout the narrative to demonstrate the tangible benefits and limitations of generative AI in practical settings.

As organizations grapple with the ethical, legal, and social implications

1

of deploying generative AI, this book equips readers with the knowledge to navigate complex challenges such as privacy concerns, algorithmic bias, and regulatory compliance. The book also provides an actionable guide for building a career in AI-driven cybersecurity, outlining key skills, certifications, and emerging opportunities in this fast-paced domain.

Furthermore, the book examines the future of generative AI in cybersecurity, exploring its role in quantum computing, autonomous systems, and global security strategies. It envisions a future where AI not only enhances organizational defenses but also transforms the cybersecurity industry into one driven by automation, collaboration, and innovation.

Generative AI in Cybersecurity: Redefining Threat Defense in the Current Era is an essential resource for cybersecurity professionals, AI practitioners, business leaders, and students who wish to harness the power of generative AI to stay ahead of emerging threats. By blending technical insights with strategic guidance, this book empowers readers to embrace generative AI as a critical tool in the fight against cyber adversaries, safeguarding digital ecosystems in the modern age.

Chapter 1: Introduction to Generative AI in Cybersecurity

Introduction

The rapid evolution of technology has brought both unprecedented opportunities and complex challenges to the cybersecurity landscape. As cyber threats grow in sophistication, traditional security measures often struggle to keep pace. This has paved the way for artificial intelligence (AI) to revolutionize cyber defense strategies. Among the many advancements in AI, generative AI stands out as a transformative force that is redefining how we approach cybersecurity in the modern era.

Generative AI represents a paradigm shift in the field of cyber defense, moving beyond traditional reactive models to proactive, intelligent systems capable of simulating, predicting, and neutralizing advanced threats. With its ability to generate realistic data, mimic attack scenarios, and identify hidden vulnerabilities, generative AI is increasingly becoming an indispensable tool for organizations aiming to secure their digital infrastructures.

This chapter provides a comprehensive introduction to the world of generative AI in cybersecurity. It begins by tracing the evolution of artificial intelligence in cyber defense, highlighting the transformative journey from basic automation to sophisticated AI-powered solutions. The chapter then defines generative AI, explaining its unique capabilities and its potential to address the limitations of existing cybersecurity frameworks.

As cybercriminals leverage AI to create more advanced threats, the need for generative AI in modern threat landscapes becomes evident. However, the adoption of generative AI is not without challenges. This chapter explores the opportunities and obstacles associated with implementing generative AI and provides insight into the trends driving its adoption across industries.

By the end of this chapter, readers will gain a clear understanding of the critical role generative AI plays in shaping the future of cybersecurity. This foundational knowledge sets the stage for subsequent chapters, where the applications, techniques, and implications of generative AI in cyber defense are explored in greater depth.

1.1 The Evolution of Artificial Intelligence in Cyber Defense

Artificial Intelligence (AI) has transformed the cybersecurity landscape over the decades, evolving from rudimentary systems to sophisticated models that enable proactive defense strategies. This section traces the journey of AI in cyber defense, highlighting its progression from static rule-based systems to dynamic, generative models capable of predicting and mitigating advanced cyber threats.

1.1.1 Early Applications of AI in Cybersecurity

The integration of AI into cybersecurity began with rudimentary rule-based systems in the late 20th century. These systems relied on predefined rules and static signatures to detect known threats, such as viruses and worms. While effective at identifying straightforward attacks, their inability to adapt to new or evolving threats posed significant limitations.

The next milestone came with the advent of machine learning (ML). Unlike rule-based systems, ML algorithms could learn from data and identify patterns, enabling the detection of anomalies in network traffic, endpoint activity, and user behavior. For example, intrusion detection systems (IDS) began leveraging ML to flag unusual activities, reducing reliance on static signature databases. The shift to ML-based solutions allowed for better adaptability, particularly in identifying previously unseen threats like zero-day exploits. However, these systems were largely reactive, focusing on detecting attacks after they occurred rather than preventing them.

1.1.2 Transition to Predictive and Proactive AI Models

The growing sophistication of cyber threats necessitated a shift from reactive to proactive defense strategies. Predictive AI models emerged as a game-changer, enabling organizations to anticipate potential threats by analyzing historical data, behavioral patterns, and contextual information.

Predictive analytics empowered cybersecurity teams to identify vulnerabilities and forecast attack vectors before exploitation. For instance, behavioral analytics tools could monitor user and system activities to detect deviations indicative of insider threats or malicious intent. Similarly, predictive models used in endpoint protection could identify potential malware based on its behavior rather than relying on a known signature.

This proactive approach also extended to threat intelligence. By analyzing vast datasets from threat intelligence feeds, predictive AI models could identify emerging trends, such as the rise of specific ransomware families, and alert organizations to prepare for potential attacks. While these advancements significantly enhanced cyber defense capabilities, the introduction of generative AI marked the next frontier.

1.1.3 Generative AI as the Next Frontier

Generative AI has revolutionized cybersecurity by introducing the ability to simulate, predict, and counteract advanced threats in ways previously unimaginable. Unlike traditional AI models, generative AI—powered by technologies such as Generative Adversarial Networks (GANs) and transformers—goes beyond detection and prediction to actively generate new data and scenarios.

Generative AI excels in creating realistic attack simulations, helping organizations test their defenses against complex threat scenarios, such as phishing campaigns, ransomware attacks, or supply chain intrusions. For example, AI can generate synthetic datasets that mimic malicious activities, enabling security systems to train and improve without exposing live environments to actual threats.

Another critical application of generative AI is its role in understanding adversarial tactics. By generating potential attack strategies, these models help organizations anticipate and counteract techniques that attackers might employ. This proactive approach is especially valuable in dealing with advanced persistent threats (APTs) and nation-state actors, where conventional defenses often fall short.

Moreover, generative AI is instrumental in cybersecurity innovation, including automated incident response and adaptive security measures. For example, by using natural language processing (NLP) models, organizations can automate responses to phishing attempts or refine security policies based on real-time feedback.

As cybercriminals also begin leveraging AI to develop more sophisticated attacks, the role of generative AI in cyber defense becomes even more critical. It represents not just a tool but a strategic asset in the ongoing battle to secure digital infrastructures against ever-evolving threats.

1.2 Generative AI Defined: A Paradigm Shift in Cybersecurity

Generative AI represents a transformative leap in the field of cybersecurity, shifting the narrative from reactive defense to proactive and predictive measures. Unlike traditional AI systems, which primarily focus on analyzing and detecting known patterns, generative AI creates data and scenarios that closely mimic real-world phenomena. This ability to generate content and simulate potential cyber threats makes it a critical innovation in addressing today's sophisticated and evolving cyberattacks.

1.2.1 What is Generative AI?

Generative AI encompasses a class of algorithms designed to create new data—such as text, images, or code—that resembles human-generated content. These systems rely on advanced neural network architectures, including Generative Adversarial Networks (GANs), Variational Autoencoders (VAEs), and transformer-based models like GPT (Generative Pre-trained Transformer).

GANs, for example, use two neural networks—a generator and a discriminator—that work in tandem to produce highly realistic outputs. While the generator creates data, the discriminator evaluates its authenticity, iteratively refining the quality of the generated content. Similarly, VAEs compress and reconstruct data, enabling the creation of variations that are statistically similar to the original input. Transformer models, on the other hand, excel at understanding context and generating coherent, contextually accurate outputs, which is especially valuable in tasks such as automated threat analysis and response.

Generative AI's unique ability to simulate real-world scenarios, anticipate threats, and generate actionable insights makes it indispensable in the modern cybersecurity landscape, where attackers constantly innovate new methods to bypass traditional defenses.

1.2.2 Distinctive Capabilities of Generative AI in Cybersecurity

Generative AI is not just an enhancement of traditional AI—it fundamentally redefines the scope and effectiveness of cybersecurity strategies. Its distinctive capabilities include:

- **Predictive Threat Modeling:** Generative AI can anticipate potential attack vectors by simulating the behavior of cybercriminals. For instance, it can generate realistic phishing emails or simulate ransomware activities, enabling organizations to test their defenses under near-real-world conditions.

- **Simulation of Zero-Day Exploits:** By mimicking previously unseen attack methods, generative AI prepares cybersecurity

7

teams to address zero-day vulnerabilities, which traditional systems often fail to recognize.

- **Enhanced Malware Detection:** Generative models synthesize a wide range of malware samples, even those that do not yet exist in the wild. By training on these synthetic datasets, cybersecurity solutions can improve their ability to detect polymorphic malware and other advanced threats.

- **Automation of Threat Response:** Generative AI can dynamically generate automated responses to attacks, reducing response times and minimizing damage. For example, it can simulate patch deployment scenarios or generate adaptive firewall rules based on ongoing attacks.

- **Adversarial Training:** By generating adversarial examples—data specifically designed to fool machine learning models—generative AI strengthens the resilience of AI-driven security systems against attempts to bypass them.

The ability of generative AI to create, simulate, and predict ensures that cybersecurity teams stay one step ahead of attackers, addressing threats before they materialize.

1.2.3 Role in Enhancing Traditional Security Mechanisms

Generative AI complements and enhances traditional security mechanisms, transforming them into more adaptive, intelligent, and effective solutions. For decades, cybersecurity systems have relied on static, rule-based models or machine learning algorithms that analyze historical data. While these approaches are effective against known threats, they struggle with novel, adaptive, and highly sophisticated attack methods. Generative AI fills this gap by bringing dynamic and forward-looking capabilities to the table.

One of the most significant advantages of generative AI is its ability to augment traditional defenses against advanced persistent threats (APTs) and polymorphic malware. APTs often involve stealthy, prolonged campaigns where attackers continuously adapt their strategies to evade detection. Generative AI can simulate these evolving tactics, helping organizations to preemptively strengthen their defenses.

Similarly, polymorphic malware, which alters its code to avoid detection, poses a significant challenge to conventional systems. By generating a variety of malware variants, generative AI allows cybersecurity solutions to train on an extensive dataset, improving their accuracy in identifying and mitigating these threats.

Moreover, generative AI enhances automation in cybersecurity operations. It enables the creation of adaptive intrusion detection and prevention systems (IDPS) that adjust in real-time to emerging threats. For example, by analyzing ongoing attacks, a generative model can suggest updates to security policies or generate custom responses to mitigate risks.

In threat intelligence, generative AI plays a pivotal role by synthesizing insights from multiple sources, such as network logs, threat feeds, and user behavior analytics. This synthesized intelligence enables cybersecurity teams to make more informed decisions, streamline incident response processes, and optimize resource allocation.

1.3 The Need for Generative AI in Modern Threat Landscapes

The increasing sophistication and frequency of cyberattacks have highlighted the need for a more advanced, adaptive, and proactive approach to cybersecurity. Traditional methods of defending against cyber threats are struggling to keep up with evolving attack techniques that leverage AI and other cutting-edge technologies. In this landscape, generative AI is emerging as a crucial tool for ensuring that organizations can protect their data, networks, and systems against modern threats. This section explores the need for generative AI in today's cybersecurity environment, focusing on the challenges posed by advanced attacks, the limitations of manual defense methods, and the ways in which generative AI can enhance proactive defense strategies.

1.3.1 The Rise of Sophisticated Cyber Threats

In recent years, the cybersecurity landscape has become increasingly complex, with cybercriminals adopting advanced tactics, techniques, and procedures (TTPs) that are difficult for traditional defense mechanisms to detect and counter. One of the most alarming developments in this area is the rise of AI-driven cyberattacks, such as deepfake phishing, AI-generated malware, and automated social engineering.

AI-Driven Attacks: AI-powered attacks are particularly dangerous because they can adapt in real-time, making them much harder to identify and mitigate. For instance, **deepfake phishing** uses AI to generate realistic, but fake audio or video messages from trusted figures within an organization, thereby tricking employees into revealing sensitive information or executing malicious actions. AI-generated malware, on the other hand, can constantly change its form, making it difficult for traditional signature-based detection systems to identify and eliminate it.

These attacks are growing in sophistication as cybercriminals gain access to powerful generative models, such as Generative Adversarial Networks (GANs), which can create realistic, undetectable cyberattacks. Furthermore, the rapid development of AI technology allows these threats to evolve faster than human analysts can detect, creating a significant challenge for cybersecurity teams.

As cyber threats become increasingly sophisticated and driven by AI, there is an urgent need for similarly advanced defense mechanisms. Generative AI's ability to simulate and predict attacks, create synthetic datasets, and enhance threat detection systems offers a powerful solution to counter these emerging challenges.

1.3.2 Challenges in Manual Threat Detection and Response

Traditional cybersecurity approaches, while effective to a certain extent, face significant challenges in dealing with the volume and complexity of modern cyber threats. Historically, security teams have relied on manual processes, including rule-based systems, signature-based detection, and human-driven threat analysis. However, these methods are becoming increasingly ineffective against advanced, fast-evolving attacks.

The Volume and Complexity of Attacks: Modern cyberattacks often involve a combination of techniques, including malware, social engineering, and network infiltration. In addition, the volume of potential threats generated every day is overwhelming. Security teams can quickly become inundated by alerts from firewalls, intrusion detection systems, and other monitoring tools, many of which are false positives or low-priority threats. Manually sifting through this data to identify and respond to the most critical attacks is time-consuming and prone to error.

Human Error and Delays in Response: Manual threat detection also suffers from inherent limitations. Human analysts may overlook critical patterns, make mistakes in their assessments, or fail to respond quickly enough to mitigate attacks in time. The complexity and variety of modern cyber threats require a level of attention and analysis that manual processes simply cannot keep up with.

Generative AI addresses these issues by automating threat detection and response processes. Through machine learning models that continually learn from data, generative AI can analyze vast amounts of information in real-time, quickly identifying potential threats based on known attack patterns and anomalies. Furthermore, AI can predict attacks before they happen by simulating various threat scenarios, enabling organizations to strengthen their defenses proactively. By automating routine threat detection and response tasks, generative AI also frees up security professionals to focus on higher-level strategy and more complex tasks.

1.3.3 Enhancing Proactive Defense Strategies

A fundamental shift is underway in the world of cybersecurity: organizations are moving from reactive to proactive defense strategies. Traditionally, cybersecurity teams would respond to attacks as they occurred, often focusing on containment and recovery rather than prevention. However, as threats become more advanced and frequent, a reactive approach is no longer sufficient. Generative AI is at the forefront of enabling this transition, offering powerful tools for predicting and preventing attacks before they happen.

Predictive Threat Modeling: One of the core strengths of generative AI is its ability to create predictive models that simulate potential attack scenarios. By analyzing historical data, trends, and emerging threats, AI can forecast the likelihood of certain attack vectors, enabling organizations to strengthen their defenses proactively. For example, generative AI can model various types of cyberattacks—such as ransomware, phishing, or DDoS (Distributed Denial of Service)—and identify the specific vulnerabilities that would be exploited in each case. This allows security teams to implement preemptive measures, such as patching vulnerabilities or reinforcing weak points in the network, before an attack occurs.

Simulating Attack Scenarios: Generative AI's ability to simulate real-world attack scenarios is another crucial aspect of its role in proactive cybersecurity. By generating synthetic cyberattacks, AI helps organizations test their defenses against scenarios that might not yet exist in the real world. These simulated attacks can be used to identify gaps in security, assess the effectiveness of existing defense mechanisms, and provide insights into how to respond to new types of threats. This "attack-first" mentality helps organizations stay ahead of cybercriminals who are constantly innovating new tactics.

Automating Threat Prevention: In addition to simulation, generative AI can also automate the implementation of defense measures. Once an attack is predicted or simulated, AI can automatically adjust security settings, deploy patches, or reconfigure firewalls to prevent the attack from being successful. By integrating AI with existing security tools, organizations can build a highly adaptive security system that responds in real-time to emerging threats without requiring human intervention.

1.4 Key Opportunities and Challenges in Adopting Generative AI

The adoption of **generative AI** in cybersecurity presents significant opportunities for enhancing defense mechanisms, but it also introduces challenges that need to be carefully managed. As generative AI continues to evolve, organizations must strategically navigate both the opportunities it offers and the risks it introduces to fully harness its potential in strengthening cybersecurity. This section explores the key opportunities and challenges that arise with the adoption of generative AI in the cybersecurity domain and discusses the balance that organizations need to strike between leveraging its benefits and mitigating its risks.

1.4.1 Opportunities

Generative AI opens up new possibilities in cybersecurity, particularly by enhancing the ability to predict, simulate, and respond to sophisticated threats. Some of the most important opportunities it provides include:

Automated Threat Simulation:

One of the primary advantages of generative AI in cybersecurity is its ability to **simulate a wide range of cyberattacks** that could potentially target an organization. By using generative models, cybersecurity teams can simulate both known and unknown (zero-day) attacks, such as phishing, ransomware, and advanced persistent threats (APTs). This proactive approach to simulation allows security professionals to test the resilience of their infrastructure and identify vulnerabilities that may not have been apparent during routine security assessments. Simulating attacks also provides a controlled environment for experimenting with new defensive techniques and tools without the risk of real-world consequences. This helps organizations stay ahead of emerging threats and refine their defensive capabilities before attacks occur in reality.

Enhanced Incident Response:

In addition to improving threat detection, generative AI can significantly enhance **incident response capabilities**. AI models can autonomously respond to security incidents by analyzing incoming threats and deciding on the best course of action in real-time. For example, if a potential ransomware attack is detected, a generative AI system could isolate the infected network segment, terminate malicious processes, and alert human security personnel for further investigation. This automation not only **reduces response time** but also helps minimize the **impact of cyberattacks** by acting faster than human responders. By continually learning from past incidents, generative AI systems can refine their response strategies, improving over time to handle new and evolving threats more effectively.

Advanced Threat Detection:

Generative AI can enhance traditional threat detection systems by enabling the **identification of novel and previously unseen threats**. While conventional cybersecurity systems rely on signature-based detection or predefined rules, generative AI analyzes large datasets to **generate synthetic threat patterns**. This allows the system to **identify zero-day vulnerabilities**, which are typically unknown to traditional defense mechanisms. AI models trained on large-scale datasets can recognize **anomalous behaviors** and patterns that deviate from the norm, identifying threats that may have been overlooked by other detection methods. Additionally, AI-powered detection systems can continue to evolve, staying current with the latest threat vectors and attack techniques as cybercriminals adapt their methods.

1.4.2 Challenges

While generative AI holds significant promise in the field of cybersecurity, its adoption comes with several challenges that organizations must address:

Ethical Concerns:

The potential for the **misuse of generative AI** for malicious purposes is one of the most significant ethical concerns. Cybercriminals can leverage generative AI to create **realistic deepfakes**, manipulate public opinion, craft **highly convincing phishing emails**, or even generate new types of malware that evade traditional detection mechanisms. These capabilities raise important **legal and ethical questions** about accountability, misuse, and the potential harm caused by such technologies. As generative AI becomes more accessible, establishing ethical guidelines and enforcing responsible AI use will become crucial to prevent the technology from being exploited for harmful purposes. Ethical concerns also extend to the development of AI models, where biases in the data used to train the systems can result in discriminatory outcomes or unfair targeting of specific groups.

Algorithmic Bias:

Another challenge in adopting generative AI is the **risk of algorithmic bias**. AI models, including generative models, are only as good as the data they are trained on. If the data is biased or incomplete, it can lead to **discriminatory outcomes** in threat detection, decision-making, and response. For example, an AI system trained primarily on data from one region or demographic may fail to accurately detect or respond to threats that affect other regions or groups. In the context of cybersecurity, algorithmic bias could mean the **underrepresentation** of certain types of attacks, potentially leaving organizations vulnerable to those specific threats. To mitigate bias, it's essential to use **diverse, comprehensive datasets** and regularly audit AI systems for fairness and accuracy.

Integration Complexities:

Integrating generative AI into existing **cybersecurity frameworks** is another major challenge. Most organizations already have a variety of security tools and systems in place, such as firewalls, intrusion detection systems (IDS), and endpoint protection platforms. **Incorporating generative AI** into these existing tools requires careful planning, expertise, and resources. AI models must be seamlessly integrated into security workflows and systems to ensure they provide value without disrupting existing operations. Additionally, there may be challenges in training personnel to work effectively with generative AI, as cybersecurity professionals need specialized skills in AI, machine learning, and data science. Organizations must invest in **skilled talent** and infrastructure to successfully adopt AI-driven solutions.

1.4.3 Balancing Opportunities and Risks

To successfully implement generative AI in cybersecurity, organizations must strike a balance between exploiting the transformative **opportunities** it offers and addressing the associated **challenges**. This requires a thoughtful, strategic approach that includes the following key steps:

Strategic Planning:

Before adopting generative AI, organizations should conduct a thorough assessment of their cybersecurity needs and **identify specific use cases** where AI can add value. Whether it's enhancing threat detection, improving incident response, or simulating attack scenarios, having a clear understanding of how AI will be applied ensures that organizations make informed decisions and achieve their desired outcomes.

Ongoing Audits and Monitoring:

AI systems should be subject to regular audits and performance evaluations. Organizations must implement continuous monitoring to ensure that AI models remain accurate, unbiased, and aligned with their objectives. This can help detect any unexpected behaviors or deviations from expected outcomes, allowing security teams to take corrective action when necessary.

Ethical Frameworks and Guidelines:

To address ethical concerns, organizations should develop and adhere to **ethical frameworks** for the responsible use of AI. This includes ensuring transparency in AI decision-making, protecting privacy, and mitigating potential biases. By adopting ethical guidelines and legal compliance frameworks, organizations can minimize the risks of AI misuse and maintain trust with stakeholders.

Employee Training and Skill Development:

As AI becomes a critical part of cybersecurity strategies, it's essential for organizations to **train their staff** to work with AI-powered systems effectively. Security teams should receive training in AI technologies, including machine learning, natural language processing, and data analysis. This ensures that AI systems are used effectively and responsibly and that human oversight remains in place when needed.

By carefully balancing these opportunities and challenges, organizations can harness the full potential of generative AI while minimizing the risks associated with its use. Through thoughtful adoption, ongoing management, and continuous improvement, generative AI can become a powerful tool in the fight against modern cyber threats.

1.5 Current Trends Driving Generative AI Adoption in Cybersecurity

The adoption of **generative AI** in cybersecurity is gaining momentum as organizations recognize its transformative potential to bolster their defense capabilities. Driven by the evolving complexity of cyber threats and the increasing demand for automated, proactive security measures, generative AI is becoming a key component in next-generation cybersecurity strategies. This section explores the current trends that are accelerating the integration of generative AI into cybersecurity practices, showcasing its growing role in the defense ecosystem and highlighting specific areas where it is having a significant impact.

1.5.1 The Increasing Role of AI in Cyber Defense

The role of **AI in cyber defense** has expanded rapidly in recent years, driven by the increasing sophistication of cyberattacks. **Traditional**

cybersecurity measures—relying primarily on signature-based detection, firewalls, and other reactive techniques—have struggled to keep pace with emerging threats. In contrast, **generative AI** offers a proactive, anticipatory approach, enabling security systems to not only detect known threats but also predict and counteract new, unknown attacks. Generative AI models, such as **Generative Adversarial Networks (GANs)** and **transformer models**, have proven to be effective in simulating adversarial attacks, creating synthetic attack data, and automatically generating responses to threats in real-time.

This capability to **tackle complex, high-volume attacks** is one of the primary reasons why AI-driven security solutions are becoming more prevalent across various industries. As **cybercriminals** continue to deploy AI-powered tools to outmaneuver traditional defenses, businesses are increasingly turning to **generative AI** to level the playing field. These AI models can create new attack patterns for defensive systems to identify and mitigate, allowing for more **dynamic and adaptable security strategies**. This shift to AI-driven defense mechanisms is enabling organizations to build **self-learning systems** that continuously improve their threat detection and mitigation capabilities.

1.5.2 Industry-Specific Applications

Generative AI is making substantial strides in a variety of industries, offering tailored solutions to meet the unique cybersecurity challenges of each sector. **Industry-specific applications** of generative AI demonstrate its versatility and its ability to address a wide range of cybersecurity concerns. Some key examples include:

Financial Services:

The financial industry faces persistent threats, such as **fraudulent transactions, account takeover** attacks, and **money laundering schemes**. Generative AI is helping financial institutions by simulating and analyzing various fraudulent activities. These systems can generate synthetic data to simulate attack vectors and test defenses against real-world fraud scenarios. Furthermore, generative AI models can detect anomalies in transaction data, identify suspicious patterns, and autonomously alert security teams. By analyzing large volumes of data and generating new attack scenarios, AI can spot fraudulent behavior more efficiently than traditional methods, reducing response times and preventing financial losses.

Healthcare:

In healthcare, the protection of sensitive patient data is paramount, especially as **healthcare providers** increasingly adopt digital health records and connected medical devices. Generative AI is being used to improve **data encryption**, **access controls**, and **anomaly detection systems** that safeguard patient data. AI models can simulate potential cyberattacks on healthcare systems, generating realistic attack scenarios and testing the resilience of existing security protocols. Additionally, generative AI can assist in identifying and mitigating risks related to **medical device security**, protecting both patient safety and privacy.

Government and Defense:

In government and defense sectors, **national security** is heavily reliant on maintaining the confidentiality, integrity, and availability of critical infrastructure. Generative AI is used to simulate cyberattacks on critical systems, analyze large-scale data breaches, and enhance overall **cyber resilience**. The ability to generate synthetic attack patterns allows security teams to anticipate and prepare for threats before they materialize, bolstering national defense systems against state-sponsored cyberattacks and **advanced persistent threats (APTs)**.

By leveraging **industry-specific applications**, generative AI can offer highly **customized solutions** that address the unique needs and regulatory requirements of each sector, enhancing both security and compliance.

1.5.3 Innovations in Generative AI Technology

Advancements in **generative AI technology** are driving the growth and effectiveness of AI-driven cybersecurity solutions. Some of the most notable innovations include:

Transformer Models and GPT:

Transformer models, such as **GPT-3** (Generative Pretrained Transformer 3), have revolutionized natural language processing (NLP) and are now being adapted for use in cybersecurity. By leveraging the power of transformers, generative AI can process vast amounts of data more efficiently and accurately, enabling the detection of **complex threats** hidden in **text-based communications** (e.g., phishing emails or social engineering attacks). GPT and similar models can generate realistic attack scenarios and simulate realistic responses, providing critical insights into vulnerabilities and attack patterns.

Multimodal AI:

Multimodal AI is an emerging trend in generative AI that integrates multiple forms of data, such as text, images, and network traffic, to provide a more comprehensive analysis of cybersecurity risks. This approach enables generative AI models to generate and analyze attack scenarios across different data modalities, offering a deeper understanding of the nature of threats and vulnerabilities. By incorporating various data types, multimodal AI enhances **threat detection**, **data classification**, and **attack simulation**, making it a highly effective tool for combating complex and multifaceted cyber threats.

Explainable AI (XAI):

One of the key challenges with AI, especially in high-stakes environments like cybersecurity, is the **black-box nature** of many AI models. **Explainable AI (XAI)** is helping to address this issue by making AI decision-making processes more transparent and understandable to human security analysts. By improving the interpretability of generative

AI systems, XAI enables cybersecurity professionals to trust AI-generated insights and take informed actions based on the AI's reasoning. This is critical for ensuring that AI systems remain accountable and that human oversight is maintained when necessary.

These technological innovations are enhancing the capabilities of generative AI, making it more adept at detecting, simulating, and responding to complex cyber threats. As AI technology continues to advance, its role in cybersecurity will become even more integral in defending against emerging attack techniques and evolving threat landscapes.

1.5.4 Collaborative Ecosystems for AI-Driven Cybersecurity

The development of generative AI in cybersecurity is not occurring in isolation; instead, **collaborative ecosystems** involving governments, academia, industry leaders, and technology providers are driving its advancement. **Collaboration** is critical for establishing **standards**, **frameworks**, and **best practices** that ensure the safe and effective deployment of generative AI in cybersecurity applications. Some key initiatives include:

Government and Private Sector Partnerships:

Governments and private organizations are working together to create **regulatory frameworks** and **standards** for AI in cybersecurity. These partnerships are aimed at ensuring that generative AI solutions are deployed ethically, securely, and in compliance with existing laws and regulations. By establishing **collaborative research** initiatives, both parties can share data, insights, and resources to accelerate the development of advanced AI technologies that enhance cybersecurity defenses.

Academic and Industry Collaboration:

Academic institutions are collaborating with industry leaders to conduct **cutting-edge research** in generative AI. By partnering with universities and research organizations, businesses can leverage the latest advancements in AI technology and benefit from the academic community's work on improving **AI ethics, bias mitigation**, and **threat simulation**. This collaboration also helps ensure that AI models are continually evolving in response to new threats and emerging cybersecurity challenges.

Open-Source Communities and Frameworks:

The growth of **open-source initiatives** in AI is enabling developers, researchers, and organizations to collaborate on the creation of **AI-driven cybersecurity frameworks**. These frameworks provide access to the latest AI tools, models, and datasets, enabling organizations to leverage **state-of-the-art generative AI technologies** without having to build them from scratch. Open-source collaborations foster innovation and make generative AI tools more accessible to businesses of all sizes, democratizing access to advanced cybersecurity solutions.

The formation of **collaborative ecosystems** ensures that generative AI is developed and deployed in a way that benefits society at large. It helps create **cross-disciplinary solutions** that harness the collective knowledge and expertise of multiple sectors to address the growing cybersecurity challenges of the digital age.

Conclusion

This chapter sets the stage for understanding the revolutionary role of generative AI in cybersecurity. By exploring its evolution, capabilities, necessity, opportunities, challenges, and current trends, readers are equipped with a solid foundation to delve deeper into how generative AI is reshaping cyber defense strategies in the modern era.

Chapter 2: Foundations of Generative AI Technologies

Introduction

In the rapidly evolving landscape of cybersecurity, **Generative AI** has emerged as a revolutionary tool that not only identifies and mitigates threats but also anticipates and simulates potential attack vectors. Understanding the foundational principles and technologies behind generative AI is essential for leveraging its full potential in cybersecurity applications. This chapter delves into the core technologies driving generative AI, offering a comprehensive overview of how these technologies work, their applications, and the ethical considerations surrounding their development.

2.1 What Is Generative AI and How Does It Work?

Generative AI refers to a subset of artificial intelligence techniques designed to generate new data or content by learning patterns from existing datasets. Unlike traditional AI, which typically involves tasks such as classification or prediction based on input data, generative AI focuses on **creating novel outputs** that mimic the properties of the data it was trained on. These outputs can span a variety of content types, such as **text, images, audio, video**, or even **code**. This capability to create entirely new and realistic content has made generative AI a transformative tool across industries, particularly in **cybersecurity**, where it is being used to simulate attacks, enhance threat detection, and automate responses.

2.1.1 Key Concepts of Generative AI

Generative AI works through a variety of foundational principles that enable its ability to produce realistic, synthetic outputs. Let's break down these concepts:

1. Training Data:

The foundation of any generative AI model is **training data**. These models learn by analyzing large, high-quality datasets that reflect the characteristics of the real-world data they aim to mimic. For instance, to generate realistic images, a model might be trained on millions of photos; to generate text, it might learn from books, articles, and other written materials.

- **Pattern Recognition:** During the training process, the AI identifies patterns, relationships, and structures within the data. For example, a generative model for text generation learns grammar, sentence structure, and vocabulary usage from vast text corpora.

- **Data Representation:** The model represents data in high-dimensional spaces, where each data point corresponds to a set of features that define its characteristics. These learned features allow the AI to create novel content that maintains coherence with the training data.

2. Generative Process:

Once the AI has learned patterns from its training data, it uses those learned distributions to **generate new outputs**. The generative process involves sampling from these distributions and transforming that into a new, realistic data point.

- **Sampling from Distributions:** The AI can generate diverse outputs by sampling from a **probability distribution** that reflects the characteristics of the training data. This allows for variability while ensuring the generated content remains similar to real-world examples.

- **Data Transformation:** Once a sample is drawn from the learned distribution, the AI transforms it into a meaningful output. For instance, a model trained on images might generate a new image, or a language model might generate coherent and contextually appropriate text based on an initial prompt.

3. Loss Function:

To improve its output quality, a generative AI model uses a **loss function** to quantify the difference between the generated content and the real data it is trying to replicate. The loss function measures how well the model's outputs match the desired characteristics, such as **accuracy, realism**, or **believability**.

- **Minimizing the Loss:** The AI model uses optimization techniques to minimize the loss function, adjusting its parameters (weights) over time to improve the generated outputs. This process involves **backpropagation**, where errors are calculated and used to update the model's internal weights.

- **Continuous Improvement:** As the model is trained, it continually improves its ability to generate realistic outputs by reducing the discrepancy between its creations and actual data.

2.1.2 Applications in Cybersecurity

Generative AI holds significant promise for advancing cybersecurity defenses and enhancing the capabilities of threat detection systems. By simulating attack scenarios and generating synthetic data, generative AI can help improve cybersecurity models, test defensive mechanisms, and ensure that security protocols are robust enough to withstand evolving threats.

1. Simulating Potential Attack Scenarios:

One of the primary uses of generative AI in cybersecurity is its ability to simulate realistic attack scenarios. By learning from existing cybersecurity threats (e.g., malware samples, phishing emails, or exploit patterns), generative models can create **synthetic attack scenarios** that might be used for training, testing, or preparing response strategies.

- **Advanced Threat Simulation:** Generative AI can produce realistic **zero-day exploits** or **advanced persistent threats (APTs)** that could test the resilience of security systems and incident response strategies. These synthetic attacks can be tailored to target specific vulnerabilities or simulate emerging threat techniques.

- **Adversarial Testing:** Security teams can use generated attacks to evaluate their network defenses, intrusion detection systems (IDS), and firewalls. These tests help identify weaknesses that real-world attackers could exploit.

2. Generating Synthetic Data for Model Training:

Training cybersecurity models, especially for threat detection and anomaly recognition, often require vast amounts of high-quality labeled data. However, obtaining real-world labeled datasets can be time-consuming, expensive, or even difficult due to privacy concerns.

- **Synthetic Data Creation:** Generative AI can create **synthetic datasets** that mimic the characteristics of real-world data, such as network traffic patterns, user behavior logs, or malware samples. These datasets can be used to **train machine learning models** that detect abnormal behavior, network intrusions, or malware infections.

- **Augmenting Datasets:** Generative AI can also **augment existing datasets** by generating additional variations of real-world data, such as new malware variants, different types of network traffic, or various phishing email designs. This expanded dataset helps improve the generalization ability of security models, making them more effective at detecting new, unseen threats.

3. Phishing Email Generation:

Phishing remains one of the most prevalent attack methods, relying on social engineering to trick individuals into revealing sensitive information, such as login credentials or financial details.

- **Creating Realistic Phishing Emails:** Generative AI, particularly models like **GPT (Generative Pretrained Transformer)**, can be trained to generate highly convincing phishing emails that resemble legitimate communications. These AI-generated emails can be used for **training** anti-phishing systems or simulating phishing attacks in order to enhance employee awareness and detection capabilities.

- **Training Anti-Phishing Models:** Generative AI can be used to generate a wide variety of phishing emails with different tactics, enabling organizations to train and refine their anti-phishing solutions. These models can mimic various types of phishing, such as spear-phishing, whaling, and social media phishing, preparing defenses for diverse threats.

4. Malware Code Generation:

Malware detection systems often face challenges due to the dynamic and ever-evolving nature of malware. Cybercriminals frequently alter or obfuscate their code to evade detection by traditional security tools.

- **Malware Variant Generation:** Generative AI can be employed to generate **new variants** of malware by learning from existing malware samples. This allows cybersecurity teams to train malware detection systems to recognize novel or polymorphic threats that may not be present in conventional malware datasets.

- **Evasion Techniques Testing:** Generated malware can also be used to test **antivirus software** and intrusion detection systems for their ability to identify sophisticated evasion techniques, such as code obfuscation or rootkits.

5. Threat Intelligence Generation:

Another key application of generative AI in cybersecurity is the generation of **synthetic threat intelligence**. Threat intelligence includes valuable information about emerging cyber threats, such as **malicious IP addresses, file hashes**, and **URLs** associated with **cybercriminal activities**.

- **Generating Threat Intelligence Feeds:** Generative AI can produce synthetic threat intelligence data that mirrors real-world attack patterns, enabling threat detection systems to stay up-to-date with evolving threats. This allows organizations to proactively defend against cyberattacks by integrating AI-generated threat data into their security operations.

- **Improving Threat Prediction:** By leveraging generative models, cybersecurity professionals can anticipate potential attack patterns and better understand adversaries' tactics, techniques, and procedures (TTPs), improving overall threat prediction and response strategies.

2.2 The Mechanics of Generative Adversarial Networks (GANs)

Generative Adversarial Networks (GANs) have become one of the most groundbreaking innovations in the realm of **generative AI**. They consist of two competing neural networks—**the generator** and **the discriminator**—which engage in a game-theoretic process, enabling them to improve iteratively. This adversarial training process is the foundation of GANs' ability to generate highly realistic data samples, making them particularly valuable in various domains, including cybersecurity.

2.2.1 The Generator and Discriminator

The fundamental mechanism of GANs revolves around two neural networks: the **generator** and the **discriminator**. Each plays a critical role in the GAN's ability to produce realistic outputs, and their interplay is what drives the model's improvement.

The Generator:

The generator's primary function is to create synthetic data that closely resembles real-world data. It starts with **random noise** as input and tries to convert it into a realistic output. Initially, the generator's outputs are far from perfect, but it progressively refines its outputs through **training**. Over time, it learns to create data that is increasingly indistinguishable from genuine data.

- **Training the Generator:** The generator is trained using feedback from the discriminator. Initially, its creations are easily identifiable as fake by the discriminator, but as it learns from the feedback, it improves its ability to generate more realistic samples.

- **Output Examples:** In the context of cybersecurity, the generator could produce fake **phishing emails, malicious network traffic**, or **synthetic attack patterns** to simulate real-world cybersecurity threats. By learning the characteristics of real attack data, the generator becomes adept at creating increasingly realistic simulations.

The Discriminator:

The discriminator's role is to evaluate the authenticity of the data generated by the generator. It is essentially a **binary classifier** that differentiates between real data (from a true source) and fake data (generated by the generator).

- **Training the Discriminator:** During training, the discriminator receives both real data (e.g., actual network traffic or legitimate emails) and fake data (e.g., generated phishing emails or simulated attack patterns). It must determine whether each piece of data is genuine or generated. The discriminator provides feedback to the generator based on its evaluation, helping the generator improve.

- **Learning to Classify:** The discriminator's goal is to become as proficient as possible at distinguishing fake from real data. As it becomes more accurate, the generator is forced to improve and produce even more realistic data in response to the discriminator's growing abilities.

Adversarial Process:

The **adversarial** nature of GANs means that the generator and discriminator are in constant competition. The generator aims to produce more convincing data, while the discriminator strives to become better at detecting fakes. This iterative process continues until the generator produces data that is highly realistic, making it difficult for the discriminator to tell the difference.

2.2.2 GANs in Cybersecurity

GANs offer a wide range of applications in **cybersecurity**, where their ability to generate realistic data can be harnessed to simulate attacks, train defense systems, and detect anomalies. By generating synthetic data, GANs can be used to overcome the limitations of **labeled datasets** and improve the **training** of cybersecurity models.

1. Phishing Attack Simulation:

One of the most notable applications of GANs in cybersecurity is **phishing attack simulation**. Phishing remains one of the most common and dangerous attack vectors, with cybercriminals using increasingly sophisticated techniques to trick individuals into disclosing sensitive information.

- **Realistic Phishing Emails:** GANs can be used to generate highly realistic phishing emails that mimic the language, style, and tactics used by actual attackers. These emails can be customized to simulate different types of phishing attacks, from **spear-phishing** to **whaling**, providing valuable training data for **anti-phishing systems**.

- **Employee Training:** By using GAN-generated phishing emails in simulated training environments, organizations can train employees to recognize phishing attempts more effectively. The advantage of using GANs for this purpose is that they allow the generation of diverse, realistic phishing campaigns that are continuously evolving in line with real-world tactics.

2. Synthetic Attack Data Generation:

Cybersecurity models, particularly those used for **threat detection**, rely heavily on high-quality training data. However, acquiring enough labeled data to train these models can be challenging, especially for **new** or **rare attack types** that have not been seen before. GANs offer a solution to this problem by generating **synthetic attack data** that can be used to train other machine learning models.

- **Training Data for Rare Attacks:** GANs can simulate rare or novel attack scenarios, such as **zero-day exploits** or advanced **persistent threats (APTs)**. By training detection systems on this synthetic data, cybersecurity teams can ensure their models are equipped to identify a broader range of attacks, including those that have yet to be discovered.

- **Continuous Model Improvement:** As new attack methods emerge, GANs can be used to generate synthetic samples of these unknown attack types, ensuring that threat detection models are always up-to-date with the latest attack strategies.

3. Anomaly Detection:

Another critical application of GANs in cybersecurity is **anomaly detection**, especially in the context of **network traffic analysis** and **intrusion detection systems (IDS)**. Traditional methods of anomaly detection are often limited by the availability of **realistic abnormal data** for training.

- **Learning Normal Behavior:** GANs can be trained on **normal network behavior** to generate realistic synthetic examples of **anomalous behavior**. For instance, a GAN might learn to simulate unusual network traffic patterns that deviate from typical traffic flows, which could indicate an ongoing **DDoS attack, data exfiltration**, or **insider threats**.

- **Enhanced IDS Training:** By generating synthetic anomalies, GANs provide a way to **train intrusion detection systems (IDS)** on a wide range of abnormal patterns without the need for actual attacks. This allows IDS models to become more robust and capable of detecting a broader array of attacks in real-time.

4. Malware Detection and Analysis:

GANs can also assist in detecting and analyzing **malware** by generating synthetic samples of malicious code. These generated samples can be used to **train malware detection systems**, improving their ability to detect new variants of malware, including those that employ **obfuscation techniques**.

- **Generating Malicious Code:** GANs can be trained on existing **malware datasets** to generate new variants of malicious code, which can then be used to test the effectiveness of antivirus programs, **sandboxing techniques**, and other malware detection systems.

- **Evolving Threats:** As new types of malware emerge, GANs can help generate synthetic malware samples for training, ensuring that detection systems are prepared for evolving threats.

5. Cybersecurity Threat Intelligence:

GANs can be used to generate synthetic **threat intelligence data**, such as fake **IP addresses, URLs,** and **file hashes** associated with **malicious activities**. This synthetic data can be used to enhance threat intelligence platforms and improve the accuracy of threat feeds.

- **Simulating Attacks:** By generating threat intelligence data that mirrors real-world attacks, GANs can help organizations identify attack patterns early on and improve their overall threat posture. This can also aid in the **early detection** of campaigns conducted by advanced adversaries.

2.3 Transformers and Their Role in Cybersecurity

Transformers have emerged as one of the most powerful architectures in modern **deep learning**, particularly within the domain of **natural language processing (NLP)**. They are capable of handling large-scale sequential data and offer significant improvements over traditional models like **recurrent neural networks (RNNs)**. The **self-attention mechanism** allows transformers to focus on the most relevant parts of the input data, enabling them to process and understand context in a more powerful and efficient way. In cybersecurity, transformers are being adapted to handle a wide variety of challenges, from **threat detection** to **incident response automation**.

2.3.1 Key Components of Transformers

Transformers consist of several key components that make them highly effective for processing complex datasets, including text and structured data. These components are particularly valuable in fields like cybersecurity, where the ability to identify subtle patterns in large datasets can be the difference between identifying a threat and missing it.

1. Self-Attention Mechanism

The self-attention mechanism is one of the most groundbreaking aspects of the transformer architecture. This mechanism allows the model to evaluate the **importance** of each input element relative to the others, regardless of its position in the sequence. For example, in text data, this allows the model to understand relationships between words, even if they are far apart in a sentence.

In the context of cybersecurity, the self-attention mechanism helps transformers process **vast datasets** such as network logs, threat intelligence reports, and system event logs. It allows the model to focus on **relevant parts of the data**, enabling it to detect anomalies, identify suspicious patterns, or spot malicious behavior that traditional models might overlook. For example, a transformer model could focus on abnormal patterns in network traffic or unusual patterns of user behavior that could indicate a potential **insider threat**.

2. Positional Encoding

Unlike traditional sequence-based models like **RNNs**, which process data in a **sequential manner**, transformers process all input data simultaneously in parallel. However, this parallel processing could cause the model to lose information about the **order** of the input elements. To address this, transformers incorporate **positional encoding**, which provides the model with information about the order of the data.

In cybersecurity, positional encoding becomes crucial when processing data like **network packets**, where the order in which packets arrive or the sequence of events is critical. For example, in a **Denial-of-Service (DoS)** attack, the sequence and frequency of incoming requests matter. Positional encoding helps the model maintain the context of such data and understand the relationship between events in a sequence.

3. Multi-Head Attention

Multi-head attention is another key component of the transformer architecture that enhances its ability to capture complex patterns in the data. Instead of focusing on one part of the data at a time, multi-head attention allows the model to simultaneously focus on multiple parts of the input sequence. This enables the transformer to gain a more comprehensive understanding of the relationships between different elements of the data.

In cybersecurity, this ability is especially valuable when analyzing multi-faceted data sources like **network traffic** or **security logs**. For example, multi-head attention can help the model identify multiple potential attack vectors at once—such as detecting both suspicious traffic patterns and unusual user activity in a system, improving the overall detection of complex threats.

2.3.2 Transformers in Cybersecurity

As transformers have demonstrated remarkable success in NLP tasks like **text generation**, **language translation**, and **question answering**, their application to cybersecurity is rapidly growing. They are being used in several critical areas to enhance the **accuracy**, **efficiency**, and **scalability** of cybersecurity solutions.

1. Threat Detection

Threat detection is one of the most prominent applications of transformers in cybersecurity. With the ability to analyze large datasets quickly and accurately, transformers excel at identifying patterns and detecting anomalies that might indicate an emerging threat. These threats can come in various forms, including **malicious code**, **suspicious network activity**, and **insider threats**.

Transformers can process vast quantities of **textual data**, including **security bulletins**, **social media feeds**, and **internal threat reports**, to detect early signs of threats. By continuously monitoring and analyzing this data, transformers can identify **new attack vectors** before they escalate, helping organizations stay ahead of potential security breaches. Additionally, transformers can also be used to analyze **logs** and **alerts** from multiple security devices and correlate them to detect complex threats, like **multi-stage cyberattacks** or advanced **persistent threats (APTs)**.

Example: A transformer model trained on network logs might be able to identify an emerging **zero-day exploit** based on subtle anomalies in traffic patterns, even if no known signature for the attack exists.

2. Incident Response Automation

Incident response is another area where transformers can significantly improve the efficiency and effectiveness of cybersecurity teams. Transformers can be used to automate responses to certain types of incidents by generating human-like responses, which can assist security teams in identifying, classifying, and responding to threats more quickly.

For example, when a potential **phishing** attack is detected, a transformer model could automatically analyze the threat, classify it, and generate a report detailing the nature of the attack, the affected systems, and recommended remediation steps. This helps reduce the time and effort required for security analysts to respond to incidents, ensuring that organizations can react to threats in real-time.

Furthermore, transformers can generate **automated alerts** that are more comprehensive and context-aware, reducing the risk of false positives and helping security teams prioritize their actions more effectively.

3. Phishing Detection

Phishing attacks continue to be one of the most prevalent and damaging forms of cyberattack. Transformers, particularly models like **GPT** (Generative Pretrained Transformer), are being used to both **detect** and **simulate phishing attempts**.

- **Detection:** Transformers can analyze the content of emails, websites, and messages to identify signs of phishing attempts, such as **suspicious URLs, fake sender addresses**, or manipulative language designed to deceive recipients into clicking malicious links. By processing large volumes of email data, transformers can spot patterns in phishing tactics and detect new phishing schemes that have not been encountered before.

- **Simulation:** Generative transformers like **GPT-3** are used to **create synthetic phishing emails** for training purposes. This allows organizations to prepare their employees for a wide variety of phishing tactics, improving **employee awareness** and reducing the likelihood of successful attacks.

Example: GPT models can be used to generate phishing email templates that are realistic and context-specific, training employees to recognize even the most convincing phishing attempts.

4. Malware Analysis

Transformers can also aid in malware analysis by processing large amounts of **binary data** or **network traffic** to detect the presence of malicious software. By analyzing the behavior of programs and their interaction with system resources, transformers can identify new variants of malware, even those that employ **obfuscation techniques** to avoid detection by traditional signature-based systems.

5. Threat Intelligence and Predictive Analytics

In addition to detecting and responding to known threats, transformers are also being used to analyze **threat intelligence** and generate **predictive insights**. By analyzing data from diverse sources such as **dark web forums**, **threat actor communications**, and **open-source intelligence**, transformers can predict potential future threats and advise on proactive security measures.

Transformers can track the activities of **advanced persistent threats (APTs)** and predict the next steps in their campaigns, giving security teams a valuable edge in the fight against sophisticated adversaries.

2.4 Comparing Generative AI with Traditional AI Approaches

While both **traditional AI** and **generative AI** aim to solve complex problems, they differ fundamentally in their approaches, capabilities, and how they interact with data. Understanding these differences is crucial, especially in fields like **cybersecurity**, where the need for adaptability, data simulation, and quick detection of novel threats has become paramount. This section explores how generative AI compares with traditional AI approaches, highlighting their unique strengths and limitations.

2.4.1 Traditional AI Approaches

Traditional AI refers to well-established models and techniques that have been used for decades to solve a variety of problems. While these approaches have been highly successful in many domains, they are generally limited when it comes to dealing with rapidly evolving and unknown challenges.

1. Supervised Learning

Supervised learning is one of the most widely used techniques in traditional AI. In this approach, AI models are trained using **labeled data**, meaning the input data comes with corresponding outputs or **labels**. The model learns to recognize patterns in the data and map them to the correct outputs.

For example, in cybersecurity, a traditional AI model might be trained using labeled examples of **spam** and **non-spam** emails. The AI will learn to identify characteristics that define each class and apply that knowledge to classify new incoming emails.

Advantages of Supervised Learning in Traditional AI:

- It is effective when there is **sufficient labeled data** available.

- It is highly accurate in environments where the data and labels are **well-defined** and **consistent**.

- The predictions and classifications made by the model are easily interpretable and reliable.

Limitations of Supervised Learning:

- It struggles with **unlabeled data**, meaning it requires extensive human intervention to label large datasets before training.

- It is less effective at handling **novel or unseen threats**, as the model can only make predictions based on previously encountered patterns.

2. Predictive Models

Traditional AI typically relies on **predictive models** to make forecasts or classifications based on patterns found in historical data. These models are built using supervised learning and are designed to predict future outcomes by identifying patterns in past data.

In cybersecurity, predictive models can be used to identify **malicious** or **benign** emails, network traffic, or even user behavior based on historical observations. For instance, a traditional AI model might be trained to predict whether an email is phishing or not based on features such as sender, subject line, and body content.

Advantages of Predictive Models:

- They can predict outcomes based on patterns in large datasets, making them valuable in environments where data is consistent.

- These models are reliable when historical data is abundant and known threats are well-documented.

Limitations of Predictive Models:

- They struggle with detecting new, **previously unseen** types of attacks that were not present in the training data.

- They are **less adaptive** to rapidly changing environments, such as evolving cyber threats.

3. Rule-Based Systems

Traditional AI often uses **rule-based systems**, which operate on predefined sets of rules. These systems take specific inputs and trigger defined actions based on those inputs. For example, in cybersecurity, a rule-based system might identify malicious network traffic by matching it against a set of known attack signatures or patterns.

Advantages of Rule-Based Systems:

- Highly effective for detecting **known threats** with well-established patterns or signatures.

- They offer **predictable behavior**, with clear cause-and-effect relationships between input and output.

Limitations of Rule-Based Systems:

- They are ineffective at detecting **unknown** or **emerging threats** that have not been included in the predefined rules.

- Maintaining and updating the rules can be labor-intensive and may require **constant tuning** to keep up with new attack methods.

2.4.2 Generative AI Approaches

Generative AI, on the other hand, represents a significant departure from traditional AI methods. Instead of merely identifying patterns within existing data, generative AI focuses on **creating new data** and generating synthetic representations of real-world scenarios.

1. Unsupervised and Semi-Supervised Learning

Unlike traditional AI, which heavily relies on supervised learning (labeled data), **generative AI** can thrive in environments where labeled data is scarce. It uses **unsupervised** or **semi-supervised learning**, where the model learns patterns, structures, and relationships from the data without needing explicit labels.

In cybersecurity, generative AI can be used to identify **anomalies** and **unknown attack vectors** by analyzing **unlabeled data**. For example, generative models like **autoencoders** or **GANs** can detect subtle deviations in network traffic that could indicate an emerging cyberattack.

Advantages of Unsupervised Learning:

- It can learn from **unlabeled** data, which is particularly useful when there is no predefined classification or when labeled data is unavailable.

- It can identify **novel** patterns or threats that were not part of the original training dataset.

- It does not require human intervention to label data, making it scalable and efficient.

2. Data Generation

Generative AI is unique in its ability to **generate new data** rather than simply analyzing or predicting based on existing data. Through techniques like **Generative Adversarial Networks (GANs)** or **variational autoencoders (VAEs)**, generative AI models can produce realistic synthetic data that mimics the properties of real-world data.

For example, in cybersecurity, generative AI can create synthetic **attack scenarios** or **malicious data** to train threat detection models. This ability to generate new data helps the AI model understand a wider range of attack patterns and improve its ability to detect previously unseen threats.

Advantages of Data Generation:

- It allows the model to be **exposed to a broader range of scenarios**, including rare and unseen events, helping it generalize better.

- It can simulate new threats, making it particularly useful for testing and training models in dynamic environments like cybersecurity.

Limitations of Data Generation:

- The quality of the generated data is highly dependent on the **training** of the generative model. If the model is poorly trained, the generated data might not be representative of real-world scenarios.

- There is a risk that **fake data** could be generated, leading to potential overfitting if not properly managed.

2.4.3 Key Differences

There are several key differences between **traditional AI** and **generative AI**, especially in how they handle data, adapt to new challenges, and contribute to solving complex problems like those found in cybersecurity.

1. Adaptability

- **Generative AI** is far more **adaptable** to novel or unknown threats. It can generate new data and identify previously unseen attack patterns, which is crucial in dynamic environments like cybersecurity where threats are constantly evolving.

- **Traditional AI** is more reliant on **predefined datasets** and **rules**, making it less adaptable to new or unknown threats. It struggles to recognize novel attack methods unless it has been specifically trained on similar patterns.

2. Data Usage

- **Generative AI** excels at **creating synthetic data** that can be used for training, testing, and simulation. This ability to generate new data helps overcome the limitations of having limited or biased real-world data.

- **Traditional AI** is more **dependent on existing data** for training and pattern recognition. It requires large amounts of high-quality labeled data, which can be difficult to acquire in fields like cybersecurity.

3. Learning Mechanisms

- **Generative AI** is capable of working with both **labeled and unlabeled data**, and it learns to generate new, realistic examples that can be used to simulate various scenarios.

- **Traditional AI** typically uses **supervised learning** and **predictive models**, which require a significant amount of labeled data to make predictions or classifications based on existing patterns.

4. Threat Detection

- **Generative AI** is better equipped for detecting **unknown or evolving threats** because of its ability to simulate and predict new data patterns, which can be used to detect novel cybersecurity attacks.

- **Traditional AI**, while effective at identifying known threats based on predefined rules or patterns, struggles to detect new or unknown attacks that it has not encountered during training.

2.5 The Role of Synthetic Data in Training AI Models

In the development of AI models, especially those aimed at tackling complex challenges like cybersecurity, data is the foundation upon which models are built. However, obtaining real-world data for training purposes can often be challenging—whether due to scarcity, sensitivity, or difficulty in acquiring high-quality, representative datasets. This is where **synthetic data** comes into play. By simulating real-world conditions, synthetic data offers a powerful way to enhance AI model training while sidestepping the limitations of real data.

2.5.1 What is Synthetic Data?

Synthetic data is artificially generated information designed to mirror the statistical properties, patterns, and structure of real-world data. Rather than relying on actual observations or real-time inputs, synthetic data is created using **generative models**, such as **Generative Adversarial Networks (GANs)** or **variational autoencoders (VAEs)**. These models produce data that resembles the original dataset in terms of its key characteristics but is entirely synthetic, meaning it does not include any actual sensitive or identifiable information.

For example, in cybersecurity, synthetic data can be generated to replicate network traffic, malicious attack patterns, or even user behavior. This simulated data can be used to train AI systems without the need for real user data or actual attacks, making it both **safe** and **secure** for use in testing, validation, and training purposes.

Key characteristics of synthetic data include:

- **Statistical resemblance** to real-world data (e.g., distribution, correlation, patterns)

- **Anonymity**, as no real user or organizational data is involved

- **Flexibility**, allows it to cover a broad spectrum of scenarios, including rare or previously unseen events.

2.5.2 Importance of Synthetic Data in Cybersecurity

In cybersecurity, synthetic data plays a critical role in overcoming some of the most pressing challenges faced by security teams and AI models:

1. Augmenting Training Data

For cybersecurity AI models to effectively detect and respond to cyberattacks, they need access to a large and varied set of training data. However, real-world data can sometimes be scarce, especially when dealing with rare or novel attack patterns. Synthetic data allows organizations to generate massive amounts of **attack data** that can be used to train threat detection models, providing AI systems with exposure to various types of attacks that may not be well-represented in historical datasets.

For instance, if a new type of malware or advanced persistent threat (APT) is emerging, there may not be enough data to train models to detect it. In such cases, synthetic data can simulate these attacks, enabling AI models to learn the characteristics and behaviors of these threats before they even occur in the real world.

2. Privacy Preservation

Privacy concerns are a significant barrier in many industries when it comes to using real-world data for training AI models. In sensitive sectors like **healthcare, finance**, or **government**, data often contains personally identifiable information (PII), protected health information (PHI), or confidential financial records. Using real data to train AI models can introduce significant risks of privacy breaches and legal violations.

Synthetic data offers a solution to this problem. Since it is artificially created and does not involve any real individual's information, it can be used to train AI models without compromising privacy. In cybersecurity, synthetic data allows security teams to build threat detection models using realistic data without the need to expose sensitive or private information.

3. Testing Defenses

Synthetic data is invaluable for testing and **simulating different attack scenarios**. In cybersecurity, where threats evolve rapidly, it's crucial for organizations to test their defenses against emerging attack methods. With synthetic data, organizations can create a wide variety of **realistic attack scenarios** that replicate sophisticated or unusual tactics, techniques, and procedures (TTPs) that may not yet be captured in real-world attack data.

For example, synthetic data can be used to simulate a Distributed Denial-of-Service (DDoS) attack, ransomware deployment, or an insider threat scenario. By running these simulations in a controlled environment, security teams can evaluate the effectiveness of their defense strategies, identify potential weaknesses, and fine-tune their systems before an actual attack takes place.

2.5.3 Benefits of Synthetic Data

The use of synthetic data brings several advantages, particularly in areas like cybersecurity where high-quality data is crucial, yet challenging to acquire.

1. Improved Accuracy

By leveraging synthetic data, AI models can be trained on more **diverse**, **representative**, and **comprehensive** datasets. This is especially beneficial in cybersecurity, where threats are constantly evolving. Models that use synthetic data can be exposed to a broader range of attack scenarios, enabling them to better recognize unusual or emerging threats. As a result, these models are more accurate in detecting and mitigating attacks in real-world settings, as they have been trained on a wide variety of potential scenarios.

For example, by generating synthetic data that mimics various **phishing attempts**, **malware variants**, and **zero-day vulnerabilities**, AI models can learn to spot these threats with greater precision, even if such attacks have not yet been encountered in historical data.

2. Cost-Effectiveness

Acquiring real-world data, especially in cybersecurity, is often **expensive** and **logistically complex**. Sensitive data must be carefully managed to ensure privacy and regulatory compliance, which can incur significant costs. Furthermore, collecting high-quality attack data is not always feasible, particularly for **rare events**.

Synthetic data provides a **cost-effective** alternative, as it can be generated in large volumes without the need for complex data acquisition processes. Organizations can avoid the expense of purchasing real-world datasets, or the challenge of managing and anonymizing sensitive data. This makes synthetic data an affordable and scalable solution, particularly for startups or smaller companies that may lack the resources to collect comprehensive real-world datasets.

3. Speed and Flexibility

Creating real-world datasets often takes time—whether through data collection efforts, logging events, or waiting for attacks to happen. In contrast, synthetic data can be generated **quickly** and **on demand**, providing organizations with the ability to rapidly produce data for training, testing, and simulation purposes. This is particularly important in industries like cybersecurity, where speed is critical in responding to new threats.

Additionally, synthetic data can be **customized** to represent any scenario, attack vector, or system behavior, allowing organizations to simulate a broad range of conditions that might be difficult to recreate with real data. This flexibility is valuable in ensuring that AI models are trained to detect not only known threats but also **novel, unknown attacks**.

4. Scalability

The scalability of synthetic data makes it an essential tool for large-scale AI model training. In traditional data acquisition processes, obtaining sufficient data to train complex AI models can be a barrier. Synthetic data, however, can be generated in vast quantities, enabling AI models to scale their learning capabilities without being constrained by the availability of real-world data.

This scalability ensures that AI models are continuously evolving, improving, and adapting to new threats as they arise. With synthetic data, organizations can create datasets that grow with the changing threat landscape, ensuring that their AI systems are always up to date.

2.6 Ethical Considerations in Developing Generative AI Systems

Generative AI presents unprecedented opportunities to enhance cybersecurity; however, its power and capabilities raise several ethical challenges that must be addressed. While the technology has the potential to revolutionize threat detection, incident response, and even attack simulations, its misuse, inherent biases, and lack of transparency can introduce significant risks. Ethical considerations must be embedded in the development process to ensure that generative AI systems are used responsibly and do not contribute to harmful or malicious activities.

2.6.1 Misuse of Generative AI

One of the most pressing ethical concerns surrounding generative AI is its potential for misuse. The very capabilities that make it powerful for cybersecurity—such as the ability to generate realistic content—can also be exploited for malicious purposes. For example, generative AI can be used to create highly realistic **deepfakes**, which could be deployed to impersonate individuals in fraudulent activities, such as **identity theft**, **social engineering attacks**, or **political manipulation**. Similarly, **AI-generated phishing emails** or malicious scripts could be produced with greater ease, increasing the sophistication of cyberattacks. This raises alarms about the widespread abuse of AI-generated content to manipulate public opinion, deceive individuals or organizations, and conduct **disinformation campaigns**.

As generative AI continues to improve, the distinction between authentic and AI-generated content becomes more blurred, making it harder for individuals and even AI-based security systems to differentiate between legitimate and malicious materials. This misuse presents a significant ethical dilemma, as the technology can be leveraged for harm, with repercussions ranging from financial loss to compromising national security.

2.6.2 Bias in Training Data

Another critical ethical issue arises from the **bias** inherent in training data used for generative AI systems. These biases can manifest in various forms, including **racial, gender, geographical**, or **socioeconomic** bias, all of which can skew the decision-making process of AI models. In cybersecurity, biased training data could result in **false positives**, where benign activities are incorrectly flagged as malicious, or **false negatives**, where actual threats are not detected.

For instance, a generative AI model trained on data that predominantly reflects specific geographic regions or user behaviors might fail to detect cyberattacks or malicious activity that falls outside of those patterns. Similarly, if an AI system's training set reflects biased data about certain online behaviors or cultures, it may inadvertently miss attacks that don't match the model's learned patterns. The ethical concern here is that biased AI can lead to **discriminatory outcomes** and undermine the effectiveness and fairness of cybersecurity solutions.

To mitigate these risks, cybersecurity professionals need to ensure that training datasets are representative of diverse real-world scenarios. This includes accounting for various attack methods across different regions, industries, and systems, and making sure that AI models are trained in a way that reflects the complexity and global nature of cyber threats.

2.6.3 Accountability and Transparency

As generative AI systems become more autonomous and capable of making decisions in real-time, **accountability** and **transparency** become critical concerns. When AI systems are responsible for detecting threats or generating responses, it is essential to determine who is accountable for their actions, especially in cases where an AI system fails or makes an incorrect decision.

For example, if a generative AI model mistakenly flags a legitimate user action as a cyberattack, causing disruption or financial loss, who is responsible for the error? Should it be the developers of the AI system, the organization using the AI, or the AI itself? This raises difficult ethical questions about responsibility and liability. Clear accountability structures need to be in place to ensure that the stakeholders involved in AI decision-making can be held responsible for its impact.

In addition to accountability, **transparency** is a critical ethical issue in AI development. Many generative AI models, especially deep learning models, are considered **"black-box"** models, meaning that it is difficult to understand how the system arrives at its conclusions. In high-stakes areas like cybersecurity, this lack of transparency is particularly troubling, as security professionals need to trust and understand the decision-making process of AI systems to make informed choices.

For instance, if a generative AI model flags a new attack as a potential threat, security analysts need to be able to understand how the AI arrived at this conclusion to assess whether the alert is valid. Without transparency, AI systems may inadvertently make decisions that are difficult to challenge, leading to **unintended consequences**, such as false positives, overlooked threats, or ethical violations.

2.6.4 Guidelines for Ethical AI Development

To ensure that generative AI systems are developed and deployed ethically, it is essential to establish comprehensive guidelines and regulatory frameworks. These frameworks should be designed to promote **transparency, accountability**, and **fairness** in AI development. They should also ensure that AI systems are used in a manner that aligns with societal values and legal standards.

Key guidelines for ethical AI development include:

- **Bias Mitigation:** Ensuring that AI models are trained on diverse, representative datasets that account for a broad spectrum of potential attack vectors, user behaviors, and environments. This will help to minimize the risk of biased outcomes.

- **Transparency in Decision-Making:** Advocating for the development of AI systems that allow for clear and understandable explanations of their decision-making processes, especially in critical applications like cybersecurity. This can help security professionals understand and trust the AI system's actions.

- **Accountability Structures:** Establishing clear accountability mechanisms, so that if an AI system causes harm, there are well-defined procedures for determining responsibility and addressing the consequences. This could involve collaboration between developers, users, and regulatory bodies.

- **Ethical Use of Technology:** Generative AI systems should be designed with ethical considerations in mind, such as preventing misuse for criminal activities like identity theft, fraud, or cyberattacks. Developers must also consider how their systems might inadvertently contribute to harmful outcomes and actively work to minimize such risks.

Furthermore, collaboration between **governments**, **academic institutions**, and **private enterprises** is essential to create globally accepted ethical standards and regulations for AI technologies. Ongoing audits and evaluations of AI systems' impact on society will also play a key role in maintaining ethical practices and ensuring that these systems are not misused or exploited.

Conclusion

In this chapter, we have explored the foundational principles behind **Generative AI** technologies, delving into key mechanisms such as **Generative Adversarial Networks (GANs)**, **Transformers**, and the role of **synthetic data** in training AI models. Each of these technologies plays a pivotal role in revolutionizing cybersecurity by enabling organizations to tackle emerging threats more proactively, generate high-quality training datasets, and automate complex tasks that were once human-dependent.

Generative AI's adaptability in simulating attack scenarios, detecting novel threats, and enhancing incident response systems has positioned it as an invaluable asset in the cybersecurity arsenal. However, as with any powerful technology, there are inherent challenges and ethical concerns that must be addressed, including **misuse**, **bias**, and **lack of transparency**. Striking a balance between harnessing its transformative potential and ensuring ethical use is essential for its successful integration into cybersecurity practices.

In the upcoming chapters, we will continue to explore the **real-world applications** of these generative AI technologies in cybersecurity, how they are being implemented across various industries, and the evolving regulatory and ethical frameworks necessary to safeguard their deployment. As the landscape of cyber threats grows more complex, understanding the core technologies behind generative AI will be essential for businesses and security professionals alike to stay ahead of potential risks while ensuring that these innovations are used responsibly and effectively.

Chapter 3: Generative AI Applications in Cybersecurity

Introduction

Generative AI has emerged as a revolutionary technology in the cybersecurity domain, offering new approaches to threat detection, vulnerability management, and the prevention of social engineering attacks. By leveraging advanced machine learning models and deep learning techniques, generative AI helps organizations stay ahead of cyber threats, identify vulnerabilities proactively, and enhance their overall security posture. This chapter explores the various applications of generative AI in cybersecurity, focusing on its impact on threat detection, malware analysis, vulnerability management, and more.

3.1 Proactive Threat Detection Using Generative AI Models

Proactive threat detection is one of the most transformative applications of generative AI in the cybersecurity domain. In traditional cybersecurity models, the focus has largely been on reactive strategies. Security systems generally work by responding to detected threats after they have already been identified or after damage has occurred. While this can help mitigate some threats, it often leads to delayed responses and greater damage, as attackers frequently have time to infiltrate networks and systems before detection. Generative AI shifts this paradigm by enabling proactive threat detection, allowing organizations to identify potential threats and vulnerabilities before cybercriminals can exploit them. This helps organizations better anticipate attacks and address weaknesses proactively rather than waiting for them to manifest in damaging ways.

Generative AI's ability to synthesize realistic attack data, predict evolving threats, and continuously learn from both known and unknown attack patterns allows security teams to stay ahead of emerging cyber threats. The following sections delve deeper into the key components that power generative AI's role in proactive threat detection.

Key Components of Proactive Threat Detection:

1. **Data Generation**:

   One of the most important aspects of generative AI is its ability to **generate realistic datasets** that replicate normal and abnormal system behaviors. Traditional detection methods primarily depend on datasets gathered from real-world attacks or system logs, which may be incomplete or outdated, especially in the case of zero-day vulnerabilities or new types of threats. Generative AI models can synthesize large volumes of data that simulate a wide range of scenarios, including normal traffic patterns, as well as potential malicious activities such as **data breaches, malware infections**, or **unauthorized access**. This data is invaluable for training machine learning models and **intrusion detection systems (IDS)**, enabling them to detect new types of attacks and previously unseen attack vectors.

   By simulating attack data, generative AI can create datasets that allow detection systems to recognize potential threats before they happen in real-world environments. This helps organizations build defenses that can **anticipate and respond to zero-day exploits** and other evolving attack methods, reducing the risks posed by previously unknown vulnerabilities.

2. **Anomaly Detection**:

   Another powerful feature of generative AI is its ability to establish baseline behaviors within a network or system, enabling it to detect anomalies or suspicious activities. In cybersecurity, **anomaly detection** is a critical function that identifies deviations from established norms, which could indicate an impending attack.

Generative AI can analyze historical data on **network traffic**, **system processes**, and **user activity** to create models of what constitutes normal behavior. Once these models are established, any deviation from these patterns can be flagged as potentially malicious. This is particularly useful for detecting threats like **data exfiltration**, where attackers attempt to send sensitive data out of an organization, or **brute-force attacks**, where attackers attempt to gain unauthorized access by guessing credentials repeatedly. Generative AI models can quickly spot these deviations, whether they are minor or major, and flag them for further investigation.

Moreover, generative AI can learn and adapt to these normal and abnormal behaviors in real-time. As the system receives more data and encounters new types of attacks, it continually refines its understanding of what constitutes **normal operation** and what signifies an attack, allowing it to better detect emerging threats without relying solely on predefined signatures.

3. **Threat Simulation:**

   Threat simulation is one of the most innovative applications of generative AI in cybersecurity. Rather than waiting for an attack to occur, generative AI can simulate potential cyberattacks, including **Advanced Persistent Threats (APTs)**, **ransomware**, or **insider threats**, to test a security system's effectiveness. Generative AI creates **synthetic attack data** that mimics real-world attack behaviors and tactics, including those that are evolving or yet to be observed.

   Security teams can leverage these simulations to understand the attack vectors that are most likely to be exploited, assess the performance of their **detection systems**, and validate their defenses in a controlled environment. For example, by generating synthetic data that simulates an **APT** using multiple stages of an attack (reconnaissance, lateral movement, exfiltration), security teams can measure the effectiveness of their intrusion detection tools and response protocols without the risks associated with live data.

Generative AI also allows security professionals to simulate the latest **tactics, techniques, and procedures (TTPs)** that adversaries may use, ensuring that the security systems are always up-to-date with the latest threats. This makes generative AI a vital tool in enhancing **red team** and **blue team** exercises, which test the offensive and defensive capabilities of an organization's cybersecurity infrastructure.

4. **Enhanced Threat Intelligence**:

Threat intelligence refers to the information collected about potential or existing cyber threats that can help organizations anticipate and defend against attacks. Traditionally, this intelligence comes from a variety of sources, such as **security feeds, threat reports**, and **malware analysis**. However, the increasing complexity of cyberattacks means that traditional sources of threat intelligence may no longer be sufficient on their own.

Generative AI can enhance threat intelligence by producing **synthetic threat intelligence reports** based on historical data patterns, attack trends, and evolving attack techniques. By analyzing data from various sources and using generative models to synthesize plausible future attack scenarios, AI can predict potential threats and provide actionable insights for proactive defense measures.

For example, generative AI can analyze a set of recent cyberattacks, identify patterns in attacker behavior, and generate

intelligence reports that predict how these tactics may evolve. This information can help security teams prepare for future attacks by adjusting their defenses to the most likely scenarios. Additionally, AI-generated threat intelligence can be used to **automatically update firewalls, intrusion prevention systems (IPS),** and other security tools with the latest attack signatures and defensive measures, ensuring that the organization is always prepared for emerging threats.

5. **Continuous Learning and Adaptation:**

One of the most significant advantages of generative AI in proactive threat detection is its ability to **continuously learn and adapt** as it encounters new data and attack patterns. Unlike traditional systems, which rely on fixed, signature-based models or predefined rules, generative AI models evolve over time as they process new information.

With each new attack or anomaly detected, generative AI systems refine their models of normal behavior and update their threat detection capabilities. This **adaptive learning** helps ensure that security systems remain effective even as attackers change their tactics and methods. The AI is not limited to a fixed set of attack signatures, meaning it can recognize and respond to previously unseen attack methods, **zero-day vulnerabilities**, and evolving **cyber threats**.

This capability is especially crucial in today's fast-changing threat landscape, where cybercriminals are constantly innovating and developing new tactics. Generative AI's ability to anticipate, learn, and adapt makes it an essential tool for **future-proofing** an organization's cybersecurity defenses.

3.2 Automated Analysis of Malware and Cyber Threats

The rapid evolution of malware and cyber threats is one of the most significant challenges facing cybersecurity professionals today. Malware analysis involves examining malicious code to understand its functionality, origin, and behavior, which is essential for developing effective defenses against cyberattacks. However, the increasing sophistication and frequency of cyber threats, along with the growing number of attack vectors, have made traditional, manual analysis methods insufficient to keep up with the pace of new malware development.

Generative AI offers a revolutionary approach to automating malware analysis, enhancing the ability to quickly identify new threats, predict future attack vectors, and adapt to the constantly evolving landscape of cyber threats. By leveraging AI-powered automation, security teams can significantly accelerate their ability to detect, analyze, and respond to sophisticated malware and cyber threats.

How Generative AI Enhances Malware Analysis:

1. **Malware Generation for Training**

   One of the most valuable capabilities of generative AI is its ability to **synthesize realistic malware samples** that replicate the characteristics of real-world threats. This is particularly useful for training security tools and AI models to recognize new variants of malware, including highly evasive **polymorphic** and **metamorphic malware**.

   o **Polymorphic Malware**: Polymorphic malware constantly changes its appearance to avoid detection by signature-based security tools. Generative AI can create synthetic variants of polymorphic malware, helping detection systems recognize its evolving forms.

   o **Metamorphic Malware**: Similar to polymorphic malware, metamorphic malware modifies its code with each iteration, making it even harder to identify using traditional detection methods. Generative AI can simulate these modifications, ensuring that detection systems remain effective as malware evolves.

By generating artificial malware samples, generative AI provides a constant stream of new training data for AI models, helping them stay up-to-date with the latest malware techniques and detection strategies.

2. **Automated Code Analysis**

   Malware code analysis is a critical part of understanding how malware operates and devising methods to neutralize it. However, with the constant development of new malware variants, manually analyzing each piece of code is becoming increasingly difficult.

   Generative AI can be trained to automatically generate **plausible variants of malicious code**, based on patterns observed in existing malware samples. This allows security tools to analyze these generated variants and gain insights into how malware evolves over time. For example, AI can generate mutated code that might attempt to bypass common defense mechanisms, such as **anti-sandbox** or **anti-virus** evasion techniques.

   This automated analysis enables security teams to quickly identify novel malware variants, even those that use advanced evasion tactics, without the need for labor-intensive manual intervention. By constantly training AI models with new variants, security systems can continuously adapt to the latest malware evolution.

3. **Behavioral Analysis**

   Traditional malware analysis methods often focus on examining **static code**, which provides limited insight into how the malware will behave in a live environment. Generative AI takes this a step further by enabling **behavioral analysis** of malware in dynamic environments.

Rather than just analyzing the static code of malware, generative AI can simulate how the malware will behave once executed in a target environment. This includes modeling how the malware interacts with:

- o **System processes**: Malware can modify or disrupt normal system operations. By simulating its interaction with the operating system, generative AI can identify behaviors such as **resource hijacking**, **file modification**, or **system shutdowns**.

- o **Memory**: Malware often resides in system memory to execute its payload. By simulating malware's memory interactions, AI can identify **memory-based attacks** such as **buffer overflows** or **code injection**.

- o **Network traffic**: Malware may attempt to communicate with external servers or exfiltrate data over the network. Generative AI can simulate how malware interacts with network traffic, identifying patterns such as **C&C (command and control) communication**, **data exfiltration**, or **DDoS (Distributed Denial of Service)** attack traffic.

This **dynamic analysis** provides a more comprehensive understanding of how malware functions in real-world environments and helps identify potential threats that traditional static analysis methods may miss. It also allows security tools to anticipate the behavior of new and unknown malware variants, improving detection and response times.

4. **Prediction of Future Threats**

One of the most powerful features of generative AI in malware analysis is its ability to predict the **future evolution of cyber threats**. By analyzing historical malware data and identifying recurring attack patterns, AI models can forecast the emergence of new threats, attack techniques, and tactics. This predictive capability is invaluable for organizations looking to stay ahead of cybercriminals and proactively bolster their defenses.

- o **Emerging Malware Trends**: Generative AI can identify trends in malware development, such as the rise of new evasion techniques, encryption methods, or attack vectors. For instance, it can predict the development of new **ransomware variants** or identify new **phishing** tactics that are gaining popularity in the cybercriminal community.

- o **New Exploitation Methods**: Generative AI can analyze vulnerabilities and predict how attackers might exploit them in future attacks. This allows security teams to prepare their defenses ahead of time by patching vulnerabilities or deploying appropriate countermeasures.

- o **Evolving Threat Landscape**: As cybercriminals adapt and refine their attack strategies, generative AI can forecast how attacks will evolve and recommend new defense strategies. For example, it may predict the increased use of **AI-powered malware** and suggest new techniques for detecting and mitigating such threats.

By leveraging these predictions, security teams can implement proactive measures to protect against emerging threats, such as updating malware signatures, strengthening defenses, or improving detection capabilities.

5. **Reducing Analyst Workload and Accelerating Response**

One of the key advantages of using generative AI in malware analysis is its ability to **automate repetitive tasks**, significantly reducing the workload of human analysts. Traditional malware analysis requires analysts to manually dissect malware samples, which can be time-consuming and prone to human error. Generative AI automates much of this process, from generating synthetic malware samples for training to analyzing new malware variants in real-time.

This automation not only accelerates the identification of new threats but also allows human analysts to focus on more complex tasks, such as responding to advanced threats, creating new defense strategies, and refining detection techniques. As a result, security teams can respond to cyber threats faster and more efficiently, reducing the impact of potential attacks.

6. **Enhanced Collaboration Between Human and AI Systems**

Generative AI doesn't replace human analysts; rather, it **augments their capabilities**. AI can handle the bulk of repetitive tasks, such as generating malware variants or scanning for known threat patterns, while human analysts focus on interpreting the results and developing sophisticated countermeasures.

This collaboration between AI and human experts helps ensure that cybersecurity systems remain effective even as malware evolves. Analysts can work alongside AI-powered tools to improve threat detection accuracy, develop new detection algorithms, and fine-tune AI models to handle complex threats that require human judgment.

3.3 Enhancing Vulnerability Management with Generative AI

Vulnerability management is a critical aspect of cybersecurity that involves identifying, assessing, and mitigating security weaknesses within an organization's systems, networks, and applications. The process is designed to minimize the risk of cyberattacks by proactively addressing potential points of failure before they can be exploited. However, as the complexity and scale of IT environments grow, traditional vulnerability management methods are becoming increasingly insufficient, often leaving systems exposed to new and emerging threats.

Generative AI offers a transformative solution for enhancing vulnerability management by improving the speed, accuracy, and effectiveness of vulnerability identification, risk assessment, and remediation. With the ability to simulate attack scenarios and provide insights into exploitation paths, generative AI helps organizations stay ahead of potential threats and address vulnerabilities more efficiently.

Applications of Generative AI in Vulnerability Management:

1. **Vulnerability Identification**

   One of the most important roles of generative AI in vulnerability management is **identifying previously unknown vulnerabilities**. Traditional vulnerability scanning tools rely on signature-based detection methods and predefined databases of known vulnerabilities, often missing newly discovered or zero-day vulnerabilities.

   Generative AI can overcome this limitation by **analyzing large codebases, system configurations, and network infrastructures** to identify potential vulnerabilities that conventional tools might not flag. Through its ability to synthesize synthetic vulnerabilities, AI can simulate potential weaknesses in systems and highlight those weak points that attackers could exploit.

   o **Code Analysis**: Generative AI can analyze software code and configurations to find vulnerabilities such as buffer overflows, improper error handling, or insecure APIs that traditional static analysis tools may overlook.

   o **Network Configuration**: By simulating network traffic and system interactions, AI can identify misconfigurations or weak access controls in network infrastructure, providing insight into potential exposure points.

- o **Database and Application Layer**: Generative AI can also analyze database schemas, stored procedures, and application code to detect SQL injection vulnerabilities, cross-site scripting (XSS), or insecure data storage practices.

By automatically generating and flagging potential vulnerabilities, generative AI accelerates the vulnerability discovery process and uncovers hidden weaknesses that might otherwise remain undetected.

2. **Prioritization of Risks**

Once vulnerabilities are identified, the next critical step in vulnerability management is **prioritizing remediation efforts**. Not all vulnerabilities present the same level of risk to an organization, so security teams must assess each vulnerability based on its **severity, exploitability**, and potential impact on business operations.

Generative AI can help prioritize risks by assessing vulnerabilities according to several factors:

- o **Exploitability**: Generative AI can predict how easily a vulnerability can be exploited by an attacker. For example, AI can evaluate whether a vulnerability requires specialized knowledge or tools to exploit, or if it could be easily leveraged in an automated attack.

- o **Asset Value**: The value of the affected asset also plays a key role in determining risk. AI models can be trained to assess the importance of the asset within the organization's infrastructure, ensuring that vulnerabilities in critical systems or high-value assets are prioritized.

- o **Business Impact**: Generative AI can analyze the potential consequences of a successful attack exploiting the vulnerability, such as loss of data, financial impact, reputational damage, or service disruption.

By combining these factors into an integrated risk assessment model, generative AI helps organizations focus their resources on the most critical vulnerabilities, ensuring that the most severe threats are addressed first.

3. **Predicting Attack Scenarios**

One of the most powerful capabilities of generative AI is its ability to **simulate attack scenarios**. After vulnerabilities are identified, it is important to understand how an attacker might exploit these vulnerabilities in the real world. Generative AI can generate synthetic attack paths and tactics, helping security teams understand the **chain of events** that could lead to a successful breach.

- o **Attack Path Simulation**: By generating synthetic attack paths, generative AI can illustrate how an attacker might move through an organization's systems, from an initial point of compromise to lateral movement and eventual data exfiltration or system takeover. This allows security teams to anticipate potential attack scenarios and fortify critical systems.

- o **Exploitation Simulation**: AI can simulate how specific vulnerabilities might be exploited, providing insights into the tools and techniques an attacker would use. This could include simulating **SQL injections, privilege escalation**, or **social engineering attacks** that exploit weak points in organizational procedures.

- o **Multi-stage Attacks**: Generative AI can also predict multi-stage attack campaigns, such as Advanced

Persistent Threats (APTs), which may involve a combination of tactics such as **phishing** for initial access, **lateral movement** within the network, and **data exfiltration** over time. By simulating these sophisticated attack strategies, AI helps organizations prepare more robust defenses.

Predicting how vulnerabilities might be exploited in real-world attacks enables organizations to take more proactive measures to block potential threats before they can escalate.

4. **Automated Patch Management**

After vulnerabilities are identified and prioritized, the next step is implementing **remediation** to fix those vulnerabilities. One of the challenges in patch management is ensuring that patches are applied quickly and efficiently without causing disruptions to critical systems or applications.

Generative AI can help streamline the patch management process by **generating automated patching strategies**. The AI can simulate the application of security patches and updates in a controlled environment to evaluate their effectiveness and ensure that they do not cause unintended side effects. This includes:

o **Patch Testing**: Generative AI can simulate the application of patches in virtual environments, testing for compatibility issues and unintended consequences. This ensures that patches do not interfere with the normal functioning of critical systems or applications.

o **Deployment Strategies**: AI can generate deployment strategies to roll out patches in stages, reducing the risk of widespread system downtime. By simulating patch rollouts, AI can help identify the optimal approach to applying patches to large, complex networks.

o **Patch Impact Assessment:** Generative AI can evaluate the potential impact of each patch on business operations, helping prioritize which patches should be deployed first and which can be delayed until later.

Automating the patch management process with generative AI ensures that security patches are applied quickly and without disrupting operations, reducing the window of exposure to attackers.

5. **Proactive Defense Strategies**

Generative AI can also assist in the development of **proactive defense strategies** by generating synthetic threat data that can be used to strengthen systems against vulnerabilities. For example, AI can generate simulated attack traffic that mimics real-world attack patterns, allowing security teams to test their defenses against the latest tactics and techniques.

By continuously feeding security systems with synthetic attack data, generative AI helps ensure that defenses are always up-to-date and capable of handling the latest threats. This enables organizations to respond to emerging vulnerabilities more quickly and effectively, reducing the overall risk of a successful cyberattack.

3.4 Social Engineering Prevention Using Generative AI

Social engineering is a psychological manipulation technique used by attackers to exploit human behavior and gain unauthorized access to systems, sensitive data, or physical locations. Unlike technical vulnerabilities, social engineering attacks target the human element, making them harder to detect and defend against using traditional security measures. **Phishing**, **spear-phishing**, **vishing** (voice phishing), and **SMiShing** (SMS phishing) are common forms of social engineering attacks that rely on deception, trust exploitation, and urgency to manipulate individuals into taking harmful actions.

Generative AI can play a pivotal role in preventing and mitigating these attacks by simulating realistic attack scenarios, generating synthetic phishing content, and enhancing employee training and awareness. By automating the creation of attack simulations and training exercises, generative AI helps organizations create a more resilient defense against social engineering threats.

How Generative AI Helps in Social Engineering Prevention

1. **Phishing Simulation**

   Phishing attacks, where cybercriminals craft deceptive emails to trick recipients into revealing sensitive information, are one of the most widespread forms of social engineering. **Generative AI** can help prevent these attacks by **automatically generating highly convincing phishing emails** that mimic the tactics used by cybercriminals. These emails are designed to look like legitimate communication, including authentic logos, brand language, and personalized details that make them appear real.

   o **Synthetic Phishing Emails**: Generative AI can generate a wide variety of phishing email types, including spear-phishing emails that are highly targeted and tailored to specific individuals or roles within the organization. This helps test the susceptibility of different user groups to specific phishing techniques.

   o **Contextual Customization**: AI can create phishing scenarios based on the organization's current activities, such as fake invoices, fake security alerts, or bogus promotions, mimicking real-life contexts where employees may be more likely to fall victim to phishing attempts.

   o **Comprehensive Training**: These phishing simulations can be deployed to employees as part of training programs or regular security assessments, helping staff recognize the characteristics of phishing emails, such as suspicious links, odd sender addresses, and grammatical errors.

Regular phishing simulations conducted with the help of generative AI can significantly improve **employee awareness** and reduce the likelihood of successful phishing attacks.

2. **Employee Training**

A **well-trained workforce** is one of the most effective defenses against social engineering attacks. Generative AI enhances employee training by creating **realistic social engineering scenarios** that mimic the full range of tactics used by cybercriminals.

- o **Diverse Attack Vectors**: In addition to phishing, AI can generate training scenarios that simulate other social engineering tactics like **vishing** (voice phishing), **SMiShing** (SMS phishing), **pretexting**, and **baiting**. These simulated attacks educate employees on how to identify suspicious behavior across multiple communication channels, such as phone calls, text messages, and emails.

- o **Scenario-Based Learning**: Generative AI can craft dynamic and varied training exercises that engage employees in **real-time decision-making** during simulated attacks. For example, an employee may be asked to respond to a phone call or a text message that mimics a vishing attempt, helping them practice identifying and responding to such threats.

- o **Behavioral Feedback**: AI-driven training tools can provide immediate feedback to employees on their actions, pointing out when they fall for a phishing attempt or fail to report suspicious behavior. This personalized feedback helps employees improve their awareness and security posture over time.

Through AI-powered training, employees develop the skills needed to spot and respond to social engineering attempts effectively, ultimately improving an organization's overall **human-layer security**.

3. **Automated Response Generation**

Once an organization has detected a social engineering attack, it is essential to respond quickly and effectively to mitigate any damage. **Generative AI** can assist in creating **automated response strategies** to phishing and other forms of social engineering.

- o **Incident Response Testing**: Generative AI can be used to simulate social engineering incidents and test an organization's **incident response protocols**. By generating different types of phishing or vishing attacks, organizations can assess their readiness to respond to such incidents in real-time, ensuring that security teams and employees know what steps to take in the event of an attack.

- o **Automated Alerts and Remediation**: AI can also automate the generation of **alerts** when suspicious social engineering attempts are detected. For example, if a phishing email is flagged by an employee or by a security system, AI can send an automated alert to the IT team, instruct employees to change their passwords, and even isolate compromised accounts.

- o **Response Playbooks**: AI can assist in generating and refining **response playbooks** that outline the steps to take when a social engineering attack is detected. These playbooks ensure a **coordinated response** across different teams, minimizing the potential impact of the attack.

By automating the response process, generative AI enables organizations to react swiftly to social engineering threats and reduce the risk of data breaches or other security incidents.

4. **Detection of Evolving Social Engineering Tactics**

Social engineering tactics are continuously evolving, with attackers constantly developing new strategies to deceive individuals. **Generative AI** is capable of **adapting to new attack methods** by learning from the latest trends in social engineering and simulating emerging attack patterns.

- o **Continuous Learning and Adaptation**: Generative AI can be trained on new datasets to recognize the latest social engineering tactics, such as increasingly sophisticated phishing attempts, **AI-generated fake voices** (vishing), or **deepfake videos**. By keeping pace with evolving threats, AI ensures that training programs and attack simulations stay up to date.

- o **Simulating New Threats**: AI can generate simulated social engineering attacks based on the latest news or vulnerabilities, such as a phishing campaign exploiting a newly discovered vulnerability or a spear-phishing attack mimicking a widely publicized corporate breach. These simulations help employees stay prepared for the latest threats.

- o **Dynamic Scenario Creation**: As cybercriminals develop new tactics or exploit new technologies, generative AI can automatically create fresh attack scenarios. These could involve **new social engineering tools**, such as phishing websites that use **AI-generated personas** to mimic company executives or fake voice assistants designed to impersonate customer service agents.

By continuously adapting to new social engineering tactics, generative AI helps security teams **stay ahead of attackers**, ensuring that employees are trained to recognize and respond to the latest forms of deception.

5. **Building Human-Layer Security with AI-Driven Insights**

    Social engineering attacks often succeed because they bypass technical defenses, relying instead on human error or manipulation. **Generative AI** enhances human-layer security by **combining technology with psychological insights** to anticipate and counteract human vulnerabilities.

    o **Psychological Profiling**: Generative AI can help identify the psychological factors that make employees susceptible to social engineering attacks, such as a sense of urgency, authority bias, or trust in a familiar colleague. By understanding these behavioral tendencies, AI can generate more targeted training scenarios that address these specific vulnerabilities.

    o **Behavioral Simulation**: AI-powered systems can simulate different employee behaviors during social engineering attacks and evaluate how susceptible different individuals are to specific tactics. This allows security teams to pinpoint which individuals or departments need additional training and tailor their efforts to reduce risk.

    o **Improving Human-Computer Interaction**: Generative AI can enhance the way humans interact with computers, ensuring that employees are trained not only to identify social engineering tactics but also to **safely**

verify information through official channels, thus reducing the chances of falling for an attack.

3.5 Predictive Analytics for Cybersecurity Using AI-Generated Data

Predictive analytics leverages data, statistical algorithms, and machine learning techniques to forecast future events, providing organizations with the ability to anticipate and mitigate potential threats before they materialize. In the realm of cybersecurity, **predictive analytics** using AI-generated data can significantly enhance an organization's ability to foresee emerging risks, identify potential cyberattacks, and proactively address security vulnerabilities. By analyzing vast amounts of historical data and utilizing AI's ability to generate synthetic datasets, organizations can predict where and when attacks are most likely to occur and take preemptive actions to prevent or minimize damage.

With the increasing complexity and frequency of cyberattacks, relying solely on reactive measures is no longer enough. **AI-generated data** and **predictive analytics** offer organizations the ability to move from reactive defense to proactive threat prevention, making security teams more agile and effective in their defense strategies.

Applications of Predictive Analytics in Cybersecurity

1. **Threat Forecasting**

   One of the most powerful applications of predictive analytics in cybersecurity is the ability to forecast **emerging threats** before they happen. Generative AI can create synthetic datasets based on **historical attack patterns**, allowing security teams to anticipate new types of attacks, identify vulnerable targets, and allocate resources more effectively.

   o **Synthetic Data Generation**: Generative AI can analyze past cyberattacks, identifying common trends and attack vectors used by threat actors. Using this data, AI can

73

create synthetic attack scenarios that mimic future threats, helping cybersecurity teams prepare for novel attack methods.

o **Attack Vector Identification**: By identifying emerging attack vectors, such as new exploits targeting specific software or hardware vulnerabilities, AI-generated data allows predictive models to forecast how these threats may evolve.

o **Cyberattack Seasonality**: Predictive models can also recognize **seasonal trends** in cyberattacks. For instance, AI can detect patterns where certain attacks are more prevalent during specific times of year or in conjunction with events like holidays, public announcements, or security conferences.

These **forecasting capabilities** allow organizations to stay ahead of evolving threats by adjusting their defenses and preparedness in anticipation of potential cyberattacks.

2. **Behavioral Prediction**

Cybersecurity is not only about identifying known threats but also about spotting **anomalous behaviors** that may signal the early stages of an attack. Generative AI can help identify these **abnormal behaviors** by analyzing vast amounts of user and network data and creating models that predict actions that deviate from the norm.

o **User Behavior Analytics (UBA)**: By studying historical user interactions, AI can predict the likelihood of an insider threat or compromised credentials. For instance, AI can track typical user behavior and alert security teams to **unusual access patterns** or **high-risk activities**, such as accessing sensitive files outside of normal work hours.

o **Network Anomalies**: Generative AI can analyze network traffic and create predictive models that identify unusual data flows or communication patterns that could signal **data exfiltration, lateral movement,** or **malware communication** within the network.

o **Threat Detection Using Behavioral Insights**: Behavioral analytics helps detect **zero-day attacks**—attacks that exploit vulnerabilities unknown to the organization—by focusing on **anomalous behaviors** rather than relying solely on signature-based detection.

These predictive capabilities help security teams spot early indicators of threats and allow for faster intervention, reducing the likelihood of significant breaches or damage.

3. **Risk Assessment**

Risk assessment is a critical aspect of any cybersecurity strategy, and generative AI can enhance this process by assessing the **likelihood of vulnerabilities being exploited** and predicting the **potential impact** of these vulnerabilities. Predictive analytics helps prioritize security efforts by identifying high-risk areas that need immediate attention.

o **Vulnerability Prioritization**: AI can analyze vulnerabilities in an organization's network, systems, or applications and predict the probability of exploitation based on past attack patterns. By assessing the **severity of vulnerabilities** and the **likelihood of exploitation,** AI helps organizations prioritize their patch management efforts and apply resources to the most critical vulnerabilities.

o **Predicting Attack Surface Expansion**: Predictive models can forecast how the attack surface of an organization may grow as new devices, services, or applications are added. This helps security teams identify areas that may become more vulnerable to attacks over time and take proactive measures to safeguard them.

- o **Resource Allocation**: By generating predictive risk assessments, AI ensures that organizations allocate security resources to the areas of greatest risk, improving the overall effectiveness of their cybersecurity investments.

Through AI-driven **risk assessment**, organizations can focus on securing their most vulnerable assets and reduce the overall attack surface, thereby enhancing their defense mechanisms.

4. **Intelligent Threat Detection**

Traditional threat detection systems often struggle to keep up with the sophistication of modern cyberattacks. **Generative AI** enhances threat detection by analyzing **trends** in **historical attack data** and using these insights to identify **malicious activities** or precursors to an attack in real-time.

- o **Early Detection of Cyberattack Patterns**: By examining past cyberattacks, AI can identify subtle patterns that are indicative of an impending attack, such as unusual access attempts or data anomalies. These predictions help security teams take proactive measures before a full-scale attack occurs.

- o **Threat Detection Models**: AI can generate predictive models that detect **emerging threats** in real-time, such as new types of malware or ransomware. These models are continuously refined based on new data, ensuring that the detection system evolves to recognize **novel attack tactics**.

- o **Precursors to Attacks**: Generative AI can spot the early warning signs or **precursors to cyberattacks**, such as abnormal system scans, login attempts from unusual locations, or data transfers that indicate a **breach in progress**. Detecting these indicators early allows for faster response times and **minimized damage**.

By implementing **intelligent threat detection** powered by generative AI, organizations can improve their ability to respond to cyberattacks swiftly and accurately, reducing the impact of potential incidents.

5. **Predictive Incident Response**

While detecting an attack early is crucial, responding to it in a timely and effective manner is just as important. Predictive analytics can help organizations optimize their **incident response plans** by forecasting the **impact** and **severity** of an attack before it fully unfolds.

   o **Scenario-Based Response Planning**: Generative AI can simulate various attack scenarios, allowing organizations to predict how different incidents may escalate and what resources will be needed to mitigate the impact. These scenarios can include **network outages**, **data breaches**, or **ransomware attacks**.

   o **Resource Optimization**: AI-generated predictions can help security teams allocate resources and personnel based on the severity of the threat, ensuring that the most critical incidents receive immediate attention.

   o **Automated Playbooks**: Predictive analytics can be used to refine **incident response playbooks**, enabling automated responses based on the predicted evolution of an attack. For example, AI can trigger pre-configured actions, such as isolating compromised systems or alerting security personnel, to minimize the attack's damage.

3.6 Tailored AI Solutions for Cloud and IoT Security

Cloud environments and IoT devices are rapidly becoming the backbone of modern digital infrastructure, offering immense convenience, scalability, and connectivity. However, this interconnectedness also makes them prime targets for cyberattacks. As the adoption of cloud services and IoT devices grows exponentially, so does the attack surface, exposing organizations to new vulnerabilities. Securing these systems requires innovative solutions that can adapt to the dynamic nature of cloud environments and the diverse range of IoT devices. **Generative AI** offers a powerful tool for creating **tailored security solutions** that address the specific challenges posed by these technologies.

Generative AI can be leveraged to enhance security across cloud and IoT ecosystems by providing automated threat detection, vulnerability testing, and the ability to simulate real-world attacks to prepare defenses. By using AI to create synthetic attack scenarios and adaptive security models, organizations can ensure that their cloud infrastructures and IoT devices remain secure in an increasingly complex and interconnected world.

How Generative AI Enhances Cloud and IoT Security

1. **Cloud Threat Simulation**

   One of the most critical aspects of cloud security is the ability to identify potential vulnerabilities before they are exploited by cybercriminals. Generative AI can help **simulate synthetic attack scenarios** in cloud environments, providing security teams with valuable insights into the weaknesses of their systems.

   o **Simulating Cloud Breaches**: Generative AI can generate synthetic attack data based on **historical attack patterns** and emerging threats. These simulations help security teams test the effectiveness of their cloud security measures and identify areas that may require additional safeguards.

o **Vulnerability Discovery**: Through simulated cloud breaches, AI can uncover hidden vulnerabilities within cloud platforms, services, and configurations, such as **misconfigurations, exposed APIs**, or **insecure authentication mechanisms**.

o **Stress Testing Security Posture**: By generating large volumes of attack traffic or simulating complex multi-stage attacks, generative AI helps security teams conduct thorough stress tests, ensuring that their cloud infrastructure can withstand real-world attack scenarios.

These cloud threat simulations provide organizations with the tools to proactively address vulnerabilities and improve the resilience of their cloud environments.

2. **IoT Device Vulnerability Testing**

The sheer number and variety of IoT devices present unique security challenges. Many IoT devices lack robust security controls, and their interconnected nature often makes them a vector for larger-scale attacks. Generative AI plays a crucial role in identifying and addressing vulnerabilities in IoT devices through comprehensive **vulnerability testing**.

o **Simulating IoT Attacks**: Generative AI can simulate various types of cyberattacks on IoT devices, including **Denial-of-Service (DoS) attacks, buffer overflow exploits**, and **man-in-the-middle (MITM) attacks**. These simulated attacks help uncover security flaws in the devices' hardware, software, and network communications.

o **Security Assessment of IoT Communication Protocols**: Many IoT devices rely on specific communication protocols (e.g., Zigbee, Bluetooth, MQTT), which may have vulnerabilities that attackers exploit. AI can simulate attacks targeting these protocols to identify weaknesses and recommend security improvements.

- o **Firmware and Software Vulnerability Identification**: Generative AI can be used to simulate attacks on the firmware or software running on IoT devices, ensuring that any weaknesses in the code are detected and addressed before the devices are deployed in real-world environments.

By using AI-generated simulations, manufacturers and security teams can thoroughly test IoT devices for vulnerabilities, helping to secure the broader IoT ecosystem.

3. **Data Privacy Testing**

Protecting sensitive data in the cloud is a top priority for organizations, especially as data privacy regulations become stricter. Generative AI can simulate **data privacy breaches** and test the strength of **encryption mechanisms** and **access control policies** in cloud environments, ensuring that data remains protected even in the event of a security breach.

- o **Simulating Data Breaches**: AI can generate synthetic data breaches to test how cloud systems handle data exposure and whether **encryption methods** and **data masking techniques** are sufficient to protect sensitive information from unauthorized access.

- o **Testing Access Controls**: Generative AI can simulate unauthorized access attempts to test the strength of **identity and access management (IAM)** controls in cloud environments. This ensures that only authorized users can access critical systems and data, and that any access violations are swiftly detected and addressed.

- o **Assessing Compliance with Data Privacy Regulations**: AI can also simulate attacks targeting compliance gaps, helping organizations ensure that their cloud infrastructure meets **data privacy regulations** such as **GDPR** or **CCPA**. These simulations help organizations identify potential compliance issues and rectify them before they result in legal penalties.

By using AI to simulate data privacy breaches, organizations can enhance their cloud data protection strategies and ensure compliance with the latest privacy standards.

4. **Adaptive Security Models**

The evolving nature of cyber threats requires a dynamic and adaptable security approach. Traditional security models often struggle to keep up with the pace of change, making it essential for organizations to implement **adaptive security models** that can evolve in real-time. Generative AI can help create these **self-learning security systems** by continuously analyzing new data and adjusting security measures as needed.

- o **Real-Time Threat Detection**: AI-powered security models can analyze network traffic, system logs, and user behavior data in real-time to detect **anomalies** that may indicate an attack in progress. These models learn from past attack patterns and adjust detection algorithms to recognize **new attack techniques** and strategies used by cybercriminals.

- o **Automated Response Mechanisms**: Generative AI can help develop adaptive response systems that automatically trigger appropriate actions based on the predicted severity of an attack. For example, AI could automatically isolate affected devices or block suspicious network traffic in response to a detected attack.

o **Dynamic Risk Assessment**: As cloud and IoT environments evolve, so too does the risk landscape. AI-powered security models can continually reassess the risk level associated with different assets, services, and devices, helping organizations allocate resources to the areas that need the most protection.

3.7 Generative AI in Ransomware Mitigation Strategies

Ransomware attacks continue to be one of the most prevalent and damaging forms of cybercrime, with devastating consequences for organizations. These attacks involve cybercriminals encrypting the victim's data and demanding a ransom for its release, often leading to significant financial losses, operational downtime, and reputational damage. Traditional security measures may struggle to keep pace with the evolving tactics used by ransomware attackers. **Generative AI** presents a promising solution for enhancing ransomware mitigation strategies by enabling earlier detection, simulating attack scenarios, and developing more effective response mechanisms.

Generative AI can play a pivotal role in combating ransomware by creating synthetic data that mimics real-world ransomware activity, allowing security systems to learn and recognize attack patterns before they occur. This capability enables organizations to build proactive defenses, ensuring that they are better prepared to handle and recover from ransomware attacks.

Applications of Generative AI in Ransomware Mitigation

1. **Ransomware Detection**

   One of the most critical aspects of ransomware mitigation is the ability to **detect ransomware infections early** before they can cause significant damage. Generative AI can help security systems identify ransomware by training them on **synthetic ransomware samples** and **attack behaviors**.

o **Generating Synthetic Ransomware Samples**: Generative AI can create realistic ransomware variants and simulate their behavior, enabling detection systems to recognize the **unique signatures** of ransomware. By training on these synthetic samples, AI models can learn to detect **indicators of compromise (IoCs)** such as specific file extensions, encryption patterns, or system behaviors that are characteristic of ransomware infections.

o **Identifying Emerging Ransomware Variants**: As ransomware attacks become increasingly sophisticated, attackers frequently modify their malware to evade detection. AI models powered by generative techniques can continuously analyze new ransomware variants, adapt to evolving tactics, and update detection systems accordingly.

o **Real-Time Monitoring**: AI models can monitor network traffic, file systems, and other system behaviors in real-time, instantly identifying potential ransomware activity. Early detection allows security teams to respond quickly, potentially stopping an attack before it spreads.

By generating synthetic ransomware samples and training detection systems to recognize these threats, generative AI strengthens an organization's ability to detect ransomware attacks before they can encrypt critical data.

2. **Attack Simulation**

One of the key challenges in ransomware defense is ensuring that an organization's incident response plans are effective and can be implemented quickly in the event of an attack. Generative AI can assist in this process by **simulating ransomware attacks** in a controlled environment, allowing organizations to test their defense mechanisms and improve their preparedness.

o **Simulating Real-World Ransomware Scenarios**: Generative AI can simulate a wide range of ransomware attack scenarios, from the initial infection to the encryption of files and the subsequent ransom demand. These simulations allow organizations to test their **incident response strategies**, identify gaps in their defenses, and refine their processes to ensure that they are prepared for a real attack.

o **Testing Backup and Recovery Protocols**: Ransomware attacks often target backup systems in an attempt to prevent recovery. Generative AI can simulate ransomware's impact on backup systems, allowing organizations to assess whether their backup strategies are resilient enough to withstand an attack and quickly restore encrypted data.

o **Evaluating Organizational Response**: By simulating a ransomware attack, AI can help assess how well the organization's security operations center (SOC) responds to the incident. This includes testing the **effectiveness of communication protocols, coordination between teams**, and the ability to **contain the attack** and minimize damage.

Through attack simulation, generative AI enables organizations to evaluate and enhance their ransomware response strategies, ensuring they can recover quickly and efficiently in the face of a real-world attack.

3. **Behavioral Analytics**

Detecting ransomware early often requires identifying **anomalous behaviors** that suggest an attack is underway. Generative AI excels in **behavioral analytics**, enabling security systems to recognize abnormal activities associated with ransomware attacks, such as unusual file access patterns or rapid encryption of files.

- o **Analyzing File System Behavior**: Ransomware often begins by scanning and encrypting files on the infected system. Generative AI models can analyze file access patterns, such as sudden spikes in read/write activity or **bulk file modifications**, which are common signs of ransomware behavior. By monitoring these activities, AI can trigger alerts when suspicious behavior is detected, enabling a faster response.

- o **Monitoring User Behavior**: In many cases, ransomware is deployed via phishing emails or social engineering tactics, making user behavior a critical indicator. Generative AI can analyze **user interaction patterns**, such as unusual login times, **unauthorized file access**, or **privilege escalation attempts**, all of which could signal the start of a ransomware attack.

- o **Detecting Lateral Movement**: Once ransomware infects one system, it often attempts to spread across the network, looking for additional targets to encrypt. AI can identify **anomalous lateral movement**, such as attempts to access files or systems outside the user's typical domain, and alert security teams to contain the attack early.

By leveraging AI-powered behavioral analytics, organizations can detect ransomware at the earliest stages and prevent widespread damage by halting the attack before it progresses.

4. **Decryption Key Generation**

Once a ransomware attack has successfully encrypted an organization's data, recovery often hinges on obtaining a **decryption key**. In some cases, **generative AI** can assist in

developing decryption algorithms or conducting **brute-force attacks** to recover encrypted files, potentially mitigating the impact of ransomware attacks.

- o **Brute-Force Decryption Algorithms**: Generative AI can simulate a **brute-force decryption attack,** where it attempts multiple decryption keys or methods to recover encrypted files. This approach can be used when attackers fail to provide a working decryption key or refuse to cooperate.

- o **Reverse Engineering Ransomware**: AI-powered systems can also analyze the ransomware code and attempt to reverse engineer its encryption mechanisms. By understanding the encryption algorithm, AI can potentially generate a **decryption key** or **develop a decryption tool** that can be used to recover locked files.

- o **Collaboration with Law Enforcement**: In cases where a ransomware group has been identified, AI can assist in deconstructing ransomware variants in collaboration with law enforcement agencies, increasing the chances of recovery without paying the ransom.

Although decrypting ransomware can be a complex and time-consuming task, generative AI provides organizations with additional tools to recover encrypted data, reducing the potential financial and operational impact.

Conclusion

Generative AI is reshaping the cybersecurity landscape by enabling proactive threat detection, automating malware analysis, enhancing vulnerability management, and preventing social engineering attacks. As the technology continues to evolve, its applications in cybersecurity will become more sophisticated, providing organizations with the tools they need to stay ahead of increasingly complex cyber threats. By integrating generative AI into their security strategies, businesses can build more resilient defense systems and better protect their sensitive data and assets.

Chapter 4: Generative AI in Advanced Threat Detection

Introduction

As cyber threats grow in sophistication, traditional defense mechanisms struggle to keep pace with the evolving landscape of cyberattacks. Generative AI provides a powerful solution for enhancing threat detection capabilities by creating models that can predict, identify, and respond to a wide range of security threats. This chapter explores how generative AI contributes to advanced threat detection, with a focus on real-time monitoring, anomaly detection, insider threat identification, AI-driven forensics, behavioral analytics, and cross-platform threat correlation. We will also examine real-world case studies to demonstrate the practical application of generative AI in combating advanced cyber threats.

4.1 Real-Time Monitoring and Detection of Anomalies

Real-time monitoring and anomaly detection are crucial to maintaining robust cybersecurity defenses. In today's increasingly complex cyber threat landscape, the ability to quickly identify abnormal activity can mean the difference between mitigating an attack early and suffering a major breach. Generative AI enhances real-time monitoring capabilities by not only automating the detection of anomalies but also by continuously improving its ability to recognize new and sophisticated attack patterns as they emerge.

How Generative AI Enhances Real-Time Monitoring

Data Generation and Simulation:

One of the core advantages of generative AI in anomaly detection is its ability to generate synthetic data sets that mimic normal system behaviors. These generated datasets serve as baselines for the AI to compare against live data streams. By establishing what "normal" activity looks like, the AI can more effectively identify irregularities such as spikes in traffic, unusual login attempts, or unauthorized file access. This comparative analysis helps organizations quickly pinpoint and respond to potential security incidents that deviate from the expected behavior.

Behavioral Anomaly Detection:

Generative AI excels in recognizing patterns of behavior that deviate from the norm. For example, if an employee suddenly accesses sensitive data they would not typically need or if network traffic spikes unexpectedly, these behavioral anomalies can trigger real-time alerts. Unlike traditional methods that may rely on predefined rules, generative AI continuously analyzes and learns from data to refine its detection capabilities, offering more dynamic and adaptive threat detection. By evaluating user activities, login behavior, and interactions with data, it provides a layer of monitoring that can catch subtle signs of potential threats.

Adaptive Learning:

One of the significant limitations of traditional anomaly detection systems is their reliance on fixed rules and manual updates to account for new attack vectors. In contrast, generative AI incorporates machine learning algorithms that evolve over time. The more data it processes, the better it becomes at detecting emerging threats. This adaptive learning process ensures that the AI models are not static and can stay ahead of cybercriminals who are constantly evolving their tactics, even when those tactics have not been previously encountered.

Early Detection of Zero-Day Attacks:

Zero-day attacks target previously unknown vulnerabilities, making them difficult to detect with traditional security methods. Generative AI is particularly effective in identifying zero-day vulnerabilities by simulating and generating potential attack scenarios. Using these simulations, the AI can spot attack vectors that have not been recognized by traditional systems, thereby allowing it to detect malicious activity before it can cause significant damage. This proactive approach to cybersecurity enables earlier intervention and reduces the risk of exploitation.

Applications of Generative AI in Real-Time Monitoring:

- **Continuous Network Traffic Monitoring**: Generative AI can be used to continuously monitor network traffic for suspicious activity, identifying unusual patterns that may indicate an attack, such as DDoS attacks or exfiltration of sensitive data.

- **Identifying Anomalous Data Access Across Multiple Systems**: AI can flag abnormal access to critical files, databases, or systems by unauthorized users or through unusual methods, helping to prevent insider threats or external breaches.

- **Detecting Malicious Insider Behavior**: By analyzing user behavior, such as login times, accessed data, and system changes, generative AI can detect signs of insider threats before they escalate into full-blown attacks.

- **Proactive Alerts About Malware Infection**: AI-driven models can spot unusual behaviors, such as the rapid encryption of files or unauthorized modifications, which could indicate a malware infection, triggering real-time alerts and automated responses.

4.2 Generative AI for Identifying Insider Threats

Insider threats represent one of the most significant and complex challenges in cybersecurity, often coming from individuals with legitimate access to critical systems and sensitive data. Unlike external threats, which conventional methods can often detect, insider threats can be subtle, gradual, and difficult to predict. These threats can arise from malicious actions, such as data theft or sabotage, or from negligent behavior, like accidentally exposing sensitive information. Traditionally, identifying insider threats has been a reactive process, often relying on alerts from static monitoring systems or human intervention after the damage is done. However, generative AI provides a proactive and dynamic solution by leveraging sophisticated algorithms to analyze vast quantities of user activity and system data in real-time.

How Generative AI Identifies Insider Threats

User Behavior Analysis:

One of the most powerful features of generative AI is its ability to create detailed profiles of user behavior. By tracking a range of activities—such as login patterns, data access, file modifications, email communications, and network interactions—AI systems can learn what constitutes "normal" behavior for each individual user. Once a baseline is established, AI models continuously monitor the user's activities to detect deviations that may signal an insider threat. For example, suppose an employee who typically accesses a limited set of files suddenly attempts to access a vast amount of sensitive data. In that case, the system can flag this as anomalous behavior, triggering an alert for further investigation.

Insider Threat Simulation:

Generative AI can simulate various insider attack scenarios to test the organization's defenses and identify potential vulnerabilities in security measures. These simulations use synthetic data to replicate malicious or accidental actions, such as an employee copying large volumes of sensitive data to external drives or attempting to disable security systems. By simulating these attacks in a controlled environment, organizations can uncover weaknesses in their monitoring and response strategies, allowing them to refine their security protocols and improve their ability to detect insider threats before they occur in the real world.

Contextual Awareness:

Context is critical when evaluating user activities, and generative AI excels at considering the broader circumstances surrounding an action.

AI models are capable of analyzing not just the behavior itself but also the context in which it occurs. For example, if a user accesses sensitive data during unusual hours, such as late at night or during non-working hours, this could be flagged as a potential red flag, even if the activity seems normal in isolation. Similarly, AI can detect when employees perform activities outside their typical work scope, such as a low-level employee trying to access high-level managerial data. Contextual awareness allows AI to assess risks more accurately and make better-informed decisions about potential threats.

Advanced Detection Techniques:

Generative AI utilizes advanced detection techniques, such as predictive analytics, to identify insider threats before they escalate into full-blown security incidents. By correlating seemingly unrelated activities across various endpoints (e.g., email usage, file access, network traffic), generative AI can detect complex patterns that may indicate malicious behavior or data exfiltration attempts. This capability enables AI to foresee potential insider attacks by identifying early warning signs, such as a combination of unusual access patterns, data copying behaviors, and attempts to bypass security controls. Predictive models based on historical user behavior and context enable the system to anticipate insider threats and take proactive action to prevent damage.

Applications of Generative AI in Insider Threat Detection:

- **Monitoring User Activities in Real-Time**: Generative AI can monitor employee behavior in real-time, providing a dynamic, ongoing assessment of whether a user is misusing privileges or engaging in suspicious activities. Continuous monitoring ensures that potential insider threats are detected as soon as they arise, preventing unauthorized access to sensitive systems or data.

- **Analyzing Abnormal Access to Sensitive Data**: One of the key indicators of insider threats is unauthorized or unusual access to sensitive data. Generative AI can detect this by analyzing patterns of data access over time and identifying anomalies. For example, if an employee typically accesses only a specific subset of files related to their role but suddenly accesses data unrelated to their job, this could trigger an alert for further investigation.

- **Predicting Potential Insider Attacks Based on Historical Behavior**: AI models can predict potential insider threats by analyzing historical data about user behavior and contextual patterns. For instance, if an employee who has demonstrated unusual behavior over time—such as accessing data outside of their normal scope, downloading large amounts of data, or accessing systems late at night—shows additional suspicious activity, AI can predict that they may be preparing for an insider attack. By leveraging these predictive capabilities, organizations can take preemptive measures, such as restricting access or initiating further investigation, to prevent an incident from occurring.

4.3 AI-Driven Forensics and Incident Investigation

Forensic investigations are a crucial aspect of modern cybersecurity, as they provide insights into how an attack occurred, the extent of the damage, and the underlying vulnerabilities that were exploited. Traditional forensic tools are typically reactive, and focused on collecting and analyzing data after an incident has already occurred. They primarily examine logs, file systems, and other sources of evidence to understand what happened during the attack. However, these tools often struggle to analyze large volumes of data quickly, and they may miss key indicators of malicious activity. Generative AI, on the other hand, transforms forensic investigations by offering advanced capabilities to process vast amounts of data, generate simulated attack scenarios, and uncover the root cause of a security breach in a more efficient and proactive manner.

How Generative AI Improves Forensics

Automated Evidence Generation:

One of the key challenges in forensic investigations is reconstructing the timeline of events that led to a breach. Traditional forensic methods involve manual log analysis, which can be time-consuming and prone to human error. Generative AI, however, can simulate cyberattack behaviors, creating synthetic logs, activity traces, and network data that help security professionals understand the sequence of events. These synthetic data points act as a detailed map of the attack, from the initial compromise to the exfiltration of sensitive information, allowing investigators to visualize the full extent of the attack. By generating artificial evidence that mimics real-world attacks, AI aids forensic teams in quickly identifying the attack's origin and the methods used by the adversary, providing a more comprehensive view of the incident.

Attack Path Simulation:

Understanding the attack path—the sequence of steps an attacker takes to move through a network—is critical for identifying the vulnerabilities that were exploited during a breach. Generative AI can recreate these attack paths by simulating how an attacker might infiltrate a system, escalate privileges, move laterally within the network, and eventually exfiltrate data. By modeling different attack scenarios, AI provides forensic teams with insights into how attackers navigate a network, which tools and techniques they use, and what security gaps were leveraged. This attack path reconstruction is essential for root cause analysis, as it helps organizations pinpoint which specific weaknesses were exploited and how those vulnerabilities can be patched to prevent similar incidents in the future.

AI-Powered Correlation:

During an incident investigation, forensic teams must sift through large amounts of data from various sources, including logs, network traffic, endpoints, and security devices. Traditional methods often require investigators to manually correlate this data, which is both time-consuming and prone to errors. Generative AI, however, can automatically correlate disparate data sources, identifying connections and relationships that may not be immediately apparent. By analyzing logs from multiple endpoints, network traffic, and security devices, AI tools can quickly identify common patterns and indicators of compromise (IoCs). These AI-driven correlations help security teams identify the attack methods used by the adversaries and uncover any lingering threats that may still be active within the system, improving the overall speed and accuracy of the investigation.

Automated Incident Response:

In the course of a forensic investigation, identifying and responding to immediate threats is crucial. AI can assist in automating incident response actions based on findings during the investigation. For example, if AI detects a compromised endpoint or unauthorized data exfiltration attempt, it can automatically isolate the affected system from the network to prevent further damage. AI can also be used to block malicious IP addresses, prevent the spread of malware, and enforce containment measures without human intervention. By automating these responses, AI reduces the time it takes to mitigate ongoing attacks, limiting the damage and enhancing the overall efficiency of the investigation process.

Applications of AI-Driven Forensics:

- **Automated Log Analysis and Detection of Hidden Attack Vectors**: AI can quickly analyze logs from various systems and detect hidden attack vectors that may not be immediately visible to traditional detection systems. By using machine learning models, AI can uncover anomalies or patterns that suggest attackers have exploited unknown vulnerabilities or employed sophisticated techniques to evade detection. Automated log analysis significantly accelerates the investigation process, helping security teams identify threats faster and more accurately.

- **Reconstructing Attack Timelines and Tracing Activities in a Post-Breach Environment**: Once an attack has occurred, forensic teams often struggle to reconstruct the exact timeline of events, especially if the attackers have taken steps to cover their tracks. AI can help by creating a clear and detailed attack timeline that shows how the attack progressed, what systems were compromised, and when specific actions were taken. This timeline reconstruction allows investigators to understand the full scope of the breach and identify critical points where security defenses failed.

- **Predicting the Attacker's Next Move**: One of the most powerful capabilities of generative AI in forensics is its ability to predict future actions based on past attack patterns. By analyzing the attacker's behavior during the incident and correlating it with historical attack data, AI models can simulate the attacker's next move and predict further escalation attempts. This foresight can be crucial for forensic teams, allowing them to prepare countermeasures and prevent additional damage as the attack unfolds. AI-driven simulations can also help in understanding the tactics and strategies employed by the attackers, improving overall incident preparedness.

4.4 The Role of Generative AI in Behavioral Analytics

Behavioral analytics is a crucial aspect of modern cybersecurity that involves monitoring and analyzing user behavior, system activity, and network interactions to identify potential threats. As cyber threats continue to evolve and become more sophisticated, traditional rule-based methods of identifying anomalies are often insufficient. Generative AI significantly enhances behavioral analytics by providing deeper insights into user and system activity, detecting subtle deviations that may otherwise go unnoticed, and forecasting potential security risks with greater accuracy. By leveraging machine learning and data-driven models, generative AI enables cybersecurity teams to not only react to threats in real-time but also anticipate and mitigate them before they result in significant harm.

How Generative AI Contributes to Behavioral Analytics

Learning Normal vs. Abnormal Behavior:

One of the core strengths of generative AI in behavioral analytics is its ability to understand what constitutes "normal" behavior within a system. By training on historical data, AI models can learn to recognize typical user activity, such as the usual times and frequency of logins, the types of systems accessed, and the typical patterns of file access or network communication. Over time, these models develop a comprehensive understanding of the baseline behavior for every user and device within the system. When deviations from this baseline occur, such as an employee logging in at unusual hours, accessing sensitive data they don't typically interact with, or transferring large amounts of data to unauthorized locations, the AI models can detect these abnormalities and flag them for further investigation. This ability to differentiate between normal and abnormal behavior is crucial in identifying early signs of a security breach.

Predicting Future Threats:

Generative AI excels not only at detecting anomalies but also at forecasting potential threats. By analyzing historical behavioral data, AI models can identify patterns and trends that suggest an increased likelihood of an attack. For example, if a user starts escalating their privileges, making lateral movements within the network, or accessing systems and applications that they normally wouldn't, AI can recognize these behaviors as precursors to an attack. Additionally, AI models can identify behaviors associated with more advanced tactics, such as insider threats or data exfiltration, by correlating unusual patterns across multiple user actions and systems. By predicting potential future threats, AI enables cybersecurity teams to take preventive measures, such as isolating affected accounts or restricting access to sensitive resources, before the attack escalates.

Anomaly Detection in Real-time:

One of the most valuable capabilities of generative AI in behavioral analytics is its ability to track and compare user and system behavior in real-time. Unlike traditional systems, which may require periodic scans or rely on predefined rules to detect threats, AI-powered models continuously monitor behavior and can identify anomalies as soon as they occur. This enables organizations to respond to potential threats much more quickly, reducing the window of opportunity for attackers to exploit vulnerabilities. For example, suppose a user suddenly starts accessing large amounts of sensitive data outside of normal working hours or begins attempting to move data to an external device. In that case, AI models can immediately generate alerts, restricting the user's access or initiating automatic containment measures to mitigate the threat.

Context-Aware Analysis:

A significant challenge in behavioral analytics is the potential for false positives. For example, if a user accesses a file they don't normally interact with, it could be flagged as suspicious. However, this activity might actually be legitimate due to a specific project or task. Generative AI improves upon this by incorporating contextual information into its analysis. This might include details such as the user's role within the organization, the devices they are using, the systems they typically access, or the time and date of the activity. By factoring in this additional context, AI models can more accurately determine whether a deviation from normal behavior is genuinely suspicious or just part of a legitimate change in activity. This reduces false positives, ensures that security teams focus their attention on genuinely suspicious behavior, and improves overall efficiency in threat detection.

Applications of Generative AI in Behavioral Analytics:

- **Detecting Insider Threats Through Anomalous User Behaviors**: Insider threats, whether malicious or accidental, are one of the most difficult types of cyber threats to detect. Generative AI is highly effective in identifying these threats by continuously monitoring user activity and detecting deviations from normal patterns. For example, if an employee who typically accesses only a small subset of files suddenly begins accessing large volumes of sensitive data, this could indicate an attempt to exfiltrate data. By monitoring for such anomalies, AI can quickly alert security teams to potential insider threats and help prevent damage before it occurs.

- **Monitoring Network Traffic and Identifying Abnormal System or Network Interactions**: AI-powered behavioral analytics can also be applied to network traffic and system interactions. By analyzing communication patterns between devices and systems, AI models can identify abnormal interactions that may indicate malicious activity. For example, if a device suddenly starts communicating with a large number of external IP addresses, this could suggest that it has been compromised and is part of a botnet. Similarly, AI can detect unusual system behaviors, such as processes attempting to communicate across network boundaries or systems accessing resources that are outside of their usual scope. Detecting these abnormal interactions in real-time allows security teams to identify and respond to potential threats quickly.

- **Tracking Unusual File Access Patterns Indicative of Data Exfiltration or Malware Activity**: Data exfiltration is a common tactic used by attackers to steal sensitive information. Generative AI models can monitor file access patterns across the organization and identify unusual activities that might signal data exfiltration attempts. For instance, if an employee suddenly accesses an unusually large amount of sensitive data or begins transferring files to an unauthorized external device, AI can raise alerts about this behavior. Additionally, AI can help identify malware activity by recognizing patterns associated with common malicious actions, such as unusual file modifications, encrypted files being moved off-network, or unauthorized file transfers.

4.5 Cross-Platform Threat Correlation Using AI Models

In today's enterprise environments, data is dispersed across multiple platforms, including on-premise systems, cloud environments, endpoints, and applications. With a vast amount of security data generated from these diverse sources, correlating and analyzing this data effectively to detect potential threats can be a complex and time-consuming task. Traditional security tools often lack the capability to combine data from these various platforms and identify threats that might span across multiple environments. Generative AI models can bridge this gap by correlating data from different sources, offering a comprehensive view of potential threats that may not be apparent when considering isolated data points. By utilizing AI for cross-platform threat correlation, organizations can significantly enhance their threat detection and response capabilities.

How Generative AI Enables Cross-Platform Threat Correlation

Unified Threat Intelligence

Generative AI excels in aggregating and correlating security data from diverse platforms such as network logs, endpoint activity, cloud-based applications, and user behavior analytics. By combining this information into a unified system, AI can build a holistic view of an organization's security environment. It processes the collected data and identifies patterns, anomalies, and potential threats that may be missed when viewing individual data sources. This holistic intelligence is key to detecting complex and advanced threats, which often span multiple systems and environments. For example, suppose suspicious user activity is detected on a cloud platform. In that case, AI can cross-reference this behavior with endpoint logs, network traffic, and other sources to determine whether it correlates with other suspicious events, providing a more comprehensive understanding of the threat landscape.

Identifying Cross-Platform Attack Strategies

Attackers frequently use a multi-vector approach to infiltrate organizations, leveraging different attack vectors such as phishing emails, web-based exploits, malware, and lateral movement across various systems and platforms. Generative AI is particularly powerful in identifying these complex, cross-platform attack strategies. By correlating disparate events across multiple systems (such as unusual user activity in cloud applications, malware detected on endpoints, or unauthorized access attempts from internal servers), AI can stitch together the individual elements of an attack into a cohesive, identifiable attack chain. This allows security teams to detect multi-stage or multi-pronged attacks, which may not be obvious when examining the individual vectors in isolation. The ability to trace and understand the entire scope of an attack—spanning across on-premise systems, endpoints, and cloud environments—improves detection accuracy and response times.

Real-Time Cross-Platform Alerts

In a modern enterprise, threats can arise in any part of the IT infrastructure at any time, making it critical for security teams to receive real-time alerts. Generative AI can issue real-time alerts by correlating events across multiple platforms and analyzing them against predefined threat models or predictive algorithms. When a potential threat is identified—whether from an endpoint, cloud service, or on-premises network—the AI model sends an immediate alert, informing security teams of the issue. This real-time cross-platform alerting ensures that potential threats are quickly detected and addressed, even if they originate from disparate systems. The speed at which these alerts are generated helps organizations respond more rapidly, reducing the window of opportunity for attackers to cause damage or exfiltrate data.

Proactive Threat Hunting

Proactive threat hunting is a critical practice for modern cybersecurity teams. Instead of waiting for an alert to trigger after an attack occurs, threat hunters actively search for signs of ongoing or future threats. Generative AI enhances this proactive approach by continuously analyzing data from multiple sources in real-time. Predictive algorithms process historical behavior and activity patterns to identify subtle indicators of potential attacks, such as unusual user behavior, network traffic anomalies, or suspicious application interactions. These early indicators might span across various platforms, making manual detection extremely challenging. By correlating these signals, AI empowers security teams to identify early warning signs of attacks that may be forming across multiple systems, enabling them to take preventive actions before the threat materializes.

Applications of Cross-Platform Threat Correlation Using AI

- **Correlating Network Traffic Data with User Activity**: AI can analyze network traffic data in conjunction with user activity to detect coordinated attacks. For example, if unusual network traffic patterns—such as large data transfers or connections to foreign IP addresses—are detected, AI can correlate this with user behavior, such as the user's role or recent actions within the network. If the activity seems out of place (e.g., a low-level employee accessing high-value assets), AI can issue alerts or recommend further investigation. This cross-correlation helps identify attacks that involve both external and internal components, such as data exfiltration or advanced persistent threats (APTs).

- **Integrating Cloud Security Monitoring with On-Premises Security Tools**: In organizations that use a hybrid model or operate in multi-cloud environments, security tools across different platforms often work in silos. AI can integrate cloud security monitoring tools with on-premises security systems to identify advanced threats. For example, suspicious cloud activity—like a user attempting to access large volumes of data or an unusual login time—can be cross-referenced with on-premise endpoint logs, firewalls, or access control systems to assess if the activity is part of a larger attack. The ability to link and correlate data from both cloud and on-premises systems helps provide a more complete picture of the threat landscape, improving detection of attacks that span across both environments.

- **Real-Time Monitoring and Correlation of Endpoint and Server Logs Across Multiple Devices and Platforms**: Organizations often rely on a range of devices and platforms, including mobile endpoints, workstations, servers, and cloud-based systems. Generative AI models can correlate logs from endpoints, servers, and other devices to detect attacks that spread across multiple devices or that involve lateral movement within the network. For example, an attacker might compromise an endpoint and then attempt to move laterally through the network to escalate privileges or access sensitive systems. By correlating logs from multiple sources, AI can detect this movement in real-time, alerting security teams to take immediate action to contain the attack and prevent further damage.

Benefits of Cross-Platform Threat Correlation Using AI

- **Comprehensive Threat Detection**: Generative AI enhances the ability to detect complex threats that span multiple systems and platforms. By correlating data from disparate sources, it can identify threats that would otherwise be missed by traditional, siloed security tools.

- **Faster Incident Response**: AI-driven cross-platform correlation provides real-time alerts, enabling security teams to respond to threats more quickly and effectively. This is particularly valuable in minimizing the damage caused by cyberattacks and reducing the time it takes to remediate incidents.

- **Enhanced Threat Intelligence**: By aggregating and correlating threat data from different sources, AI can create a unified threat intelligence framework that helps organizations stay ahead of evolving attack techniques. This enhanced intelligence improves an organization's ability to predict and defend against future attacks.

- **Increased Efficiency in Threat Hunting**: AI's predictive capabilities allow security teams to proactively hunt for threats, rather than relying solely on reactive measures. By continuously analyzing data and identifying subtle indicators of attacks, AI empowers security teams to anticipate threats and strengthen their defenses.

4.6 Case Studies: AI-Supported Threat Detection in Real Life

Generative AI has proven to be a game-changer in the cybersecurity landscape, offering real-time threat detection, anomaly identification, and proactive defense strategies. Below are several real-world case studies that illustrate the power of AI in enhancing threat detection and response.

Case Study 1: AI-Powered Threat Detection in a Financial Institution

A leading global financial institution was facing a surge in advanced phishing and credential stuffing attacks. These types of attacks targeted their customers and employees, aiming to gain unauthorized access to critical accounts and sensitive data. The traditional security measures were not sufficient to stop the sophisticated and evolving attack methods.

Solution:

The institution adopted a generative AI-driven security solution that continuously monitored user behavior and network traffic. By implementing machine learning algorithms designed to detect deviations from normal user behavior, the AI system was able to analyze historical data, identifying patterns indicative of potential threats.

Outcome:

The AI solution successfully identified multiple targeted phishing attempts before they could escalate into full-scale attacks. The system was also capable of correlating suspicious activity across the institution's network, tracing the origin of the attacks. As a result, the security team could isolate the source and mitigate the risks, reducing both financial losses and reputational damage. The generative AI model helped the financial institution identify threats that traditional systems would have missed, improving both detection and response time.

Case Study 2: Insider Threat Detection in a Technology Firm

A global technology company was concerned about the potential risks posed by insider threats. The organization noticed irregular patterns of access to sensitive company data by a select group of employees, raising alarms about possible data theft, espionage, or sabotage. However, the challenge was identifying and confirming these threats without disrupting normal business operations.

Solution:

The company implemented an AI-based behavioral analytics solution that analyzed historical data, creating profiles of typical user behavior. The generative AI model continuously monitored user activities and compared them against established behavior patterns to identify anomalies. The system was specifically designed to detect deviations in access to sensitive files, systems, or applications, which might indicate potential insider threats.

Outcome:

The AI model successfully detected suspicious activities early by identifying unusual access to sensitive data that was outside the scope of the employee's role. This early warning enabled the security team to intervene before any actual breach occurred. The AI system's ability to accurately distinguish between legitimate and malicious behavior allowed the company to prevent a potential data breach, reducing the risk of insider sabotage and preserving valuable intellectual property.

Case Study 3: Cross-Platform Threat Correlation in a Cloud-Only Environment

A rapidly growing cloud-based company faced an increasing number of cyberattacks targeting various components of its cloud infrastructure. These attacks often spanned multiple platforms, including endpoints, cloud services, and web applications, making it difficult for the security team to gain a clear understanding of the scope of the attacks and their potential impact. The organization sought an innovative approach to address this issue.

Solution:

The company integrated a generative AI model for cross-platform threat detection across its entire infrastructure. The AI solution was designed to correlate data from various sources, including cloud-based resources, endpoints, and on-premises services. The AI model utilized predictive analytics to analyze patterns across different environments and detect threats that might involve multiple attack vectors.

Outcome:

The generative AI system was able to identify an attack chain that involved a phishing email, followed by malware deployment on an endpoint, and lateral movement across cloud systems. By correlating data from multiple platforms, the AI model helped the security team understand the full scope of the attack in real-time. With actionable insights from the AI model, the security team was able to promptly contain the breach, mitigate damage, and restore normal operations. The ability of AI to detect threats across diverse platforms not only enabled quicker responses but also reduced the risk of further exploitation.

Case Study 4: AI-Enhanced Endpoint Security in an Enterprise Organization

A multinational organization with a large fleet of endpoints, including desktops, laptops, and mobile devices, faced significant challenges in protecting against malware and ransomware attacks. While the traditional endpoint protection software had been effective to a certain extent, it lacked the ability to analyze complex attack patterns and respond proactively to evolving threats.

Solution:

The organization implemented a generative AI-driven endpoint protection system that could analyze and predict suspicious activity in real-time. By monitoring device behavior, network connections, and user activities, the AI model used historical data to detect anomalies that might indicate malicious actions. Additionally, the system applied machine learning techniques to refine its understanding of normal behavior continuously, enhancing its detection capabilities over time.

Outcome:

Within a short period, the AI solution identified and neutralized several malware and ransomware attempts before they could encrypt files or exfiltrate sensitive information. The generative AI model successfully predicted potential attack strategies, allowing the organization to take preventative measures. As a result, the organization minimized downtime and avoided significant financial losses associated with ransomware attacks.

Case Study 5: AI-Driven Threat Detection in a Healthcare Organization

A healthcare organization was struggling with protecting sensitive patient data from cyberattacks while ensuring compliance with stringent regulatory requirements such as HIPAA. The healthcare provider faced an uptick in data breaches and unauthorized access attempts, some originating from both external attackers and malicious insiders.

Solution:

The healthcare organization deployed an AI-powered threat detection system that continuously monitored network traffic, user access patterns, and interactions with sensitive medical records. The AI system was specifically tuned to detect violations of data access policies, unusual user behavior, and access patterns that could signal a breach of sensitive information.

Outcome:

The AI system successfully identified several insider threats involving unauthorized access to medical records, as well as external attempts to exploit vulnerable systems. In one instance, the system detected an anomalous user login after business hours, triggering an immediate investigation. The AI-driven solution enabled rapid response, preventing the exposure of sensitive health information. By using AI for real-time monitoring and threat detection, the healthcare organization improved its security posture and ensured better compliance with privacy regulations.

Case Study 6: AI-Assisted Threat Detection in a Retail Environment

A large e-commerce company was facing an increasing number of cyberattacks aimed at exploiting vulnerabilities in its payment processing systems. These attacks often involved sophisticated tactics such as SQL injection, carding, and credential stuffing, which put customer data at risk and undermined the organization's reputation.

Solution:

The e-commerce company implemented a generative AI-based threat detection system to monitor transactions and user interactions across its online platform. The AI model utilized machine learning to detect patterns of fraudulent behavior, such as multiple failed login attempts, unusual transaction volumes, or behavior consistent with bot activity. The system was capable of analyzing transaction data in real-time, identifying risks as they emerged.

Outcome:

The AI system successfully detected and blocked several fraud attempts before customer data could be compromised. In one instance, the AI model identified a pattern of suspicious transactions that suggested a credential stuffing attack. By correlating these patterns with other user behaviors, the system immediately flagged the activity, preventing fraudulent transactions and minimizing the potential for customer data exposure. The integration of generative AI improved the company's ability to defend against sophisticated online attacks, ensuring better protection for customer data.

Conclusion

Generative AI is revolutionizing advanced threat detection by enabling organizations to proactively identify and mitigate cybersecurity risks through real-time monitoring, insider threat detection, AI-driven forensics, and behavioral analytics. By leveraging AI's ability to simulate attacks, predict emerging threats, and correlate data across platforms, security teams can respond faster and more accurately to potential breaches, enhancing overall defense mechanisms. As cyber threats continue to evolve, the integration of generative AI will be essential for organizations looking to stay ahead and strengthen their cybersecurity posture.

Chapter 5: The Dark Side of Generative AI

Introduction

Generative AI has rapidly evolved, becoming a powerful tool across various industries, from healthcare to entertainment, by automating tasks and creating innovative solutions. However, as with any technology, its potential for misuse has raised significant concerns. In the wrong hands, generative AI can be weaponized for malicious purposes, giving rise to a new wave of cyber threats. This chapter delves into the darker side of generative AI, exploring how cybercriminals exploit its capabilities for phishing, deepfake attacks, synthetic identity fraud, and more. It also highlights the emerging challenges of securing AI systems from adversarial attacks and offers strategies for mitigating the risks posed by these malicious uses.

5.1 Generative AI in the Hands of Cybercriminals

Generative AI has become a double-edged sword in the realm of cybersecurity. While it holds immense potential for innovation and automation, it has also found a dark side, as cybercriminals are increasingly exploiting this technology to enhance the effectiveness and scale of their attacks. The ability of generative AI to produce realistic, human-like content—whether it's text, images, or videos—has enabled malicious actors to launch sophisticated and often undetectable attacks. As cybercriminals leverage this powerful tool, the landscape of cyber threats continues to evolve, making traditional defense mechanisms less effective against these new, AI-driven techniques.

AI-Powered Phishing Attacks

One of the most prevalent ways that cybercriminals are using generative AI is in phishing attacks. Phishing is a form of social engineering where attackers impersonate trusted entities, such as banks, government agencies, or colleagues, to trick victims into revealing sensitive information like usernames, passwords, or financial details. While traditional phishing attacks relied on generic, often unconvincing emails, generative AI allows attackers to create highly personalized and realistic messages.

Using AI, cybercriminals can scrape publicly available data from social media profiles, blogs, and other online sources to craft messages that are tailored to the victim's interests, preferences, and behavior. These personalized emails are more likely to bypass spam filters and convince the target that the message is legitimate. For example, an AI might generate an email that appears to be from the victim's bank, featuring accurate details about recent transactions or account activity, making it difficult for the victim to discern the scam.

The ability to automate this process using AI also enables attackers to scale their operations, targeting a larger number of individuals while maintaining the illusion of personalization. With generative AI, the time and effort needed to craft individual phishing emails are drastically reduced, allowing cybercriminals to reach more victims with a greater chance of success.

Deepfake Technology and its Malicious Use

Another alarming misuse of generative AI is in the creation of deepfakes—highly realistic videos or audio clips that can manipulate or fabricate events and statements. Deepfake technology leverages AI to synthesize audio and video content that mimics real people, making it possible to create convincing but entirely false depictions of individuals.

In the hands of cybercriminals, deepfakes can be weaponized for a range of malicious purposes. For example, criminals may use AI to generate fake videos of CEOs or public figures making controversial statements, which can lead to reputational damage, financial losses, or political upheaval. In some cases, deepfake videos have been used in blackmail schemes, where the attacker threatens to release the fabricated content unless the victim pays a ransom.

Moreover, deepfakes are often used to deceive people into performing actions that benefit the attacker. For instance, a cybercriminal could create a deepfake video of a company executive requesting wire transfers or other financial transactions, fooling employees into carrying out fraudulent instructions. This form of social engineering, enabled by AI, makes deepfake-based attacks increasingly difficult to detect, as the content appears genuine and is often indistinguishable from real interactions.

Synthetic Identity Fraud and Credential Harvesting

Synthetic identity fraud is another area where generative AI is having a significant impact. Criminals use AI to combine real and fake personal information to create entirely new, fabricated identities. These synthetic identities are designed to appear legitimate, making them difficult for financial institutions and regulatory bodies to detect.

Using generative AI, attackers can create convincing profiles that include names, addresses, dates of birth, and other personal details—often using information stolen from various sources. These synthetic identities are then used for a variety of fraudulent activities, including applying for loans, opening bank accounts, and committing tax fraud. AI allows these attacks to be automated and scaled, meaning cybercriminals can generate thousands of synthetic identities in a short period of time, which significantly increases the chances of their success.

AI-driven credential harvesting is another tactic enabled by generative AI. Cybercriminals can use AI to analyze vast amounts of data from previous data breaches, identifying patterns in user behavior and preferences. This allows attackers to create highly effective phishing campaigns or social engineering schemes that trick individuals into giving away their login credentials or other sensitive information. Once acquired, these credentials are used to gain unauthorized access to accounts, often leading to identity theft or financial theft.

The Growing Challenge for Cybersecurity

The rapid evolution of generative AI means that cybercriminals can now carry out attacks on an unprecedented scale, with a level of sophistication that traditional security measures are ill-equipped to handle. The ability to generate realistic and personalized content has made it more challenging for both individuals and organizations to differentiate between legitimate and fraudulent communications. Additionally, the automation of these processes allows cybercriminals to launch widespread campaigns with minimal effort and time investment.

As generative AI continues to improve, the potential for abuse only grows. Attackers can now create content that is indistinguishable from real communications, making it much harder for security professionals to detect threats before they escalate. The sophistication of AI-powered attacks means that relying solely on traditional cybersecurity solutions—such as antivirus software and firewalls—will no longer be enough to protect organizations from these evolving threats.

5.2 AI-Driven Phishing and Deepfake Attacks

AI-driven phishing and deepfake attacks represent some of the most alarming threats in today's cybercrime landscape, fueled by the power of generative AI. Phishing attacks, once reliant on basic tactics such as generic, spammy emails, have evolved into sophisticated, highly targeted scams. Similarly, deepfake technology, which creates hyper-realistic fake media, is increasingly being used to manipulate victims. These AI-powered attacks are far more dangerous than their traditional counterparts, as they exploit human trust and the growing difficulty of distinguishing real from fake content.

AI-Enhanced Phishing Attacks

Phishing remains one of the most common forms of cybercrime, and AI has significantly enhanced the efficacy and scale of these attacks. Traditionally, phishing scams were broad and generic—messages would be sent to thousands of individuals in the hope that a few would take the bait. These attacks were often easy to spot due to poor grammar, suspicious links, and unprofessional content. However, with the help of generative AI, attackers can now craft highly personalized and convincing phishing messages that are much harder to detect.

Generative AI enables attackers to scrape vast amounts of publicly available data from social media, websites, and even breached databases. This data can include personal information such as names, job titles, contact details, interests, and even past interactions, allowing attackers to craft highly targeted phishing messages. For instance, AI can use natural language processing (NLP) to analyze a victim's social media posts and emails to generate a message that mimics their writing style and tone, making the phishing attempt more credible.

Moreover, AI can analyze a victim's network to determine the best approach for a phishing attack. For example, by identifying key relationships within a company, the AI can generate emails that appear to come from trusted colleagues or executives, increasing the likelihood of success. By customizing the attack in such a way, attackers can bypass traditional email filters and social engineering defenses, making their tactics significantly more dangerous.

The Role of AI in Bypassing Security Measures

AI-driven phishing attacks are more difficult for traditional security tools to detect. Conventional phishing detection systems often rely on predefined signatures, keyword matching, and heuristics to identify malicious content. However, AI-generated phishing emails can bypass these mechanisms due to their highly personalized nature. Traditional spam filters are also less effective against these targeted attacks, which are crafted to appear as legitimate communication.

Human vigilance is an essential part of identifying phishing attempts, but even the most experienced professionals can be deceived by the increasing sophistication of AI-driven phishing. As attackers use generative AI to refine their tactics, businesses and individuals are left vulnerable to a wider range of threats. This shift underscores the need for updated training and new security technologies to keep up with AI-driven cybercrime.

Deepfake Technology and Its Malicious Use

While phishing is primarily focused on obtaining sensitive information, deepfake attacks take a different approach—creating fabricated audio, video, or images that are nearly indistinguishable from reality. Deepfake technology uses generative AI models, particularly deep learning algorithms, to create realistic manipulations of media. Cybercriminals can use deepfakes to impersonate public figures, executives, or even everyday employees, tricking their targets into following malicious instructions.

One notorious example of deepfake technology used for financial fraud occurred when a cybercriminal impersonated the voice of a CEO through deepfake audio. The attacker successfully convinced an employee to initiate a transfer of $243,000 to a fraudulent account. This form of fraud, known as "voice phishing" or "vishing," is particularly effective because it leverages the authority of a senior executive, combined with the trust that employees place in their leaders.

Deepfake technology is also being used to conduct various types of fraud, such as identity theft, extortion, and blackmail. Criminals can create videos or audio clips that depict a victim in compromising or defamatory situations, then use the threat of releasing these fakes to extort money or gain other benefits. This form of manipulation, which preys on human emotions and reputations, is difficult to combat since it involves authentic-looking media that can be easily distributed online.

How AI-Driven Deepfake Attacks Bypass Detection

The sophistication of deepfake technology has reached a level where even experts struggle to discern real from fake content. As generative AI continues to advance, the quality of deepfake audio, video, and images improves, making them more challenging to detect with conventional methods. Current detection tools often struggle to differentiate between real and fabricated media, especially when the deepfake mimics a public figure or authority figure that the victim trusts.

For example, many deepfake detectors focus on identifying inconsistencies in video or audio, such as unnatural facial movements, mismatched lip sync, or audio distortions. However, as AI models improve, these telltale signs are becoming less apparent. This has led to an arms race between attackers using AI to create more convincing deepfakes and security professionals trying to develop more sophisticated detection algorithms.

The potential consequences of deepfake attacks are significant, ranging from financial fraud to reputational damage, and they present an entirely new set of challenges for cybersecurity teams. The growing use of deepfakes for impersonation and fraud underscores the need for new methods of authentication and verification, particularly in industries where trust and authority are paramount.

Combating AI-Driven Phishing and Deepfake Attacks

Given the growing threat of AI-driven phishing and deepfake attacks, businesses and individuals need to take proactive steps to safeguard themselves. First, increasing awareness about these new threats is crucial. Users must be trained to recognize the signs of phishing emails and be cautious of unsolicited communication, even if it appears to come from a trusted source. Training programs should focus on teaching employees how to verify suspicious emails or requests, such as by contacting the sender directly using known contact details rather than responding to the message itself.

For deepfake attacks, organizations can implement multi-factor authentication (MFA) as an additional layer of protection. MFA can help mitigate the risk of credential theft, even if an attacker successfully impersonates a trusted individual. Businesses should also adopt video and voice verification systems that are difficult for AI to manipulate. Additionally, AI-powered deepfake detection tools are emerging, and integrating these technologies into security systems can help identify fraudulent media before it reaches the intended recipient.

5.3 Synthetic Identity Fraud and Credential Harvesting

Synthetic identity fraud is a rapidly growing threat, amplified by the capabilities of generative AI. It involves the creation of entirely new, fabricated identities that combine real and fake information, which are then used to carry out illegal activities. By leveraging generative AI, cybercriminals can automate the process of creating synthetic identities, making them harder to detect and allowing them to scale their operations. This chapter delves into how AI is enabling synthetic identity fraud and credential harvesting, along with the challenges it poses to traditional security measures.

The Mechanics of Synthetic Identity Fraud

Synthetic identity fraud occurs when criminals combine real data (e.g., a real Social Security number or date of birth) with fabricated information (e.g., fake names, addresses, and other personal details) to create a new identity. This synthetic identity is then used to perform fraudulent activities such as applying for loans, opening bank accounts, or committing tax fraud.

Generative AI plays a crucial role in making this process more efficient and scalable. Through machine learning algorithms and data scraping, cybercriminals can generate synthetic identities that mimic real individuals. These identities are often created by combining real, publicly available data (such as names, birth dates, and even publicly available social media profiles) with AI-generated fake data that fills in the gaps. As a result, synthetic identities can appear highly credible and evade detection by traditional security systems that rely on pattern recognition or basic identity verification methods.

Automating the Generation of Synthetic Identities

One of the key advantages of using generative AI in synthetic identity fraud is the ability to create these identities at scale. AI-powered tools can generate thousands of unique identities in a fraction of the time it would take a human to manually fabricate one. This automation makes it much more difficult for security systems to spot trends or anomalies in identity data.

Moreover, the AI tools used by criminals can be trained to ensure that these synthetic identities appear legitimate, thus bypassing conventional security measures like database matching and human verification. By using machine learning models that analyze existing identity patterns, AI can generate synthetic data that matches the formatting, structure, and behavior of legitimate identities. This enables fraudsters to create highly convincing and difficult-to-detect synthetic personas that can be used to carry out illegal activities over extended periods of time.

Credential Harvesting and Its Role in Synthetic Identity Fraud

Once a synthetic identity is established, cybercriminals can proceed to harvest credentials—either through social engineering techniques or by directly exploiting vulnerabilities in databases and online systems. Credential harvesting involves stealing login information, passwords, security questions, and other personal details that can be used to gain unauthorized access to accounts or systems. AI plays a significant role in automating this process as well.

AI-driven credential harvesting typically leverages sophisticated phishing campaigns or brute-force attacks to gather sensitive information. These attacks can be further refined by using AI to analyze user behavior patterns, making the harvesting process more efficient. Once attackers have collected enough credentials, they can use them to perpetrate fraud, take over financial accounts, or commit identity theft.

Credential harvesting not only makes synthetic identity fraud more effective but also allows criminals to access a wider range of financial and personal resources. For example, stolen credentials can be used to apply for loans, access bank accounts, or conduct high-value transactions, amplifying the financial damage caused by synthetic identities.

Impact on Financial Institutions and Organizations

The creation and use of synthetic identities have severe consequences for financial institutions, businesses, and individuals. When synthetic identities are used to open fraudulent accounts or apply for loans, it can lead to significant financial losses. Financial institutions, unable to differentiate between real and synthetic identities, may inadvertently approve fraudulent transactions, which can lead to defaults, chargebacks, and reputational damage.

For organizations that handle sensitive data, synthetic identity fraud also represents a major security risk. In addition to financial losses, the infiltration of fake identities can compromise data privacy and undermine the integrity of internal systems. This can lead to long-term issues, such as regulatory fines, data breaches, and the erosion of customer trust.

Synthetic Identity Fraud in Money Laundering

One particularly concerning use of synthetic identities is in money laundering schemes. Criminals can create fake identities to open bank accounts, which they then use to funnel illicit funds. Since these synthetic identities are often difficult to trace, they allow criminals to launder money without raising red flags with financial institutions or law enforcement.

Generative AI can significantly enhance money laundering efforts by automating the process of creating synthetic identities that are difficult to detect. These identities can be used to set up a chain of transactions that move illicit funds through multiple accounts, often crossing international borders, making it harder for authorities to track the flow of money. Financial institutions, which typically rely on human verification and conventional data analysis techniques, are often overwhelmed by the sheer volume and complexity of these transactions, making it increasingly difficult to prevent money laundering activities that rely on synthetic identities.

The Role of AI in Enhancing Fraud Detection and Prevention

While AI has made synthetic identity fraud more prevalent, it is also being used to enhance fraud detection and prevention efforts. Financial institutions and cybersecurity firms are employing AI-driven systems to detect suspicious patterns of behavior and identity anomalies that might indicate synthetic identity creation. For example, machine learning models can be trained to identify discrepancies in the data, such as unusual combinations of personal information or inconsistencies in account activity, which might suggest that an identity is fabricated.

In addition, advanced AI tools can be used to detect the use of stolen or compromised credentials, helping to reduce the success of credential harvesting attempts. By leveraging AI to analyze vast amounts of transaction and login data, institutions can identify potential fraud risks more quickly and accurately than with traditional methods.

5.4 Adversarial Attacks on AI Systems

Adversarial attacks are a form of cyberattack that exploits the vulnerabilities inherent in machine learning and AI models by subtly manipulating the inputs, leading to incorrect or malicious outputs. These attacks are designed to confuse or deceive AI systems by introducing small, often imperceptible changes to data that can drastically alter the system's behavior or decision-making process. As AI systems become more integrated into critical applications, adversarial attacks pose an increasing risk, particularly in sectors such as cybersecurity, finance, autonomous vehicles, and fraud detection. In this section, we will explore how generative AI is leveraged in adversarial attacks and the potential consequences of these attacks on AI systems.

The Mechanics of Adversarial Attacks

Adversarial attacks typically involve the introduction of small perturbations or modifications to the input data, which cause the machine learning model to make erroneous predictions or classifications. These changes are often so minor that they are not noticeable to humans but are sufficient to confuse the AI system.

For instance, in the case of a facial recognition system, attackers might subtly alter an image by changing pixel values in a way that makes the AI misidentify the person. This could be done by adding noise or shifting the pixels in specific patterns, which would not be detectable by the human eye but could lead the AI to recognize or classify the person in the image incorrectly.

The effectiveness of adversarial attacks stems from the weaknesses in machine learning models that arise from their reliance on specific data patterns and correlations. AI systems, especially those trained using large datasets, can become overfitted to certain features, making them vulnerable to adversarial examples that exploit those weaknesses. This results in AI models being less robust and more susceptible to manipulation by attackers.

Generative AI's Role in Creating Adversarial Examples

Generative AI, particularly Generative Adversarial Networks (GANs), plays a crucial role in enabling adversarial attacks. GANs consist of two neural networks: a generator and a discriminator. The generator creates new data samples while the discriminator evaluates them against real data. Over time, the generator learns to produce increasingly realistic and convincing data, which can be used for various purposes, including generating adversarial examples.

In the context of adversarial attacks, GANs can be used to create inputs specifically designed to deceive AI systems. These inputs may be manipulated images, videos, or audio clips that are engineered to bypass the detection mechanisms of AI-powered systems. For example, attackers can use generative models to create images that look normal to the human eye but are crafted to confuse AI models into misclassifying them.

AI-generated adversarial examples are particularly dangerous because they can be used to bypass security systems, content moderation filters, and fraud detection tools. By weaponizing generative AI, attackers can target and manipulate AI systems, rendering them ineffective and undermining their trustworthiness.

Real-World Examples of Adversarial Attacks

Adversarial attacks have already been demonstrated in several real-world applications, highlighting their potential to disrupt AI-powered systems. One notable example is in the field of autonomous vehicles, where small changes to images from sensors or cameras can trick the vehicle's AI system into misinterpreting its surroundings. This could lead to dangerous situations, such as a self-driving car failing to recognize a stop sign or pedestrian, resulting in accidents.

Another example is in AI-powered security systems, where adversarial attacks can be used to bypass facial recognition or biometric authentication systems. By creating subtle modifications to photos or videos, attackers can impersonate someone else or gain unauthorized access to restricted areas. These types of attacks are especially concerning in security-sensitive environments, such as airports, government buildings, or private facilities.

Adversarial attacks can also target AI-powered fraud detection systems. Cybercriminals can use generative AI to create patterns that mimic legitimate transactions, effectively bypassing fraud detection systems. This can lead to unauthorized transactions, financial theft, and other fraudulent activities that are difficult to trace or prevent.

The Impact of Adversarial Attacks on AI Systems

Adversarial attacks can have significant consequences on the reliability and effectiveness of AI systems. When these attacks succeed, they can undermine the trust placed in AI models and reduce their operational efficiency. The potential impact of adversarial attacks extends beyond individual systems to industries and sectors that rely heavily on AI for decision-making and security.

For example, in healthcare, adversarial attacks could manipulate medical imaging systems, causing incorrect diagnoses and treatment plans. In finance, these attacks could result in erroneous trading decisions or the mismanagement of funds. The manipulation of AI systems used in autonomous vehicles or robotics could lead to dangerous accidents and damage public trust in AI technology.

The evolving nature of adversarial attacks also presents challenges for organizations working to develop secure and resilient AI models. As generative AI becomes more sophisticated, adversarial examples will continue to evolve, requiring constant adaptation and improvement of defense mechanisms.

Mitigating Adversarial Attacks on AI Systems

To address the growing threat of adversarial attacks, researchers and organizations are working on developing defensive strategies that can make AI models more robust. One approach is adversarial training, where models are exposed to adversarial examples during the training process, helping them learn to recognize and resist manipulations. This method allows AI systems to become more resistant to subtle changes in input data and better equipped to detect adversarial examples.

Another promising approach is the use of regularization techniques, which can help prevent overfitting and make models less sensitive to small changes in data. By incorporating these techniques, AI models can be made more generalized and less likely to be tricked by adversarial inputs.

Additionally, the use of explainable AI (XAI) can help increase transparency and trust in AI systems. By providing insights into how AI models make decisions, organizations can identify potential vulnerabilities and address them before they are exploited in adversarial attacks.

Continuous monitoring of AI systems is also critical for detecting and responding to adversarial attacks in real-time. By employing anomaly detection systems and behavior monitoring, organizations can quickly identify abnormal activities that may indicate an ongoing attack.

5.5 Mitigating Risks of Malicious Use of Generative AI

As generative AI technologies continue to evolve and become more accessible, the potential for malicious use also increases. Cybercriminals can exploit generative AI to create highly convincing phishing attacks, deepfakes, synthetic identities, and adversarial examples, all of which can have significant security implications. To mitigate these risks, a combination of strategic, technological, and regulatory measures must be put in place to ensure that AI technologies are used responsibly and securely. In this section, we will explore key strategies for reducing the risks associated with the malicious use of generative AI.

1. AI Ethics and Governance

One of the first steps in mitigating the risks of malicious AI use is to establish a comprehensive framework for AI governance. AI governance refers to the processes, rules, and policies put in place to manage the development, deployment, and use of AI technologies. By establishing ethical guidelines, organizations can ensure that generative AI is used for beneficial purposes while minimizing the potential for misuse.

AI ethics and governance frameworks should address key concerns such as:

- **Accountability:** Ensuring that individuals or organizations deploying AI systems are held responsible for the outcomes of those systems, particularly when misuse occurs.

- **Transparency:** Encouraging the development of AI systems that are explainable and whose decision-making processes can be understood by humans, enabling better oversight and identification of harmful uses.

- **Privacy Protection:** Safeguarding user data and ensuring that AI applications do not violate privacy rights, especially when handling sensitive information.

- **Compliance:** Ensuring that AI applications adhere to legal, regulatory, and industry-specific standards, such as data protection laws (GDPR, CCPA) and cybersecurity regulations.

Establishing AI ethics and governance practices can help build trust in AI systems and ensure that their deployment aligns with broader societal values and norms.

2. Advanced AI Detection Tools

As generative AI becomes more advanced, so do the techniques for creating convincing malicious content. To combat this, it is crucial to invest in AI-based detection tools that can identify AI-generated content and distinguish it from legitimate material.

Some advanced detection tools include:

- **Deepfake Detection:** Deepfake detection software leverages machine learning algorithms to analyze video and audio content for signs of manipulation. These tools can identify inconsistencies in lighting, speech patterns, facial movements, and audio-visual synchronization that may indicate a deepfake. Detecting these signs early can help prevent the spread of harmful content, such as fake news or fraudulent impersonations.

- **Synthetic Identity Detection:** AI systems can also be trained to spot synthetic identities by analyzing patterns in data such as Social Security numbers, birthdates, and credit history. By monitoring and flagging inconsistencies or anomalies in the creation of digital identities, organizations can reduce the risk of fraud and identity theft.

- **Phishing Email Detection:** AI-powered email security systems can be used to detect phishing emails generated by malicious AI. These systems analyze the content of incoming emails to identify common signs of phishing, such as suspicious URLs, urgent language, and impersonation attempts.

By implementing these detection systems, organizations can quickly identify and neutralize threats posed by generative AI, helping to protect users and sensitive data from malicious actors.

3. Security Awareness and Training

As generative AI becomes more sophisticated, cybercriminals are finding new ways to exploit human vulnerabilities. To combat these threats, it is essential to invest in security awareness and training programs that educate employees and individuals on how to identify AI-driven threats.

Training programs should include:

- **Recognizing AI-generated Phishing:** Employees should be trained to spot AI-generated phishing emails that appear more personalized and convincing. By learning how to recognize suspicious emails and verifying sources before clicking on links or downloading attachments, individuals can prevent falling victim to phishing attacks.

- **Identifying Deepfakes and Synthetic Identities:** Awareness programs should also include lessons on how to identify deepfake videos and audio clips, as well as synthetic identities used in fraudulent activities. Training employees to question the authenticity of suspicious communications, especially from unfamiliar sources, can help reduce the likelihood of these attacks succeeding.

- **Social Engineering Awareness:** Teaching individuals how to recognize and resist social engineering tactics, such as pretexting and baiting, is critical for preventing attacks that rely on manipulating human behavior to gain access to sensitive information.

By fostering a culture of vigilance and cybersecurity awareness, organizations can reduce the likelihood of employees falling victim to malicious AI-driven attacks.

4. Collaboration Between AI Developers and Security Experts

One of the most effective ways to mitigate the risks of malicious AI use is by fostering collaboration between AI developers and security professionals. By working together, these two groups can design and implement AI systems that are more resilient to adversarial attacks and malicious exploitation.

Key areas for collaboration include:

- **Developing Robust AI Models:** AI developers and security experts should collaborate on creating models that are more robust to adversarial inputs. This includes using techniques such as adversarial training, where AI models are exposed to adversarial examples during their development to help them learn how to resist manipulation.

- **Improving Data Security:** Both AI developers and security experts should prioritize data security throughout the AI development lifecycle. This involves securing training datasets, ensuring data privacy, and implementing encryption to prevent unauthorized access to sensitive information used by AI systems.

- **Real-Time Monitoring:** Once AI systems are deployed, it is essential to monitor them for vulnerabilities or signs of exploitation continuously. This collaboration can help detect AI-driven attacks early, allowing organizations to take swift action before the damage becomes widespread.

By creating a multidisciplinary approach to AI development and security, organizations can create more resilient AI systems that are less susceptible to malicious use.

5. Regulatory and Legal Measures

Governments and regulatory bodies must play a pivotal role in regulating the use of generative AI to prevent its malicious exploitation. The rapid advancement of AI technology has outpaced regulatory frameworks, making it essential for policymakers to create guidelines that govern its ethical and secure use.

Important regulatory and legal measures include:

- **Stricter Penalties for Misuse:** Governments should enforce stronger penalties for cybercriminals who misuse generative AI, including fines, imprisonment, and other legal consequences. This would serve as a deterrent to those considering using AI for malicious activities such as identity theft, fraud, and disinformation campaigns.

- **AI Usage Guidelines for Companies:** Regulatory bodies can create guidelines for companies and organizations that develop or deploy AI technologies. These guidelines should focus on ensuring that AI systems are designed with security in mind, addressing issues such as transparency, accountability, and the prevention of malicious use.

- **Data Privacy and Protection Laws:** Governments should implement and enforce stricter data protection laws to ensure that personal and sensitive data is safeguarded when used by AI systems. This includes regulations around consent, data storage, and the sharing of data with third parties.

Effective regulation is crucial in mitigating the risks of malicious AI use while promoting the responsible development and deployment of these technologies.

Conclusion

Generative AI is transforming the cybersecurity landscape, but it also brings significant risks when in the hands of malicious actors. Cybercriminals are leveraging the power of AI to enhance phishing, deepfake attacks, synthetic identity fraud, and adversarial manipulation of AI systems. These malicious uses present unprecedented challenges for cybersecurity professionals, who must adapt quickly to detect and mitigate AI-driven threats.

However, while generative AI poses new risks, it also offers powerful tools for combating cybercrime. By developing advanced detection tools, fostering ethical AI governance, and investing in education and awareness, organizations can better defend against the malicious use of AI. The dark side of generative AI is a reality that cybersecurity professionals must acknowledge, but through proactive measures, its risks can be mitigated to ensure that AI is used for good and not for harm.

Chapter 6: Building Generative AI-Powered Cyber Defense Systems

Introduction

As the complexity and sophistication of cyberattacks increase, traditional cybersecurity methods often fall short in detecting and mitigating threats effectively. Generative AI, with its ability to analyze patterns, adapt to new data, and automate tasks, offers a transformative approach to cyber defense. This chapter explores how generative AI can be harnessed to build robust cyber defense systems, focusing on its integration into Security Operations Centers (SOCs), threat intelligence platforms, incident response automation, and real-time data processing for proactive security.

6.1 Integrating Generative AI into Security Operations Centers (SOCs)

Security Operations Centers (SOCs) are the command hubs for monitoring, detecting, and responding to cybersecurity threats. Integrating generative AI into SOCs significantly improves their capabilities by enhancing detection, reducing false positives, automating repetitive tasks, and prioritizing threats effectively. Below are detailed subtopics illustrating how generative AI can transform SOCs.

6.1.1 Advanced Threat Detection

The foundation of any SOC lies in its ability to detect threats early and accurately. Generative AI offers powerful tools for advanced threat detection by:

- **Analyzing Vast Data Volumes**: Generative AI models can process terabytes of log data, including network traffic, application logs, and endpoint activity, to identify hidden anomalies and patterns indicative of threats.

- **Dynamic Pattern Recognition**: Unlike traditional methods, generative AI can dynamically adapt to new attack patterns, enabling it to detect zero-day exploits or novel malware variants.

- **Behavioral Analysis**: By studying baseline user and system behaviors, AI models can flag deviations that suggest compromised accounts or insider threats.

Example: Identifying Advanced Persistent Threats (APTs)

A generative AI-powered SOC identified a low-and-slow attack by correlating seemingly unrelated anomalies in user login behavior and file access patterns over several months. This led to early containment and prevented significant data exfiltration.

6.1.2 Reducing False Positives

False positives are a persistent challenge for SOCs, often leading to alert fatigue among analysts. Generative AI addresses this issue by:

- **Correlating Data**: AI systems contextualize alerts by cross-referencing them with historical data, threat intelligence feeds, and known indicators of compromise (IoCs).

- **Adaptive Learning**: Generative AI learns from past incidents to improve its understanding of what constitutes a true threat versus benign activity.

- **Streamlining Alert Management**: By focusing only on high-confidence alerts, AI reduces the volume of false positives, allowing analysts to concentrate on real threats.

Benefit: Enhanced Analyst Productivity

With fewer false positives to investigate, SOC analysts can allocate their time to higher-priority incidents, leading to faster remediation and improved overall efficiency.

6.1.3 Incident Prioritization

Every SOC faces the challenge of prioritizing incidents based on their severity and potential impact. Generative AI excels in this domain by:

- **Severity Assessment**: Using predictive models and natural language processing (NLP), generative AI evaluates the potential impact of an incident based on its context, affected assets, and threat type.

- **Risk-Based Prioritization**: AI aligns incident priorities with an organization's risk tolerance, critical assets, and compliance requirements.

- **Automated Recommendations**: Generative AI provides recommendations for immediate actions, such as isolating affected systems or initiating forensic analysis based on the assessed severity.

Example: Predicting Lateral Movement

Generative AI detected unusual login attempts on critical servers and flagged the incident as high priority due to its potential to escalate into lateral movement within the network.

6.1.4 SOC Automation

Automation is key to managing the growing volume and complexity of cyber threats. Generative AI can automate several SOC processes, such as:

- **Log Analysis**: AI systems can process logs in real-time, identifying anomalies and generating summary reports for human review.

- **Alert Triage**: Low-risk or repetitive alerts can be handled automatically, with AI escalating only significant threats to human analysts.

- **Basic Remediation**: Generative AI can execute predefined playbooks to remediate threats, such as blocking IP addresses, resetting user credentials, or isolating infected devices.

Efficiency Gains: Faster Mean Time to Detect and Respond (MTTD and MTTR)

Organizations that implemented AI-driven automation in their SOCs reported significant reductions in MTTD and MTTR, enhancing their overall cybersecurity posture.

6.1.5 AI-Powered Threat Hunting

Threat hunting involves proactively searching for hidden threats within an organization's environment. Generative AI enhances this capability by:

- **Simulating Attacker Behavior**: Generative AI models can mimic attack scenarios, helping analysts anticipate potential vulnerabilities and entry points.

- **Continuous Threat Hunting**: AI enables 24/7 threat hunting, identifying and flagging suspicious activities that human analysts might miss.

- **Enhanced Correlation**: AI can link disparate pieces of evidence, such as suspicious file downloads and unauthorized system accesses, to uncover hidden threats.

Case Study: Financial Sector Threat Hunting

A leading financial institution leveraged generative AI to enhance its threat-hunting capabilities. AI models trained on historical breach data proactively identified potential vulnerabilities in the organization's systems. As a result, the SOC team was able to implement patches and additional security controls, preventing exploitation by attackers.

6.2 Generative AI in Threat Intelligence Platforms

Threat intelligence platforms play a critical role in equipping organizations with actionable insights to anticipate and mitigate cyber threats. The integration of generative AI into these platforms revolutionizes how threat intelligence is collected, analyzed, and disseminated. By enhancing threat prediction, tailoring intelligence to specific needs, and providing deeper malware insights, generative AI empowers organizations to stay ahead of evolving cyber threats.

6.2.1 Enhancing Threat Pattern Generation

Generative AI excels at creating simulated attack patterns based on historical data, enabling organizations to prepare for emerging threats.

- **Scenario Modeling**: By analyzing past incidents and attacker behavior, generative AI generates hypothetical attack scenarios, offering organizations a proactive approach to threat mitigation.

- **Zero-Day Preparation**: AI models can simulate potential zero-day vulnerabilities based on historical patterns, helping security teams prepare defenses before they are exploited.

- **Adversary Emulation**: AI can mimic the tactics, techniques, and procedures (TTPs) of specific threat actors, allowing teams to test their defenses against realistic attack simulations.

Example: Emulating Advanced Persistent Threats (APTs)

Generative AI helped a healthcare organization model APT attacks targeting patient data, enabling the team to identify weak points in their infrastructure and implement preemptive measures.

6.2.2 Custom Threat Intelligence Feeds

One size does not fit all when it comes to cybersecurity. Generative AI enables the creation of custom threat intelligence feeds tailored to an organization's unique needs.

- **Industry-Specific Intelligence**: Generative AI curates threat data relevant to specific industries, such as finance, healthcare, or manufacturing, addressing unique risks.

- **Infrastructure-Specific Feeds**: Organizations can receive intelligence tailored to their technology stack, highlighting vulnerabilities in their specific configurations.

- **Risk Profile Alignment**: Generative AI generates intelligence feeds based on an organization's risk tolerance, prioritizing threats that could cause the most damage.

Benefit: Precision Targeting

With custom feeds, organizations receive actionable insights that directly align with their operations, reducing time spent filtering irrelevant information.

6.2.3 Advanced Malware Analysis

Understanding and predicting the evolution of malware is a critical aspect of threat intelligence. Generative AI facilitates this by:

- **Generating Malware Variants**: AI models can create variations of known malware, helping organizations understand how attackers may modify their code to evade detection.

- **Identifying Evasion Techniques**: By analyzing malware samples, generative AI can identify potential methods used by attackers to bypass security mechanisms.

- **Improved Defense Strategies**: Security teams can design more resilient defenses by studying the AI-generated insights on potential malware behavior.

Example: Proactive Defense Against Polymorphic Malware

An AI-powered threat intelligence platform simulated hundreds of variations of a known ransomware strain, allowing a retail organization to adapt its endpoint protection systems and mitigate the risk of infection.

6.2.4 Dynamic Threat Correlation and Global Insights

Generative AI enables dynamic correlation of real-time threat data with external intelligence feeds, providing a comprehensive view of the global threat landscape.

- **Real-Time Analysis**: AI processes and correlates data from multiple sources, including open-source intelligence (OSINT), dark web monitoring, and proprietary feeds, to identify emerging trends.

- **Global Trend Identification**: Generative AI recognizes global attack patterns and campaigns, enabling organizations to align their defenses with broader threat trends.

- **Attack Campaign Detection**: AI models correlate data to identify ongoing or potential attack campaigns targeting specific industries or geographies.

Example: Detecting Global Supply Chain Attacks

A manufacturing organization leveraged generative AI to identify a global supply chain attack trend, allowing it to implement additional security controls to protect its ecosystem from third-party vulnerabilities.

6.2.5 Predictive Threat Modeling

One of the most powerful applications of generative AI in threat intelligence is its ability to predict future threats based on historical and real-time data.

- **Indicator of Compromise (IoC) Prediction**: Generative AI identifies IoCs associated with new or evolving threats, such as ransomware campaigns or phishing schemes.

- **Proactive Countermeasures**: Security teams can implement defenses before threats materialize, minimizing the risk of damage.

- **Predictive Analysis of Attack Campaigns**: AI forecasts the progression of attack campaigns, helping organizations stay one step ahead of attackers.

Example: Predicting Ransomware Attacks

Generative AI models trained on historical ransomware data identified IoCs for emerging campaigns. A financial institution used these insights to block suspicious activities, preventing a costly ransomware incident preemptively.

6.3 Automation of Incident Response with Generative AI

Incident response is at the core of an organization's ability to manage and mitigate cybersecurity threats effectively. With the integration of generative AI, this process becomes faster, more efficient, and less prone to human error. Generative AI automates various stages of the incident response lifecycle, from detection to recovery, providing a proactive and adaptive defense against modern cyber threats.

6.3.1 Real-Time Detection and Analysis

Generative AI enhances the speed and accuracy of identifying security incidents by processing vast amounts of data in real-time.

- **Root Cause Analysis**: AI models analyze logs, user behavior, and network traffic to pinpoint the origin of an attack and its entry points.

- **Scope Identification**: By correlating data from multiple sources, generative AI determines the extent of the attack, including affected systems, data, and users.

- **Impact Prediction**: AI predicts the potential impact of an incident, enabling security teams to prioritize high-risk threats for immediate action.

Example: Analyzing Ransomware Attacks

An organization using AI-powered tools detected ransomware behavior by analyzing unusual file encryption activities, allowing immediate containment before the attack spread.

6.3.2 Playbook Automation for Rapid Response

Security playbooks outline predefined actions for responding to incidents. Generative AI automates the execution of these playbooks, ensuring consistent and timely responses.

- **Orchestrated Actions**: AI executes multiple response steps simultaneously, such as isolating affected devices, disabling compromised accounts, and initiating backups.

- **Error Reduction**: Automated playbook execution minimizes the risk of human error during critical moments.

- **Dynamic Playbooks**: AI adapts playbooks to the specifics of an incident, customizing actions to fit the situation.

Example: Automated Response to Distributed Denial of Service (DDoS) Attacks

An AI-powered incident response system detected a DDoS attack and automatically diverted traffic through a cloud-based mitigation service, reducing downtime and operational impact.

6.3.3 AI-Generated Recommendations for Incident Management

Generative AI provides actionable recommendations for containment, eradication, and recovery based on the characteristics of the attack.

- **Containment Strategies**: AI recommends isolating compromised systems, blocking malicious IPs, or terminating suspicious processes.

- **Eradication Steps**: AI identifies root causes and suggests steps to eliminate threats, such as deploying patches or removing malicious files.

- **Recovery Guidelines**: Post-incident, AI assists in restoring normal operations by guiding system restoration, data recovery, and vulnerability management.

Example: Addressing Insider Threats

When an insider threat was detected, generative AI suggested revoking the user's credentials, reviewing access logs, and conducting a forensic analysis, helping the organization mitigate the risk effectively.

6.3.4 Continuous Learning and Adaptation

Generative AI improves with each incident by learning from the response process, ensuring better handling of similar events in the future.

- **Incident Pattern Recognition**: AI identifies recurring attack patterns, enabling quicker detection and response in future incidents.

- **Playbook Optimization**: By analyzing past responses, AI refines automated playbooks for greater efficiency and accuracy.

- **Enhanced Threat Intelligence Integration**: AI integrates lessons from incidents into broader threat intelligence, improving organizational defenses.

Benefit: Adaptive Defense Strategies

Continuous learning enables organizations to stay ahead of attackers by evolving defenses based on real-world incidents.

6.3.5 Real-World Application: Autonomous Phishing Response

A global retail organization leveraged generative AI to combat phishing attacks.

- **Detection**: When a phishing email was detected, the AI identified the threat, analyzed its content, and flagged it as malicious.

- **Containment**: The AI quarantined affected accounts, preventing further spread.

- **Recovery and Training**: AI provided users with detailed guidance and training resources to recognize phishing attempts, reducing the likelihood of future incidents.

Outcome: Enhanced Phishing Defense

This automated system reduced response times from hours to minutes, minimizing potential damage and improving user awareness.

6.4 Building Resilient and Adaptive Defense Systems

To combat the rapidly evolving cyber threat landscape, organizations require cyber defense systems that are both resilient and adaptive. Resilience ensures systems can withstand and recover from attacks, while adaptability allows them to evolve and stay ahead of emerging threats. Generative AI plays a transformative role in creating such defense systems, leveraging its predictive, analytical, and creative capabilities to fortify cybersecurity frameworks.

6.4.1 Dynamic Defense Mechanisms

Generative AI enables the development of defenses that evolve in real-time based on changes in the threat environment.

- **Real-Time Configuration Adjustments**: AI can automatically adjust firewall rules, intrusion detection systems (IDS), and access controls based on the latest threat intelligence.

- **Threat Anticipation**: Using predictive analytics, generative AI can anticipate attack vectors and deploy countermeasures preemptively.

- **Automated Vulnerability Patching**: AI-driven systems can identify vulnerabilities and apply patches dynamically, reducing the window of exposure.

Example: AI-Adaptive Firewalls

An organization implemented a generative AI-powered firewall that adjusted its rules dynamically, blocking suspicious IP addresses during a wave of credential-stuffing attacks.

6.4.2 Adversarial Training for Advanced Threat Preparedness

Generative adversarial networks (GANs) provide a powerful tool for training AI systems by simulating both attack and defense scenarios.

- **Simulated Attacks**: GANs can mimic sophisticated cyberattacks, such as ransomware or zero-day exploits, allowing AI models to learn and improve their defenses.

- **Strengthened AI Models**: By exposing defense systems to diverse attack patterns, GANs create more robust models capable of handling real-world scenarios.

- **Improved Incident Response**: Adversarial training enhances the accuracy of AI-generated recommendations for mitigating complex threats.

Highlight: AI-Driven Penetration Testing

Organizations are increasingly using generative AI for automated penetration testing. These systems simulate how attackers exploit vulnerabilities, providing insights that strengthen defenses before real-world attacks occur.

6.4.3 Behavioral Analysis for Threat Detection

Generative AI continuously monitors and analyzes the behavior of users, systems, and applications to detect anomalies.

- **Insider Threat Detection**: AI identifies unusual user behavior, such as accessing unauthorized files or logging in from uncharacteristic locations.

- **Compromised Account Identification**: Generative AI can detect subtle changes in account behavior that may indicate compromise, such as altered access patterns.

- **Real-Time Anomaly Detection**: By comparing current behavior to baseline profiles, AI flags potential threats immediately.

Example: Identifying Insider Threats

A healthcare provider used generative AI to monitor access to patient records. The system flagged an employee accessing an unusually high number of files, leading to the discovery of an insider threat.

6.4.4 Failover and Recovery Strategies

Generative AI enhances system resilience by developing intelligent failover and recovery mechanisms to minimize the impact of attacks.

- **Automated Contingency Planning**: AI generates detailed failover plans that ensure business continuity during system outages.

- **Data Backup Strategies**: Generative AI optimizes data backup and restoration processes, reducing recovery times after an attack.

- **Resilient Architecture Design**: AI models simulate various attack scenarios to identify weaknesses in system architecture and recommend improvements.

Benefit: Proactive Business Continuity

With AI-driven recovery strategies, organizations experience minimal downtime and reduced data loss during cyber incidents.

6.4.5 Predictive Maintenance for Cyber Defense Systems

Generative AI enhances the reliability of cyber defense infrastructure through predictive maintenance.

- **System Health Monitoring**: AI analyzes logs and performance metrics to predict hardware or software failures.

- **Proactive Issue Resolution**: Before failures occur, AI recommends maintenance actions, ensuring uninterrupted operations.

- **Enhanced Security Infrastructure**: Continuous optimization of security tools and platforms reduces vulnerabilities.

Example: AI-Powered Predictive Maintenance

A financial institution used generative AI to monitor its security infrastructure. The AI identified potential hardware failures in its intrusion detection system and recommended proactive replacements, preventing downtime.

6.5 Real-Time Data Processing for Proactive Security

Proactive security is essential for staying ahead of cyber threats in a fast-paced digital landscape. The ability to process vast amounts of data in real-time enables organizations to detect, analyze, and respond to potential threats before they cause harm. Generative AI, with its unparalleled data processing capabilities, empowers security teams to make swift, informed decisions by turning raw data into actionable insights.

6.5.1 Streaming Analytics for Rapid Threat Identification

Generative AI can handle continuous data streams from various sources, providing real-time insights into potential threats.

- **Network Traffic Analysis**: AI monitors data from firewalls, routers, and switches to detect suspicious patterns or anomalies.

- **Endpoint Security**: Real-time analytics on endpoint activities enable the detection of malware or unauthorized access attempts.

- **Cloud Environment Monitoring**: AI processes logs and activity data from cloud platforms, identifying unusual behaviors such as unauthorized API calls or excessive resource utilization.

Example: Dynamic Threat Detection

An e-commerce platform integrated generative AI with its network monitoring tools. The AI flagged abnormal traffic spikes during a DDoS attack, allowing the organization to activate mitigation strategies instantly.

6.5.2 Anomaly Detection for Early Threat Warning

Generative AI excels at detecting anomalies by establishing a baseline of normal network and system behavior.

- **Behavioral Analytics**: AI identifies deviations, such as unusual login locations, excessive data downloads, or irregular application usage.

- **User Entity Behavior Analytics (UEBA)**: Generative AI-powered UEBA tools detect insider threats and compromised accounts by analyzing user behavior.

- **Real-Time Alerts**: AI systems notify security teams the moment anomalies are detected, enabling immediate investigation.

Highlight: Mitigating Insider Threats

A financial services company implemented generative AI for behavioral analytics. The AI identified an employee transferring sensitive files to a personal email account, preventing a potential data breach.

6.5.3 Predictive Security for Preemptive Action

By analyzing historical data and identifying trends, generative AI empowers organizations to anticipate and address vulnerabilities before they are exploited.

- **Threat Trend Analysis**: AI predicts emerging threats by analyzing global cyberattack patterns and attack vectors.

- **Vulnerability Management**: AI identifies weak points in the system and recommends timely patching or upgrades.

- **Risk Scoring**: Generative AI assigns risk scores to assets, guiding security teams in prioritizing critical infrastructure.

Example: Ransomware Prevention

A manufacturing company used generative AI to analyze previous ransomware attacks in its industry. The AI identified common IoCs (Indicators of Compromise) and advised preventive measures, such as disabling vulnerable services.

6.5.4 Integration with IoT and Edge Devices

The proliferation of IoT and edge devices introduces new vulnerabilities and data processing challenges. Generative AI enables organizations to process data directly at the edge, ensuring faster threat detection and response.

- **Low-Latency Processing**: AI-powered edge devices analyze data locally, reducing the latency associated with centralized processing.

- **IoT Security**: Generative AI monitors IoT devices for unusual activity, such as unexpected firmware updates or unauthorized access attempts.

- **Real-Time Decision Making**: AI systems deployed on edge devices enable immediate actions, such as isolating compromised devices from the network.

Highlight: Securing Smart Cities

A smart city project deployed generative AI at the edge to monitor traffic systems. When an IoT sensor detected unauthorized access, the AI system disconnected the compromised device, preventing further intrusion.

6.5.5 Case Study: AI-Enhanced Network Security in Healthcare

A healthcare provider adopted generative AI to enhance its network security by monitoring data traffic and detecting anomalies in real-time.

- **Implementation**: The AI system was integrated with the provider's existing SIEM platform, analyzing logs and network activity.

- **Incident**: The AI detected unusual traffic patterns, including a spike in outbound data transfers, signaling a potential breach.

- **Outcome**: The security team acted immediately, isolating the affected system and preventing the exfiltration of sensitive patient data.

6.5.6 Benefits of Real-Time Data Processing with Generative AI

1. **Proactive Threat Detection**: Real-time processing enables organizations to detect threats before they escalate into incidents.

2. **Improved Response Times**: Generative AI reduces the time required to analyze and respond to threats, minimizing damage.

3. **Enhanced Decision-Making**: AI-generated insights provide clarity and precision in addressing cybersecurity challenges.

4. **Scalable Solutions**: Generative AI can handle vast amounts of data, making it suitable for complex environments like IoT and cloud networks.

5. **Cost Efficiency**: Automated monitoring and analysis reduce the need for extensive manual intervention, optimizing resource utilization.

Conclusion

Generative AI offers unprecedented opportunities to revolutionize cybersecurity by enabling more effective threat detection, streamlined incident response, and adaptive defense mechanisms. By integrating generative AI into SOCs, threat intelligence platforms, and real-time data processing systems, organizations can build cyber defense systems that are resilient, adaptive, and proactive. However, successful implementation requires collaboration between AI experts, security professionals, and regulatory bodies to ensure that these systems are not only effective but also ethical and compliant. As cyber threats continue to evolve, generative AI will play an essential role in safeguarding the digital landscape.

Chapter 7: Generative AI in Cloud Security

Introduction

Cloud environments are a cornerstone of modern digital infrastructure, enabling scalability, flexibility, and innovation. However, these environments are also prime targets for cyberattacks due to their complexity and vast attack surface. Generative AI emerges as a transformative technology in securing cloud ecosystems, enabling proactive threat detection, advanced authentication mechanisms, and enhanced compliance management.

7.1 Addressing Cloud-Specific Threats with Generative AI

The adoption of cloud computing has introduced transformative benefits for businesses but has also brought along unique security challenges. Cloud environments operate on a shared responsibility model, where the cloud provider secures the infrastructure while organizations must secure data, applications, and user access. The dynamic and scalable nature of cloud platforms also increases the risk of misconfigurations, data leaks, and advanced cyberattacks. Multi-tenancy risks, where multiple customers share the same physical resources, further complicate security, creating potential vulnerabilities if proper isolation is not enforced.

Generative AI, with its ability to process massive datasets and learn patterns, plays a pivotal role in addressing these challenges. It empowers organizations to maintain a secure cloud environment by enabling intelligent threat detection, automated misconfiguration resolution, and adaptive defenses to safeguard sensitive information and resources.

Below are some of the primary ways in which generative AI addresses these cloud-specific threats.

7.1 1 Identifying Misconfigurations

Misconfigurations in cloud environments are a significant cause of vulnerabilities, often leading to data breaches, unauthorized access, and other security incidents. These misconfigurations can stem from improper settings, lack of adherence to best practices, or human errors during deployment. Generative AI excels at identifying and mitigating these risks by performing real-time configuration analysis, highlighting issues, and suggesting remediation strategies.

7.1.1.1 Exposed S3 Buckets

S3 buckets and other cloud storage solutions are often left publicly accessible due to improper permissions. Generative AI scans these storage configurations continuously to detect such exposures.

- **Proactive Identification**: By analyzing access control lists (ACLs) and policies, AI can flag storage buckets that are publicly accessible or have overly permissive settings.

- **Automated Mitigation**: AI can recommend or apply fixes, such as restricting access to authorized users or enabling server-side encryption to protect stored data.

7.1.1.2 Overly Permissive IAM Roles

Improperly configured IAM roles can allow users or services to access resources beyond their needs, increasing the likelihood of privilege escalation attacks. Generative AI can address this issue by:

- **Dynamic Role Assessment**: Continuously evaluating IAM policies to detect permissions that exceed operational requirements.

- **Policy Optimization Suggestions**: Generative AI suggests modifications to IAM roles, enforcing the principle of least privilege by restricting access to only what is necessary.

- **User Activity Monitoring**: By analyzing user behavior, AI can detect and flag unauthorized attempts to use excessive privileges.

7.1.1.3 Improper Network Rules

Firewalls, security groups, and network access control lists (ACLs) are crucial for cloud security but can be misconfigured, leading to open ports or unrestricted access. Generative AI addresses this by:

- **Scanning Security Group Rules**: AI identifies network rules that allow traffic from untrusted sources or leave critical ports exposed.

- **Cross-Referencing Known Threat Patterns**: By integrating with threat intelligence feeds, AI can flag rules that match known attack vectors.

- **Adaptive Firewall Management**: Generative AI enables real-time updates to firewall rules based on emerging threats, automatically closing vulnerabilities before they are exploited.

7.1.2 Preventing Data Exfiltration

Data exfiltration poses a significant threat to organizations using cloud environments, as attackers often attempt to transfer sensitive data out of a secure network. This risk is particularly heightened in cloud ecosystems due to the large volume of traffic, distributed environments, and potentially misconfigured security controls. Generative AI excels at preventing data exfiltration by continuously monitoring and analyzing outbound traffic patterns, identifying suspicious activities, and enabling proactive responses.

Analyzing Outbound Traffic Patterns

Generative AI can process massive volumes of network data in real-time to identify irregularities in outbound traffic. By leveraging advanced models trained on historical traffic patterns, it can distinguish between legitimate data transfers and potential exfiltration attempts.

- **Dynamic Baseline Establishment**: AI establishes a baseline for normal traffic behavior specific to the organization and flags deviations.

- **Example**: Detecting large outbound data transfers to unfamiliar or blacklisted IP addresses, which could indicate an attempt to exfiltrate sensitive information.

- **Real-Time Alerts**: Security teams are notified immediately when unusual traffic is detected, allowing for swift mitigation actions, such as blocking the transfer or quarantining the affected resources.

Threat Contextualization

Generative AI integrates with threat intelligence feeds to provide context to outbound traffic anomalies.

- **Geolocation Analysis**: The system flags traffic heading to regions associated with cybercrime or known threat actors.

- **File-Type Monitoring**: AI inspects data payloads to identify attempts to transfer sensitive files, such as proprietary documents, source code, or customer data.

Automated Containment

Generative AI can trigger automated containment responses when a potential data exfiltration event is detected.

- **Traffic Isolation**: Redirecting suspicious traffic to a secure sandbox environment for further analysis.

- **Session Termination**: Automatically shutting down sessions associated with suspicious activities, preventing further data loss.

7.1.3 Securing Multi-Cloud Architectures

The adoption of multi-cloud strategies—leveraging platforms such as AWS, Azure, and Google Cloud—offers flexibility and scalability but also creates complex security challenges. Each platform comes with its own security controls, configurations, and monitoring tools, which can result in fragmented security management. Generative AI provides a unified and intelligent approach to securing multi-cloud architectures, ensuring consistent policies, threat detection, and response across all platforms.

Unified Security View

Generative AI consolidates security data from multiple cloud platforms into a centralized dashboard.

- **Centralized Threat Intelligence**: AI aggregates and normalizes logs, alerts, and telemetry data from AWS, Azure, Google Cloud, and other platforms to provide a holistic view of the organization's security posture.

- **Cross-Platform Anomaly Detection**: By analyzing data from all cloud environments, AI identifies threats that might not be evident when monitoring platforms in isolation.

- **Example**: Detecting coordinated attacks that exploit vulnerabilities across multiple cloud providers.

Policy Harmonization

Each cloud platform has unique security configurations and access controls, making it challenging to enforce consistent security policies. Generative AI simplifies this process by:

- **Automating Policy Translation**: Translating high-level security policies into platform-specific rules for AWS Security Groups, Azure Network Security Groups, and Google Cloud Firewalls.

- **Policy Drift Detection**: Continuously monitoring configurations across platforms to detect and resolve inconsistencies.

Inter-Cloud Data Protection

Data often moves between cloud environments in multi-cloud setups, increasing the risk of data leakage. Generative AI strengthens inter-cloud data security by:

- **Encryption Enforcement**: Ensuring all inter-cloud data transfers use secure encryption protocols.

- **Data Access Monitoring**: Tracking data access and transfers across platforms to prevent unauthorized access.

Proactive Threat Mitigation

Generative AI enables proactive defenses by correlating security events across cloud platforms and identifying global attack campaigns.

- **Example**: If a phishing campaign targets Azure-hosted services, AI can predict potential spillover risks to the organization's AWS and Google Cloud assets, enabling preemptive measures.

Simplifying Multi-Cloud Compliance

Generative AI assists with meeting compliance requirements across different cloud platforms by automating:

- **Audit Preparation**: Generating reports that include evidence of compliance for each platform.

- **Regulatory Mapping**: Aligning configurations with standards such as GDPR, HIPAA, or PCI-DSS, regardless of the cloud provider.

By securing multi-cloud environments with generative AI, organizations can leverage the best features of multiple cloud platforms without compromising on security or operational efficiency.

7.2 Real-Time Data Monitoring and Anomaly Detection

In the rapidly changing and complex cloud environments, real-time data monitoring is essential for identifying and mitigating potential security threats before they cause significant damage. Generative AI excels in processing and analyzing vast amounts of data in real-time, providing security teams with actionable insights and enabling swift responses to emerging threats.

7.2.1 Continuous Monitoring

Generative AI continuously monitors cloud environments, processing a massive influx of log data from various sources such as virtual machines (VMs), containers, serverless functions, and network traffic. This allows it to detect potential threats and security issues in real-time.

Cloud Workload Protection

Cloud workloads, which include VMs, containers, and serverless functions, are prime targets for cybercriminals. Generative AI monitors these resources for anomalous behavior, such as:

- **Abnormal Resource Usage**: Identifying unusual spikes in CPU, memory, or network usage, which may indicate a compromised workload.

- **Suspicious Processes**: Detecting unexpected processes running within containers or VMs that could be a sign of a malicious actor.

- **Unauthorized Access**: Monitoring for unauthorized access or privilege escalation within cloud-hosted workloads, ensuring that only legitimate users or processes interact with critical systems.

Threat Correlation

Generative AI can cross-reference activities across different regions, accounts, or cloud services to identify potential coordinated attacks that might not be evident when isolated. This is especially important in multi-cloud and hybrid environments where resources span across multiple platforms.

- **Cross-Region Activity**: Identifying suspicious activity in one region that may be part of a broader attack affecting multiple cloud regions or data centers.

- **Account Anomalies**: Detecting unusual patterns of cross-account or inter-service communication that could indicate lateral movement by an attacker.

- **Multi-Cloud Correlation**: Generating insights across AWS, Azure, Google Cloud, and on-premises systems to spot cross-platform attacks that individual cloud-native tools may miss.

7.2.2 Behavior-Based Anomaly Detection

Generative AI uses machine learning models to establish normal behavioral baselines for users, applications, and workloads within cloud environments. By understanding typical activities, AI can then detect deviations from these patterns that may signal malicious actions.

Examples of Anomalies

Behavior-based anomaly detection helps security teams focus on potential threats that deviate from expected patterns, such as:

- **Unusual Login Times or Locations**: If a user logs in at an unusual time of day or from an unfamiliar location, it may indicate that an attacker has gained access to their account.

- **Unexpected API Calls to Critical Services**: AI detects when applications or users make unexpected or unauthorized API calls to critical cloud services, which could suggest exploitation attempts or privilege abuse.

- **Abnormal Data Transfer Volumes**: Large, unexpected data transfers from cloud servers or storage systems could indicate that an attacker is exfiltrating sensitive information.

Establishing Baselines

Generative AI creates detailed baselines for:

- **User Behavior**: Learning typical patterns for login times, IP addresses, device types, and access privileges for individual users.

- **Application Behavior**: Analyzing normal application behaviors, such as API request frequencies, database queries, and interaction with cloud services, to detect outliers.

- **Workload Behavior**: Monitoring serverless functions, containerized applications, and VMs to establish what constitutes typical workload behavior under different circumstances.

Contextualization

When deviations from normal behavior are detected, AI uses contextual data (such as historical information and threat intelligence feeds) to determine whether the anomaly is truly suspicious or a false positive. For example, a login from a new geographical location could be normal if the user is traveling or working remotely but flagged as suspicious if the login follows a known breach pattern.

7.2.3 Automated Threat Remediation

Generative AI integrates seamlessly with Security Orchestration, Automation, and Response (SOAR) platforms, enabling automated threat mitigation actions in response to detected anomalies. Automation significantly reduces the time it takes to respond to threats, which is crucial in preventing or minimizing damage caused by security incidents.

Example: Automatically Revoking Access for Compromised Credentials

If generative AI detects abnormal behavior associated with user credentials—such as access from a new location or unexpected API calls—it can trigger an automated response:

- **Revoking Access**: The AI can automatically revoke the affected user's access to critical systems, preventing further malicious activity.

- **User Notification**: The affected user is immediately notified, providing information about the suspicious activity and recommending steps to reset credentials or secure their account.

- **Password Reset**: The AI can initiate a password reset for the affected account to prevent further access from compromised credentials.

- **Quarantining Affected Resources**: If suspicious activities are associated with a particular resource (e.g., a server or database), the AI can isolate the resource to contain the potential impact of an attack.

Automating Playbooks

AI-powered automation can integrate predefined security playbooks, which outline specific steps that must be taken in response to certain types of incidents. For example:

- **Phishing Attack Playbook**: Automatically quarantine suspicious emails, alert the security team, and reset passwords for any compromised accounts.

- **DDoS Attack Playbook**: Trigger an automated response to scale resources up or engage anti-DDoS services to mitigate the impact of the attack.

- **Insider Threat Playbook:** Automatically revoke access, lock accounts, and initiate a forensic investigation into potentially compromised users.

Continuous Feedback Loop

As generative AI systems detect and respond to incidents, they continuously learn from each event, refining their models and improving their threat detection and remediation capabilities. Over time, this leads to more accurate anomaly detection and quicker, more effective automated responses.

By enabling continuous monitoring, behavior-based anomaly detection, and automated remediation, generative AI enhances cloud security operations, ensuring that organizations can respond to emerging threats faster and more effectively while minimizing the burden on human security teams.

7.3 Enhancing Secure Access and Authentication

As cloud environments continue to grow and evolve, managing secure access and identity becomes increasingly complex. Generative AI offers advanced, adaptive mechanisms for ensuring robust access control and identity management, balancing security with user convenience. By leveraging real-time data and intelligent analysis, AI transforms the traditional access management models into dynamic, context-sensitive systems that enhance both security and user experience.

7.3.1 AI-Driven Multi-Factor Authentication (MFA)

Multi-factor authentication (MFA) is a fundamental security measure that requires users to provide multiple forms of verification before gaining access to critical resources. Generative AI enhances MFA systems by introducing adaptive and dynamic approaches that respond to risk levels, improving both the security and user experience.

Risk-Based MFA

Traditionally, MFA requires users to provide two or more forms of authentication, such as something they know (password), something they have (phone or token), or something they are (biometric data). With generative AI, MFA can be adapted based on the risk level associated with a specific login attempt.

- **Dynamic Authentication Prompts**: If a login attempt is detected from an unfamiliar location, new device, or atypical time, AI can increase the authentication requirements. For instance, AI may prompt for additional verification such as:

  - **Biometric Authentication**: Facial recognition or fingerprint scanning to ensure the legitimacy of the user.

  - **Secondary OTP (One-Time Password)**: AI may require a one-time password sent to the user's mobile device or email for added security.

  - **Behavioral Biometrics**: AI can assess factors like typing speed, mouse movements, or unique device identifiers as part of the authentication process.

Adaptive Authentication

Generative AI continuously monitors user behavior, learning the typical patterns of login times, locations, and devices. It adjusts authentication requirements in real-time based on deviations from the established baseline. For example:

- **Low-Risk Scenarios**: If the system detects an access request from a known device and familiar location, it may streamline the MFA process, allowing seamless access for the user.

- **High-Risk Scenarios**: If a request comes from an unusual device or location, the AI triggers additional security measures, such as biometric authentication or multi-step verification, to ensure the authenticity of the user.

7.3.2 Context-Aware Access Control

Context-aware access control takes security to the next level by considering real-time contextual factors to determine whether access should be granted. Generative AI can dynamically enforce access control policies based on a combination of factors, ensuring that only authorized individuals can access sensitive data or systems.

Examples of Contextual Factors

Generative AI integrates multiple contextual elements to adjust access controls, enhancing security while improving usability. Key factors include:

- **Device Security Posture**: AI evaluates the security health of the device being used to access cloud resources. For instance:

    o **Device Compliance**: If the device lacks the latest security patches or has an outdated antivirus, AI may deny access or prompt the user to secure their device before granting access.

    o **Endpoint Protection**: If the device is not protected by an endpoint detection and response (EDR) solution, the AI might restrict access to critical systems until the device meets specific security standards.

- **Geographic Location**: AI can identify the geographic location from which an access request is originating. If the location deviates from the user's normal behavior or raises flags (e.g., access from a high-risk country), additional authentication measures may be required.

    o **Access Control Based on Location**: AI can dynamically adjust policies based on the geographic location, denying access from regions known for high cybercrime activity while allowing it from trusted locations.

- **Time of Access**: The timing of access requests is another factor that AI takes into consideration. If an employee typically works from 9 AM to 5 PM and attempts to access sensitive resources at midnight, the AI may flag this request for further verification.

  o **Access Time Restrictions**: AI can enforce time-based access control, where users are only allowed to access certain systems or data during specific hours based on their role or pattern of use.

Real-Time Evaluation

Generative AI continuously assesses these contextual factors in real-time, ensuring that access control policies are flexible and responsive to the current risk environment. This allows organizations to maintain secure systems while providing users with a smooth experience, even when their context changes.

7.3.3 Passwordless Authentication

As traditional passwords become a major security liability due to their vulnerability to phishing, brute-force attacks, and reuse across multiple services, passwordless authentication methods are gaining traction. Generative AI enhances passwordless authentication by using behavioral biometrics and contextual data to authenticate users in a seamless and highly secure manner.

Behavioral Biometrics

Generative AI can analyze users' unique behavioral patterns to verify their identity. This biometric approach allows organizations to eliminate passwords without sacrificing security.

- **Typing Patterns**: AI can track the way a user types, including speed, rhythm, and pressure applied on the keyboard, as part of the authentication process.

- **Mouse Movements**: The way a user moves their mouse (speed, direction, and patterns) can also serve as a biometric indicator for identity verification.

- **Touchscreen Interactions**: For mobile users, AI can assess swipe patterns, touch pressure, and the way users interact with their devices to authenticate them.

Contextual Authentication

Beyond behavioral biometrics, AI considers additional contextual factors to ensure the right person is attempting to access the system. For instance:

- **Location and Device Analysis**: If a login attempt is made from a familiar device and location, AI can quickly validate the user's identity based on behavioral biometrics alone.

- **Risk-Based Decisions**: If an anomaly is detected, such as a login attempt from an unfamiliar device or location, AI may request additional verification, such as a one-time code sent to the user's registered phone or email.

Seamless User Experience

AI-powered passwordless authentication not only enhances security but also improves the user experience. Traditional password resets or recovery procedures are eliminated, reducing friction for users while ensuring that only legitimate individuals can access sensitive systems.

Integration with Existing Systems

Generative AI can be easily integrated with existing authentication systems and identity management platforms, allowing for the gradual transition to passwordless authentication without requiring major overhauls of the organization's infrastructure.

7.4 AI-Driven Compliance and Governance in Cloud Environments

In highly regulated industries, maintaining compliance and adhering to governance standards are crucial for avoiding legal penalties, ensuring data protection, and maintaining customer trust. Generative AI plays a pivotal role in simplifying compliance management by automating monitoring, policy creation, and auditing processes, all while ensuring that organizations meet regulations such as GDPR, HIPAA, ISO 27001, and others.

7.4.1 Automated Compliance Monitoring

Automated compliance monitoring powered by generative AI is essential for organizations looking to maintain constant adherence to regulatory standards in dynamic cloud environments. Traditional compliance monitoring is often reactive, relying on periodic audits that can miss critical violations. Generative AI offers continuous, real-time compliance monitoring, allowing for immediate detection of policy violations and rapid remediation.

Continuous Monitoring of Cloud Resources

Generative AI uses real-time data analysis to monitor cloud environments for compliance issues constantly. By continuously scanning infrastructure and data configurations, AI can instantly identify violations such as:

- **Unencrypted Sensitive Data**: AI algorithms can detect sensitive data (such as personal health information or financial records) stored or transmitted without encryption, which could violate regulations like GDPR or HIPAA.

- **Non-Compliant Data Retention Policies**: AI monitors data retention practices and flags any instances where data is kept beyond its legal retention period or stored inappropriately.

- **Unauthorized Access**: AI can identify unusual user access patterns, such as an employee accessing data they are not authorized to view, triggering an automatic compliance violation alert.

Automated Reporting

Generative AI can generate detailed compliance reports for auditors, showing not only violations but also a history of actions taken to correct issues. These reports can include:

- **Summary of Violations**: Detailed summaries of non-compliance incidents with relevant timestamps, actions taken, and any user activity associated with the violation.

- **Audit Trails**: AI creates an immutable audit trail for all compliance-related activities, ensuring transparency and accountability in the organization's processes.

Proactive Remediation

AI not only detects compliance issues but also can trigger automatic remediation. For example:

- **Triggering Alerts**: When a violation is detected, AI sends immediate alerts to the appropriate teams, ensuring that corrective measures are taken swiftly.

- **Automated Remediation**: In some cases, AI can automatically rectify certain issues, such as encrypting data that was previously unencrypted or disabling unauthorized user access.

7.4.2 Policy Generation and Enforcement

Generative AI makes policy creation and enforcement significantly easier for organizations, ensuring that their cloud environments comply with a wide variety of industry standards. AI can be used to generate security policies tailored to an organization's specific regulatory requirements and automatically enforce these policies to ensure consistent compliance.

Policy Generation

AI can analyze an organization's operational and regulatory requirements and automatically generate cloud security policies that are compliant with relevant standards. These policies may include rules for:

- **Data Protection**: Defining encryption, data access control, and storage guidelines that meet standards like GDPR or HIPAA.

- **Access Controls**: Enforcing policies that ensure only authorized users have access to sensitive data or systems, adhering to regulations like SOC 2 or ISO 27001.

- **Data Residency**: Defining geographic restrictions to ensure that data is stored only in countries or regions with strong data protection laws, such as the European Union or certain U.S. states like California (CCPA).

Policy Enforcement

Once policies are generated, generative AI continuously monitors cloud environments to ensure adherence to these policies and immediately enforces actions to prevent non-compliance. For instance:

- **Blocking Data Transfers**: If an organization needs to prevent the transfer of data to regions with inadequate data protection laws, AI can automatically block any unauthorized data transfers to these regions.

- **Denying Unauthorized Access**: AI can identify and block attempts by users to access data or systems they are not authorized to, ensuring that data access complies with privacy regulations.

Adaptive Policy Enforcement

Generative AI can also adapt policies dynamically in response to changing regulations or organizational needs, ensuring that compliance remains up-to-date. For example, as new versions of HIPAA or GDPR are released, AI systems can automatically update policies to reflect new requirements, eliminating the need for manual adjustments.

7.4.3 Reducing Audit Fatigue

Compliance audits are often labor-intensive and time-consuming, requiring large amounts of data to be manually analyzed and reported. Generative AI significantly reduces audit fatigue by automating many aspects of the auditing process, making it faster, more efficient, and less prone to human error.

Aggregating Logs for a Unified View

During an audit, auditors often need to review logs from a variety of sources across different systems. Generative AI simplifies this process by aggregating logs from multiple cloud services into a unified view, saving time and effort for auditors.

- **Centralized Log Management**: AI systems automatically collect logs from various cloud resources, such as virtual machines, databases, and network traffic, and consolidate them into a single location for easy access and analysis.

- **Intelligent Log Categorization**: AI can categorize logs based on relevance to the audit, highlighting incidents that are most likely to be of concern from a compliance perspective.

Identifying Key Events Relevant to Compliance Standards

AI helps auditors by automatically identifying key events and incidents that are critical to compliance standards. For example:

- **Data Access Events**: AI highlights instances where sensitive data was accessed outside of normal business hours or by unauthorized users.

- **Non-Compliant Configurations**: AI flags changes to configurations that may put the organization at risk of non-compliance, such as the disabling of encryption or the opening of firewalls.

- **Policy Violations**: AI can recognize violations of established compliance policies, such as failure to adhere to data residency requirements, and bring them to the auditor's attention.

Streamlining Audit Processes

By automating repetitive tasks and providing intelligent insights, AI reduces the manual effort required for audits, making the process more efficient. The use of AI-driven tools ensures that:

- **Audit Results Are Presented Clearly**: AI-generated reports and dashboards present audit findings in a clear and concise manner, enabling auditors to focus on high-priority issues.

- **Real-Time Audit Readiness**: Continuous monitoring and reporting ensure that organizations are always audit-ready, reducing the stress and urgency associated with preparing for audits.

Minimizing Human Error

By automating data aggregation, log analysis, and event identification, AI reduces the potential for human error during audits. This ensures that organizations can confidently present their compliance posture to auditors, knowing that critical violations and risks have not been overlooked.

7.5 Case Studies: Successful Applications in Cloud Security

Generative AI is increasingly being leveraged by organizations across various industries to enhance cloud security. Below are several real-world case studies illustrating how generative AI addresses security challenges in multi-cloud environments, healthcare, and e-commerce, providing valuable insights into the practical applications of AI in cloud security.

7.5.1 Case Study: Financial Institution's AI-Driven Cloud Security

A global financial institution operating across multiple cloud platforms—AWS, Azure, and Google Cloud—adopted generative AI to strengthen its cloud security posture while ensuring compliance with stringent financial regulations.

Challenges

The financial institution faced several key challenges in managing its multi-cloud environment:

- **Compliance Across Multiple Cloud Providers**: The institution had to meet the compliance standards set by financial regulatory bodies, such as GDPR, PCI DSS, and SOC 2, while managing workloads across AWS, Azure, and GCP.

- **Secure Access for Remote Employees**: With a large remote workforce, maintaining secure access to sensitive financial data while ensuring seamless user experience was a significant concern.

Solutions

Generative AI played a pivotal role in addressing these challenges:

- **IAM Role Misconfigurations**: AI continuously analyzed Identity and Access Management (IAM) roles across all cloud environments. It detected overly permissive roles and flagged potential misconfigurations, preventing privilege escalation. This proactive security measure minimized the risk of unauthorized access to critical financial data.

- **Real-Time Anomaly Detection**: AI-powered anomaly detection algorithms monitored API calls in real-time, identifying suspicious activity, such as unusually large data requests or calls from unfamiliar IP addresses. When the system flagged an attempt to exfiltrate sensitive customer data, it automatically blocked the data transfer and alerted security teams.

- **Automated Compliance Reports**: To streamline compliance efforts, generative AI generated real-time compliance reports based on audit trails, which were automatically updated. This reduced the time and resources typically needed for audit preparation, cutting down the cost of manual reviews and minimizing the risk of human error.

Outcome

- **Enhanced Security**: Generative AI ensured the financial institution maintains a strong security posture, reducing the likelihood of data breaches or regulatory violations.

- **Operational Efficiency**: By automating compliance reporting and threat detection, AI freed up security teams to focus on more strategic activities, ensuring faster response times and lowering the operational costs of manual oversight.

7.5.2 Case Study: Healthcare Organization's Data Protection

A leading healthcare provider adopted generative AI to protect patient data in the cloud, ensuring compliance with the Health Insurance Portability and Accountability Act (HIPAA) while also addressing insider threats and data breaches.

Challenges

The healthcare provider faced several challenges:

- **Compliance with HIPAA**: Ensuring that sensitive patient data, including medical records, remained encrypted and was accessed only by authorized individuals in accordance with HIPAA regulations.

- **Managing Large Volumes of Sensitive Data**: The organization handled a massive volume of data, making it difficult to track every instance of data access and transfer, especially when managing remote access to sensitive information.

Solutions

Generative AI helped mitigate these risks by implementing the following solutions:

- **Data Transfer Monitoring**: AI continuously monitored data transfers within the cloud environment, ensuring that all sensitive patient data was properly encrypted both in transit and at rest. Unauthorized data access attempts were immediately flagged, ensuring compliance with HIPAA's strict data protection regulations.

- **AI-Driven Behavioral Analytics**: Generative AI implemented behavioral analytics to monitor staff activity within the cloud environment. The system learned normal usage patterns for healthcare workers and flagged deviations, such as accessing records outside of a user's normal working hours or accessing unnecessary patient data. In one instance, the AI identified a potential insider threat and prevented a data breach.

- **Automated Alerts and Remediation**: When AI detects any irregularities, such as suspicious login attempts or attempts to access non-authorized data, it immediately triggers alerts to security teams and automated remediation workflows. This included actions like temporarily locking accounts, blocking certain data transfers, or escalating issues to higher-level security personnel.

Outcome

- **Reduced Risk of Data Breaches**: By proactively detecting and mitigating insider threats and ensuring data encryption, generative AI significantly reduced the risk of a potential data breach involving sensitive patient data.

- **Enhanced Compliance**: The healthcare provider could maintain a strong compliance posture, meeting HIPAA requirements while minimizing the overhead traditionally associated with compliance audits.

7.5.3 Case Study: AI-Powered Authentication for E-Commerce

An e-commerce giant faced challenges in balancing user security and a smooth user experience during high-traffic sales events. To address these issues, the organization turned to generative AI to enhance its authentication systems while minimizing friction for customers.

Challenges

The e-commerce platform faced several challenges during peak shopping periods:

- **Balancing Security with User Experience**: High-traffic events like Black Friday or holiday sales generated millions of transactions, and ensuring secure access without causing delays or frustration for users was a critical concern.

- **Fraud Prevention**: The platform needed to prevent fraudulent transactions while ensuring legitimate customers could easily access their accounts and make purchases.

Solutions

Generative AI provided several solutions to these challenges:

- **AI-Powered MFA**: To enhance security without compromising user experience, the e-commerce platform adopted AI-driven Multi-Factor Authentication (MFA). During high-risk logins (e.g., from new locations or devices), the system dynamically adjusted authentication requirements, prompting users to provide additional verification, such as biometric authentication or a secondary code, only when necessary.

- **Passwordless Authentication**: The platform integrated generative AI to implement passwordless authentication using behavioral biometrics, such as analyzing typing patterns or mouse movements. This allowed customers to quickly log in without the need to remember or type passwords, significantly improving the user experience while maintaining a high level of security.

- **Fraud Detection and Prevention**: AI continuously monitored transaction patterns for signs of fraudulent activity. For example, if a user suddenly made large purchases from multiple locations within a short timeframe, the AI would flag this as suspicious and prompt additional verification.

Outcome

- **Improved User Experience**: The e-commerce platform achieved a seamless login process, particularly during high-traffic events, where customers did not experience delays or frustration with additional security measures.

- **Enhanced Security**: By implementing AI-powered MFA and passwordless authentication, the platform significantly reduced the risk of account takeover and fraudulent transactions while maintaining a user-friendly experience.

Conclusion

Generative AI is revolutionizing cloud security by addressing unique challenges, enabling real-time monitoring, enhancing authentication, and automating compliance processes. As cloud environments continue to grow in complexity, the role of generative AI will become increasingly pivotal in ensuring robust and adaptive defenses. Organizations leveraging these AI-driven capabilities gain a competitive edge by reducing risks, improving operational efficiency, and safeguarding their most valuable assets in the cloud.

Chapter 8: Generative AI for Insider Threat Detection

Introduction

Insider threats—whether malicious or unintentional—pose significant risks to organizations. These threats can originate from employees, contractors, or partners with access to critical systems and data. Detecting insider threats has become increasingly complex as organizations scale and implement remote work models, multi-cloud environments, and diverse access controls. Generative AI can significantly enhance an organization's ability to identify, mitigate, and prevent insider threats through advanced behavioral analysis, anomaly detection, and real-time response capabilities.

8.1 Identifying Behavioral Patterns with Generative AI

Traditional methods of detecting insider threats rely heavily on predefined rules and signatures, which may not account for evolving or new threat vectors. Generative AI, on the other hand, enables organizations to identify behavioral patterns indicative of potential malicious activity by continuously learning from vast amounts of data.

Behavioral Profiling

Generative AI uses advanced machine learning models to create behavioral profiles for users, devices, and applications. These models learn "normal" behavior patterns for individuals based on a variety of factors, such as:

- **Login Patterns**: Frequency of login attempts, times of day, and geographical location.

- **Resource Access**: Which systems, files, or applications users frequently interact with.

- **File Manipulation**: Patterns of file access, uploads, downloads, or deletions.

Anomaly Detection

Once the baseline of normal activity is established, the generative AI system continuously monitors ongoing actions to detect anomalies. For example, if an employee who typically accesses a specific set of customer records suddenly accesses sensitive financial data, this could trigger an alert. Additionally, if a user who normally logs in from one geographic location attempts to access from another, this would be flagged for investigation.

- **Example**: An employee's pattern of accessing sensitive data late at night without prior history of doing so triggers an alert, which the AI flags for review by the security team.

Dynamic Behavioral Modeling

Generative AI's advantage lies in its ability to adapt and refine behavioral profiles over time. As a user's role or the organization's needs evolve, the AI system continuously adjusts the baseline behavior models, improving its ability to detect subtle or changing insider threats.

8.2 Detecting Data Exfiltration and Unusual Activity

Data exfiltration is one of the most dangerous outcomes of an insider threat, often leading to significant breaches of confidential or proprietary information. Generative AI enhances the detection of potential data exfiltration attempts by analyzing traffic patterns, monitoring user behavior, and identifying abnormal activities that may signal an unauthorized data transfer.

Data Transfer Monitoring

Generative AI uses advanced algorithms to monitor outbound data flows, comparing real-time activity with established baselines. Any data transfers that deviate from normal patterns—such as transferring unusually large volumes of data, especially to external or untrusted locations—are flagged as potential exfiltration attempts.

- **Example**: A user who typically accesses small amounts of data may suddenly attempt to transfer a large volume of sensitive financial records to an external server. This triggers an immediate alert.

Unusual Access Patterns

By continuously monitoring user and entity activity, AI can detect instances where insiders are accessing files or systems that are not typically part of their workflow. Unusual access, particularly to critical systems or unencrypted data, is often a key indicator of potential malicious intent or negligence.

- **Example**: An employee in the marketing department accessing confidential financial reports or sensitive engineering documents would be flagged for review by AI systems trained to recognize this anomaly.

Behavioral Flags

Generative AI can also detect behavioral changes that could indicate the preparation for data exfiltration. These may include:

- **Multiple failed login attempts** or unusual success rates.
- **Uncommon network access points** (e.g., the use of a VPN or proxy server).
- **Unusual file transfers** outside normal business hours.

Real-Time Data Exfiltration Detection

Generative AI can perform real-time analysis of ongoing activities, helping detect potential exfiltration attempts as they happen. With integrated alerting mechanisms, AI ensures that potential threats are immediately flagged, investigated, and mitigated before data is fully exfiltrated.

8.3 Enhancing User and Entity Behavior Analytics (UEBA)

User and Entity Behavior Analytics (UEBA) is an advanced security approach that leverages AI to monitor and analyze the behavior of users, devices, and entities across the network. Generative AI significantly enhances UEBA systems by providing more dynamic, adaptive, and accurate threat detection.

Contextual Behavior Analysis

Generative AI adds a layer of contextual understanding to UEBA. It not only tracks what users are doing but also assesses the context in which they are performing these actions. For example, an employee accessing sensitive data during normal working hours from a company-issued device may be deemed legitimate. However, accessing the same data outside of working hours or from an unknown device could be flagged as suspicious.

- **Example**: UEBA systems powered by generative AI can detect changes in user behavior, such as increased file downloads, accessing files from different departments, or attempts to bypass security controls, all of which may indicate preparatory actions for a data breach.

Entity Behavior Profiling

Generative AI helps UEBA systems create profiles for entities—devices, applications, and networks—that are integrated into the enterprise ecosystem. By assessing the normal behavior of entities, such as system accesses, application interactions, and network communications, AI can flag anomalous activities that deviate from the norm.

- **Example**: An AI model could learn that a particular database is usually accessed during office hours and that high-level database administrators typically only interact with it. If an entity outside this profile attempts to access the database after hours, it will trigger an anomaly detection alert.

Real-Time Threat Detection and Prevention

Generative AI enhances UEBA by continuously analyzing data and detecting malicious behavior in real-time. When abnormal behavior is identified, the AI system can either automatically respond (e.g., locking down the user account or limiting access) or escalate the issue for human intervention, minimizing the potential damage caused by insider threats.

8.4 Preventing Insider Threats in Remote Work Environments

As organizations increasingly embrace remote and hybrid work models, securing remote access to cloud environments becomes a critical component of the cybersecurity strategy. Insider threats in remote work environments can be difficult to detect because users are not operating within the usual network perimeter, making it easier to bypass traditional security mechanisms.

AI-Powered Remote Access Monitoring

Generative AI enhances remote work security by continuously monitoring user activity across different access points—whether employees are working from home, a coffee shop, or any location outside the corporate network. By analyzing user behavior, AI can detect signs of abnormal activities, such as unauthorized access to company systems or attempts to download sensitive data from unsecured devices.

- **Example**: A remote worker who typically accesses company systems via a corporate VPN may suddenly access systems from an unfamiliar device or location. AI would flag this access attempt for review, even if the user had valid credentials.

Risk-Based Authentication for Remote Workers

Generative AI can also implement risk-based authentication (RBA) to enhance security for remote workers. Depending on the context of a remote session—such as the location, device type, or time of access—the AI may require additional verification, like biometric authentication or a one-time password.

- **Example**: If an employee logs in from an unusual geographical location or a new device, the AI system might trigger an additional layer of authentication before granting access, thus minimizing the risk of a compromised account.

Real-Time Data Loss Prevention (DLP) for Remote Work

Generative AI can integrate with data loss prevention (DLP) tools to monitor the movement of sensitive information within remote work environments. If an employee attempts to share confidential documents through unsecured channels or emails, AI-driven DLP systems can automatically block or encrypt the data.

- **Example**: If a remote worker tries to transfer customer data to a personal email account, the AI-powered DLP system would prevent the transfer and flag the action for further investigation.

Behavioral Risk Assessment for Remote Workers

By leveraging historical data and real-time behavioral analysis, generative AI can assess the level of risk associated with remote employees. If an employee shows signs of suspicious activity—such as accessing large volumes of data or trying to bypass security protocols—AI can trigger automatic remediation actions, such as limiting access or flagging the activity for human review.

- **Example**: An AI system might detect that a remote worker is accessing large amounts of financial data during odd hours and automatically alert the security team for investigation.

Conclusion

Generative AI represents a powerful tool in the detection and mitigation of insider threats, providing organizations with enhanced capabilities for identifying unusual behaviors, preventing data exfiltration, and safeguarding sensitive information in remote work environments. By leveraging machine learning models that continuously adapt to new data, AI offers organizations the ability to stay ahead of evolving threats, respond in real-time, and reduce the impact of insider-related security breaches. As insider threats continue to evolve, adopting AI-driven security measures will be essential for organizations seeking to maintain a proactive and dynamic defense posture.

Chapter 9: Generative AI for Offensive Cybersecurity

Introduction

Offensive cybersecurity techniques, such as red teaming and penetration testing, are essential for identifying vulnerabilities before malicious actors can exploit them. Generative AI is increasingly becoming a key tool in offensive cybersecurity due to its ability to simulate complex attack scenarios, improve testing efficiency, and enhance the effectiveness of security teams. However, the use of AI in these contexts also raises ethical concerns, especially with the potential for misuse in unethical hacking activities. This chapter explores how generative AI is transforming offensive cybersecurity, its applications, and the ethical challenges that come with it.

9.1 Red Teaming and Penetration Testing with Generative AI

Red teaming and penetration testing are proactive security measures used to assess an organization's security posture. Generative AI enhances these techniques by automating and streamlining complex tasks, enabling security teams to identify vulnerabilities faster and with greater accuracy.

Automating Attack Simulation

Generative AI can automate various phases of red teaming and penetration testing, significantly improving the speed and efficiency of these activities. Traditional penetration tests involve manual exploration of vulnerabilities, often consuming considerable time and resources. With generative AI, automated tools can rapidly identify attack vectors, simulate attack scenarios, and test security defenses without human intervention.

- **Example**: A generative AI model could simulate advanced persistent threats (APTs), testing how an organization's network responds to long-term, multi-phase attacks. It would mimic sophisticated tactics used by adversaries to identify weaknesses in intrusion detection systems, firewalls, and incident response plans.

Adapting to New Attack Techniques

Generative AI excels at adapting to evolving attack strategies by learning from new data and patterns. Traditional red teaming often focuses on pre-configured scenarios, but AI can generate unique attack strategies based on real-time intelligence. This enables offensive security teams to stay ahead of emerging threats and adapt their testing efforts accordingly.

- **Example**: If AI detects a new zero-day vulnerability in a widely used application, it can immediately generate custom attack scenarios to exploit this vulnerability in a test environment, allowing the team to evaluate the impact before attackers can exploit it in the wild.

Enhanced Social Engineering Simulations

Generative AI can also improve social engineering attack simulations, such as phishing, spear-phishing, or pretexting. By analyzing the behavior of targeted individuals and understanding organizational structures, AI can generate highly personalized and convincing attack scenarios. This allows red teams to assess an organization's human defenses and identify weaknesses in employee awareness and training.

- **Example**: AI could generate highly tailored spear-phishing emails based on data gathered from publicly available sources, such as social media profiles and company websites, to test whether employees fall for these advanced tactics.

Continuous Testing

Unlike traditional penetration tests that occur at fixed intervals, AI can provide continuous testing by simulating attacks across a network in real-time. This continuous testing allows organizations to maintain a proactive security posture and identify vulnerabilities as soon as they arise.

- **Example**: Generative AI could continuously probe an organization's web application for security flaws and automatically alert the security team to any vulnerabilities discovered, allowing for swift mitigation before a real attacker can exploit them.

9.2 Exploiting Generative AI for Simulated Attacks

Generative AI can be used to simulate complex and sophisticated cyberattacks, enabling security professionals to evaluate how their systems would react under various threat scenarios. By simulating these attacks, security teams can identify weaknesses in their defenses and take proactive steps to strengthen them.

Simulating Advanced Persistent Threats (APTs)

Generative AI is particularly effective at simulating APTs, which are long-term, stealthy cyberattacks that target organizations to gain access to sensitive data. AI can replicate the tactics, techniques, and procedures (TTPs) of real-world adversaries, allowing organizations to test their ability to detect and respond to these types of threats.

- **Example**: AI could simulate an attacker infiltrating an organization through a spear-phishing email, gaining access to the network, escalating privileges, and maintaining persistence by deploying backdoors or using stolen credentials over an extended period. Security teams could then assess the effectiveness of their defense mechanisms against such sophisticated threats.

Brute Force and Credential Stuffing Attacks

Generative AI can be used to simulate brute force attacks on systems, where AI generates and tests large numbers of possible passwords to gain unauthorized access to user accounts. This can help security teams understand how resilient their systems are to automated login attacks and how effective their rate-limiting and multi-factor authentication (MFA) mechanisms are.

- **Example**: Using AI, an attacker could simulate a credential stuffing attack by taking data leaks from breached websites and trying those credentials against an organization's login portals. This enables security teams to understand how vulnerable their users are to reused or weak passwords.

Ransomware Attack Simulations

Generative AI can be used to simulate ransomware attacks, including the encryption of data and demand for ransom. This allows organizations to evaluate the preparedness of their backup systems, response plans, and user training against such threats.

- **Example**: AI could simulate a ransomware attack that encrypts critical files on servers, spreads through the network, and attempts to exfiltrate sensitive data to an external server. The attack would test an organization's data recovery capabilities and its ability to prevent or detect ransomware before it spreads.

Simulating Insider Threats

Generative AI is also capable of simulating insider threats, whether from malicious or negligent employees. AI can create scenarios where an insider attempts to steal data, escalate privileges, or intentionally disrupt services, enabling security teams to assess the effectiveness of their internal monitoring and access control systems.

- **Example**: AI could simulate an insider threat where a disgruntled employee uses their access to steal customer data or install malicious software. Security teams can evaluate how effectively their internal monitoring systems identify suspicious activities and how quickly they can respond to mitigate the impact.

9.3 Ethical Concerns in Offensive Use of Generative AI

While generative AI has the potential to revolutionize offensive cybersecurity practices, its use raises several ethical concerns that must be carefully considered. Offensive cybersecurity techniques, if misused, can have unintended consequences or be exploited for malicious purposes.

Risks of AI-Generated Cyberattacks

Malicious actors can use generative AI to develop new attack strategies, automate phishing campaigns, or create sophisticated malware that can evade traditional security systems. This poses a significant threat to both individuals and organizations. Ethical hackers must be cautious not to use generative AI for offensive activities that can harm others or lead to unlawful behavior.

- **Example**: A red team could use generative AI to create convincing phishing emails or malware that could inadvertently harm innocent individuals or cause reputational damage to the targeted organizations.

Lack of Consent in Attack Simulations

When using generative AI for penetration testing and red teaming, ethical considerations arise around obtaining consent. Security teams must ensure they have the proper authorization to simulate attacks on networks and systems, especially when the tests may involve sensitive customer data or mission-critical operations.

- **Example**: Conducting simulated cyberattacks on a third-party vendor without their knowledge or consent could result in unintentional disruptions or breach of contractual obligations.

Potential for AI Misuse

While generative AI can be a valuable tool for ethical hackers, it could also be used to develop malicious scripts or automated attacks without proper oversight. Organizations need to implement safeguards to prevent their AI systems from being repurposed for unethical activities, such as launching attacks against unsuspecting targets or amplifying cybercrime efforts.

- **Example**: A generative AI model designed for red teaming could be repurposed by malicious hackers to automate large-scale cyberattacks, such as DDoS attacks, without the need for human intervention.

Transparency and Accountability

There is a need for transparency and accountability in how generative AI is used for offensive cybersecurity activities. Security professionals and organizations must maintain clear records of all actions taken, ensuring that the AI tools are used within the scope of authorized testing and are not being exploited for unauthorized purposes.

- **Example**: A penetration tester must ensure that all AI-generated attack scenarios are documented and approved by the organization's security leadership to ensure ethical compliance.

9.4 Leveraging Generative AI for Risk Assessment and Vulnerability Prioritization

Generative AI can also be leveraged to improve risk assessment and vulnerability prioritization, enabling organizations to focus on the most critical security gaps that pose the highest risk to their infrastructure.

Automated Vulnerability Scanning and Assessment

Generative AI can automate the scanning of systems, applications, and networks for vulnerabilities. Traditional vulnerability scanners often rely on predefined rules and signatures, but AI can generate new scanning strategies based on evolving attack vectors and known exploits, ensuring that security assessments remain up-to-date.

- **Example**: An AI system might be programmed to scan a cloud environment for misconfigurations, unpatched software, or exposed services, using evolving threat intelligence to generate targeted assessments and mitigate vulnerabilities before they are exploited.

Risk Score Generation

AI models can assign risk scores to vulnerabilities based on their potential impact, exploitability, and likelihood of being targeted. These scores help security teams prioritize which vulnerabilities should be addressed first, enabling more efficient use of resources and reducing the overall risk exposure.

- **Example**: AI could assign a higher risk score to vulnerabilities in publicly exposed APIs or outdated software versions that have known exploits, helping security teams prioritize remediation efforts.

Predictive Risk Assessment

Generative AI can predict future risk scenarios by analyzing historical data, emerging threat trends, and patterns in cybersecurity incidents. This predictive capability allows organizations to address vulnerabilities before they are exploited proactively.

- **Example**: By analyzing historical attack data and real-time threat intelligence, AI could predict which vulnerabilities are most likely to be targeted in the future and provide early warnings to security teams, allowing for proactive mitigation.

Tailored Risk Mitigation Recommendations

Based on its findings, generative AI can provide customized recommendations for mitigating vulnerabilities, ensuring that organizations focus their efforts on solutions that are most relevant to their specific security posture.

- **Example**: AI might recommend patching specific vulnerabilities in a company's cloud infrastructure, enabling timely remediation to prevent potential breaches without overwhelming the security team with unnecessary actions.

Conclusion

Generative AI is transforming offensive cybersecurity, providing powerful tools for red teaming, penetration testing, and risk assessment. By automating complex tasks, generating realistic attack scenarios, and offering predictive insights, AI enables security teams to better prepare for and defend against evolving threats. However, with its power comes the responsibility to use AI ethically and responsibly, ensuring it is only used for legitimate security purposes. As AI technology continues to evolve, cybersecurity professionals need to remain vigilant about the ethical implications of their work and prioritize responsible usage in all cybersecurity activities.

Chapter 10: Ethical and Regulatory Considerations

Introduction

As generative AI technologies become an integral part of cybersecurity operations, they bring with them profound ethical, legal, and regulatory challenges. The use of AI in security operations not only enhances efficiency but also raises concerns about the responsible deployment of such advanced technologies. This chapter delves into the ethical and regulatory considerations of using generative AI in cybersecurity, focusing on issues such as legal compliance, data privacy, and the development of responsible AI frameworks.

10.1 The Ethics of Generative AI in Cybersecurity

Generative AI's role in cybersecurity brings forward ethical concerns that must be carefully navigated to ensure that AI tools are used for the benefit of organizations, users, and society as a whole.

The Potential for Misuse

One of the primary ethical concerns is the potential for misuse. While generative AI can be used for legitimate purposes like threat detection and defense, it also has the potential to be weaponized. Malicious actors can exploit AI to automate cyberattacks, craft sophisticated phishing schemes, or even generate malicious software like ransomware. Ethical hackers, who are entrusted with using AI for testing and improving security, must remain vigilant about preventing AI from being used for harm.

- **Example**: AI could be misused by hackers to design more effective DDoS attacks or to automate social engineering schemes, putting organizations at risk. Ethical guidelines must be established to ensure AI is only used for defensive and authorized testing purposes.

Transparency in AI Decision-Making

Generative AI systems operate based on data inputs and learned patterns, but these systems are often opaque in how they make decisions. Transparency in AI decision-making is critical, especially when AI tools are used for making security decisions such as identifying threats or recommending actions. The lack of explainability, or "black-box" nature, of AI models could lead to a loss of trust among users and stakeholders.

- **Example**: In security operations, AI may flag an employee's behavior as suspicious, but without transparency in how this conclusion was reached, it may result in unfair or inaccurate actions, such as false positives that harm user experience or privacy.

Bias and Fairness

AI systems are trained on data, and if that data is biased, the AI model may perpetuate or amplify those biases. In the context of cybersecurity, this could mean AI systems unfairly flag certain groups or individuals as potential threats based on biased training data. Ethical use of generative AI requires ensuring fairness in the data used for training, as well as actively monitoring AI models to mitigate bias.

- **Example**: An AI model trained on historical data from a specific region may unfairly flag users from other regions as suspicious, leading to inaccurate threat assessments.

Accountability in AI Deployment

With AI becoming more autonomous in cybersecurity decision-making, accountability becomes a crucial issue. Organizations must ensure that there is clear responsibility for actions taken by AI systems, especially in critical decisions that could have legal, financial, or reputational impacts.

- **Example**: If an AI-driven security system wrongly blocks access to essential data or services, it is vital to have a clear line of accountability to ensure that corrective actions can be taken promptly.

10.2 Legal Implications of Using Generative AI in Security Operations

The use of generative AI in security operations introduces various legal considerations that organizations must address to stay compliant with laws and avoid potential liabilities.

Intellectual Property Concerns

Generative AI can create new content, including malware simulations or novel attack vectors, which may raise intellectual property (IP) concerns. AI systems may generate solutions or strategies based on proprietary data, which could potentially lead to the violation of IP rights if not handled appropriately.

- **Example**: AI-driven vulnerability scanning tools may detect security gaps that are not publicly known and may generate reports that include sensitive proprietary information, which could inadvertently lead to IP breaches if shared outside of authorized channels.

Liability for AI-Generated Outcomes

Another legal issue involves liability for the outcomes of AI-generated actions, particularly when AI is involved in identifying or responding to threats. If an AI system makes an incorrect decision, leading to data breaches or other incidents, questions arise regarding who is legally responsible for the consequences.

- **Example**: If a generative AI system used in penetration testing inadvertently disrupts an organization's services, resulting in downtime or financial loss, the question of liability becomes critical, especially if the incident is linked to an AI-generated attack simulation.

Compliance with Industry-Specific Regulations

Generative AI must comply with the regulatory frameworks specific to different industries. For instance, healthcare organizations must ensure that AI systems used for cybersecurity adhere to HIPAA regulations, while financial institutions must ensure that their use of AI complies with data protection laws such as the GDPR or the CCPA. Failing to align with these regulations could expose organizations to legal risks.

- **Example**: A financial institution using AI-powered fraud detection systems must ensure that customer data is processed in accordance with data protection laws such as the GDPR, which mandates that data be handled in a lawful, transparent, and accountable manner.

Cross-Jurisdictional Issues

As organizations increasingly deploy AI systems across multiple jurisdictions, they must consider the legal implications of operating in different legal landscapes. Some countries may have stricter data privacy regulations or limitations on AI usage, requiring organizations to ensure their security practices comply with the laws of each jurisdiction.

- **Example**: A multinational corporation using generative AI to analyze cybersecurity data across borders may encounter legal challenges when transferring data between countries, particularly if one country's laws prohibit the export of certain types of personal data.

10.3 Data Privacy Challenges with Generative AI Systems

Data privacy is one of the most critical challenges when integrating generative AI into cybersecurity systems. The capabilities of AI systems to process vast amounts of data raise concerns about how personal, sensitive, or proprietary data is handled, stored, and protected.

Handling Sensitive Data

Generative AI often requires access to large datasets to learn patterns and identify threats. In the process, sensitive data such as personal information, financial details, and intellectual property may be exposed to AI models. Organizations must ensure that these models comply with strict data protection regulations to prevent unauthorized access to sensitive data.

- **Example**: If AI is used for malware detection by analyzing network traffic, it may unintentionally access and process sensitive user data such as emails, passwords, or financial transactions, creating data privacy risks.

Data Anonymization and Encryption

One of the ways to mitigate data privacy risks is through anonymization and encryption. When using generative AI for security purposes, it is critical to anonymize data wherever possible to ensure that personal or sensitive data is not exposed. Additionally, encryption techniques must be used to protect the data when AI models are trained or when they operate in a live environment.

- **Example**: Before feeding data into a generative AI system for analyzing potential security threats, it should be anonymized so that no personally identifiable information (PII) is involved in the learning process, reducing the risk of privacy breaches.

Data Retention and Deletion

AI systems often require continuous data input, but organizations must implement strict data retention and deletion policies to ensure compliance with data privacy laws. Storing data longer than necessary could violate regulations like GDPR, which mandates that data should be retained only as long as needed for its original purpose.

- **Example**: An AI-powered security system that monitors user activity must have a mechanism to automatically delete or anonymize data after a specified retention period, ensuring that the organization is not holding onto unnecessary personal data.

Bias and Privacy Risks

AI systems that process data are vulnerable to bias, which can lead to privacy violations. If generative AI systems are trained on biased datasets, they may disproportionately affect certain demographic groups, leading to privacy concerns.

- **Example**: AI systems trained on biased data may flag certain individuals or groups as security threats based on biased criteria, which could result in discriminatory surveillance or privacy invasions.

10.4 Adapting Regulatory Frameworks for Generative AI

As generative AI continues to evolve, so must the regulatory frameworks that govern its use. Policymakers need to adapt existing regulations or introduce new ones to address the challenges and risks associated with the use of AI in cybersecurity.

Updating Data Protection Laws

Data protection regulations, such as GDPR and CCPA, need to evolve to account for the unique challenges posed by generative AI. For example, regulations must be updated to address how AI systems process and learn from data, ensuring that organizations are transparent about their data usage and that individuals' privacy rights are safeguarded.

- **Example**: New regulations may be required to establish standards for AI explainability, data transparency, and the use of AI in monitoring or surveillance.

Establishing AI Governance Standards

Governments and regulatory bodies should create standards for AI governance, focusing on accountability, transparency, and ethical usage. These standards would ensure that AI systems are designed, developed, and deployed responsibly, with clear oversight mechanisms in place.

- **Example**: Regulatory bodies could introduce certifications or accreditation programs for AI systems used in cybersecurity to ensure that they meet ethical and legal standards.

International Cooperation on AI Regulations

As AI technology transcends borders, international cooperation is essential to create harmonized regulations. Global regulatory frameworks should address cross-jurisdictional issues, including the transfer of data and the export of AI technologies, ensuring that AI systems used in cybersecurity adhere to internationally accepted standards.

- **Example**: Collaborative efforts between countries could lead to the establishment of a global framework for AI accountability, ensuring that AI technologies are deployed responsibly and safely across jurisdictions.

10.5 Guidelines for Responsible AI in Cyber Defense

To ensure the ethical and lawful use of generative AI in cybersecurity, organizations must adhere to best practices and guidelines that emphasize responsibility and accountability.

Developing Ethical AI Policies

Organizations should develop clear, comprehensive ethical AI policies that govern the use of AI in cybersecurity. These policies should address transparency, fairness, accountability, and privacy, ensuring that AI systems are used responsibly and in compliance with relevant regulations.

- **Example**: A cybersecurity organization might create an AI ethics committee to oversee the development, deployment, and use of

AI tools in security operations, ensuring that they align with ethical standards and best practices.

Ensuring Explainability and Transparency

It is essential for AI models to be transparent in how they operate and make decisions. Organizations should prioritize the development of explainable AI models that allow stakeholders to understand the reasoning behind AI-driven security decisions.

- **Example**: AI-powered threat detection systems should provide detailed logs and explanations of the rationale behind detecting specific threats or flagging unusual behavior, ensuring transparency for security teams and affected users.

Regular Auditing and Monitoring of AI Systems

Ongoing monitoring and auditing of AI systems is critical to ensure they are functioning as intended. Regular audits help detect and rectify issues such as biases, errors, or deviations from expected performance, ensuring that AI systems continue to operate ethically and within legal boundaries.

- **Example**: A company may conduct periodic audits of its AI-powered intrusion detection systems to ensure that they are not inadvertently flagging legitimate user activity as suspicious.

Collaboration with Ethical Hacking Communities

Engaging with ethical hackers and cybersecurity communities can help identify and mitigate risks associated with AI systems. By collaborating with external experts, organizations can gain valuable insights into the ethical deployment of AI in cybersecurity.

- **Example**: Organizations can partner with white-hat hackers to run penetration tests on AI-driven cybersecurity tools, identifying vulnerabilities or ethical concerns before they are exploited.

Conclusion

While generative AI holds great potential for enhancing cybersecurity, it also introduces significant ethical and regulatory challenges. By developing clear guidelines, adhering to legal standards, and ensuring transparency and fairness in AI systems, organizations can harness the benefits of AI while safeguarding against its potential misuse.

Chapter 11: Careers in Generative AI and Cybersecurity

Introduction

The integration of generative AI into cybersecurity is reshaping the way organizations protect their assets and detect cyber threats. This chapter explores the emerging career opportunities, the skills required, certifications and training programs, how to build a portfolio, and the future of cybersecurity careers in the era of generative AI. With AI-driven security tools becoming a crucial part of modern defense strategies, the demand for professionals with expertise in both cybersecurity and AI is skyrocketing.

11.1 Emerging Career Opportunities in AI Cybersecurity

As the cybersecurity landscape evolves, so too do the roles and responsibilities of professionals working in the field. The advent of generative AI has led to the emergence of new job titles and career opportunities that combine traditional cybersecurity skills with advanced AI knowledge. Below are some of the key career opportunities in AI cybersecurity.

AI Cybersecurity Analyst

AI cybersecurity analysts focus on leveraging generative AI models to detect and respond to emerging cyber threats. These professionals are responsible for deploying AI-driven security tools, analyzing outputs from AI models, and enhancing threat detection systems to proactively prevent breaches.

Key Responsibilities:

- Implementing AI-based security tools for threat detection and prevention.

- Analyzing AI-generated alerts to assess risk and potential breaches.

- Integrating AI models with traditional security systems to enhance overall defense.

Generative AI Security Engineer

Generative AI security engineers develop AI systems and models specifically for enhancing cybersecurity operations. This role involves building AI-driven security solutions such as anomaly detection, intrusion prevention, and automated incident response systems.

Key Responsibilities:

- Designing and developing generative AI models tailored to cybersecurity applications.

- Collaborating with cybersecurity teams to integrate AI tools into existing infrastructures.

- Continuously optimizing AI models for better accuracy and performance in detecting cyber threats.

AI Penetration Tester (Red Team)

AI penetration testers (or Red Team members) use generative AI to simulate advanced cyberattacks, identify vulnerabilities, and assess the security posture of an organization. This role requires knowledge of both AI and cybersecurity attack strategies.

Key Responsibilities:

- Simulating sophisticated AI-driven attacks to test system vulnerabilities.

- Developing and using AI models to identify security weaknesses in real-time.

- Creating automated penetration testing scripts based on generative AI techniques.

AI-Powered Threat Intelligence Specialist

Threat intelligence specialists using AI tools analyze vast amounts of data to predict and identify emerging cyber threats. Generative AI can be applied to synthesize information from various sources, helping to forecast potential attacks before they happen.

Key Responsibilities:

- Gathering, analyzing, and interpreting data from AI-powered threat intelligence tools.

- Developing predictive models to forecast new attack vectors using generative AI.

- Communicating intelligence to leadership teams for proactive defense measures.

Ethical AI Security Consultant

With ethical concerns surrounding AI usage in cybersecurity, ethical AI security consultants help organizations implement AI tools responsibly. This role focuses on ensuring that generative AI models are used in compliance with legal and ethical standards.

Key Responsibilities:

- Advising organizations on the ethical use of AI in cybersecurity.

- Conducting audits and ensuring AI systems meet compliance and regulatory standards.

- Developing AI governance frameworks to mitigate risks associated with AI misuse.

AI Cybersecurity Researcher

Researchers in AI cybersecurity focus on advancing the development and application of generative AI in security. This role involves studying the intersection of AI and cybersecurity to innovate and improve existing security solutions.

Key Responsibilities:

- Conducting research on AI-based threat detection models.

- Publishing papers and presenting findings on the effectiveness of AI in cybersecurity.

- Developing new algorithms and approaches to detect and mitigate cyber threats.

11.2 Skills Required for Generative AI Roles in Cybersecurity

To thrive in the growing field of generative AI in cybersecurity, professionals must possess a combination of technical and soft skills. Below is an overview of the essential skills needed for these roles.

1. AI and Machine Learning Expertise

Generative AI is based on machine learning (ML) and deep learning techniques. Professionals in AI cybersecurity roles must have a strong understanding of how AI algorithms work, including supervised and unsupervised learning, neural networks, reinforcement learning, and generative adversarial networks (GANs).

Key Areas of Knowledge:

- Machine learning algorithms and frameworks (e.g., TensorFlow, PyTorch).

- Deep learning techniques for anomaly detection and pattern recognition.

- Natural language processing (NLP) for analyzing text-based threats.

2. Cybersecurity Knowledge

A deep understanding of cybersecurity fundamentals is necessary for professionals working with AI in security. They must be familiar with network security, cryptography, threat detection, incident response, and security protocols.

Key Areas of Knowledge:

- Network security concepts (e.g., firewalls, intrusion detection systems).

- Common cyberattack techniques and attack vectors (e.g., malware, phishing).

- Cybersecurity frameworks and best practices (e.g., NIST, ISO 27001).

3. Programming and Coding Skills

Programming is essential for designing, implementing, and troubleshooting AI models used in cybersecurity. Common programming languages include Python, Java, and R, with an emphasis on Python for its dominance in AI development.

Key Areas of Knowledge:

- Proficiency in Python, C++, or Java for AI development.

- Familiarity with AI libraries (e.g., Keras, OpenCV, Scikit-learn).

- Understanding of data structures and algorithms for optimizing security solutions.

4. Data Analysis and Visualization

Generative AI models rely heavily on data. AI cybersecurity professionals must be adept at analyzing large datasets and visualizing the results to identify trends and insights relevant to threat detection and prevention.

Key Areas of Knowledge:

- Data preprocessing, cleaning, and normalization techniques.

- Visualization tools like Matplotlib, Tableau, or Power BI for displaying results.

- Statistical analysis and predictive modeling techniques.

5. Ethical and Legal Understanding

Given the sensitivity of both AI and cybersecurity, professionals must have a firm understanding of ethical considerations, regulatory compliance, and legal implications related to AI systems used in security.

Key Areas of Knowledge:

- Data privacy laws (e.g., GDPR, CCPA).

- Ethical concerns surrounding AI use in security.

- Legal frameworks around cybersecurity and AI governance.

6. Problem-Solving and Critical Thinking

AI professionals must be capable of applying logical and critical thinking to solve complex problems, especially when AI systems make autonomous decisions. This includes identifying false positives, troubleshooting system anomalies, and fine-tuning AI models for optimal results.

11.3 Certifications and Training Programs for Generative AI Security Experts

Several certifications and training programs can help individuals acquire the skills needed for careers in AI cybersecurity. These certifications validate expertise in both AI and cybersecurity and are widely recognized in the industry.

AI-Specific Certifications

- **Certified Artificial Intelligence Professional (CAIP)**: Focuses on AI fundamentals, machine learning algorithms, and their application in business and cybersecurity.

- **AI & Machine Learning for Cybersecurity by Stanford University**: Offers training in applying AI and ML algorithms for threat detection and security applications.

- **Google Cloud Professional Machine Learning Engineer**: Focuses on designing and implementing AI models, including for security-related tasks.

Cybersecurity Certifications

- **Certified Information Systems Security Professional (CISSP)**: Provides broad knowledge of cybersecurity principles, including AI's role in threat detection and security.

- **Certified Ethical Hacker (CEH)**: Focuses on penetration testing and ethical hacking, with a focus on using AI-driven tools in security operations.

- **CompTIA Security+**: A foundational certification covering core security concepts, including risk management, network security, and AI's growing role in cybersecurity.

Hybrid AI and Cybersecurity Programs

- **Certified AI Security Expert (CAISE)**: This certification combines AI and cybersecurity knowledge, focusing on AI-driven security solutions, attack simulations, and penetration testing.

- **AI and Machine Learning for Cybersecurity Specialization (Coursera)**: A comprehensive training program that blends machine learning, deep learning, and cybersecurity best practices.

11.4 Building a Portfolio in Generative AI Cybersecurity

Building a strong portfolio is essential for standing out in the competitive field of generative AI in cybersecurity. A portfolio should showcase hands-on experience, projects, and problem-solving capabilities.

1. Participate in AI and Cybersecurity Challenges

Engage in online platforms that offer challenges and competitions, such as Kaggle, CTF (Capture the Flag), and AI-focused cybersecurity hackathons. These competitions provide practical experience and can be added to your portfolio.

2. Contribute to Open-Source Projects

Contributing to open-source AI security projects or developing your own projects demonstrates initiative and expertise. Platforms like GitHub offer a great space for showcasing your work.

- **Example**: Develop an AI model for detecting phishing emails and share it as an open-source project on GitHub.

3. Publish Case Studies or Research Papers

Publishing articles or case studies about your work on generative AI in cybersecurity can showcase your thought leadership. Write about AI-driven threat detection models or penetration testing simulations using AI.

4. Build a Personal Website or Blog

Create a professional website to showcase your resume, certifications, portfolio projects, and achievements. Regularly updating a blog with insights on AI in cybersecurity can also enhance your visibility in the field.

11.5 The Future of Cybersecurity Careers in the Generative AI Era

As generative AI continues to evolve, so will the careers in cybersecurity. The future promises to be dynamic, with AI playing an increasingly central role in automating threat detection, improving incident response, and evolving security strategies.

Automation and AI-Driven Security

AI-powered tools will automate more aspects of cybersecurity, requiring professionals to focus on strategic decision-making, governance, and oversight. Security analysts will need to adapt to overseeing AI systems, fine-tuning models, and ensuring ethical usage.

The Role of Hybrid Professionals

The future will see more hybrid roles emerging, combining skills in both AI and cybersecurity. Professionals who can bridge the gap between these two fields will be in high demand, particularly those who understand AI's application to threat prevention and response.

Growth of AI in Proactive Cyber Defense

Generative AI will likely play a key role in proactive cybersecurity measures, predicting attacks before they happen. As cybersecurity increasingly shifts to predictive models, experts will need to harness generative AI's power to build resilient defense systems.

A Collaborative Future

Collaboration between cybersecurity teams and AI researchers will become essential. Cybersecurity professionals will work closely with AI specialists to develop tools that adapt to emerging threats and continuously improve defense mechanisms.

Conclusion

The intersection of generative AI and cybersecurity presents abundant career opportunities, but it also requires continuous learning and adaptation. Building expertise in both fields, obtaining relevant certifications, and gaining hands-on experience will be essential for those who wish to succeed in this rapidly evolving domain.

Chapter 12: Generative AI Tools and Frameworks for Cybersecurity

Introduction

Generative AI tools and frameworks are transforming how organizations defend against cyber threats, detect anomalies, and improve overall security operations. This chapter provides an overview of essential open-source AI tools, commercial platforms, and security-specific AI solutions that leverage generative AI to improve cybersecurity practices. We will also explore cloud-based solutions and guide you through selecting the most appropriate tools for your organization.

12.1 Open Source Tools: TensorFlow, PyTorch, and Hugging Face

Open-source frameworks play a pivotal role in the development of generative AI applications. These tools provide robust, scalable environments for building and deploying machine learning models, including those used for cybersecurity.

TensorFlow

TensorFlow, developed by Google, is one of the most widely-used frameworks for machine learning and deep learning. It is an open-source library designed for training and deploying AI models. TensorFlow supports a variety of tasks such as natural language processing (NLP), anomaly detection, and predictive analytics—all of which are essential in cybersecurity.

Key Features:

- **Versatility**: TensorFlow supports deep learning, neural networks, reinforcement learning, and more.

- **Scalability**: TensorFlow is designed to scale across multiple GPUs, making it suitable for handling large datasets in real-time security monitoring.

- **Model Deployment**: TensorFlow offers TensorFlow Serving, a tool to serve and deploy machine learning models efficiently in production environments.

- **Cybersecurity Use Cases**:

  o **Anomaly detection** in network traffic.

  o **Threat prediction** using historical data.

  o **Behavioral analysis** of users and entities.

PyTorch

PyTorch, developed by Facebook's AI Research lab, is another open-source deep learning framework widely used for developing AI models. It is known for its ease of use, flexibility, and speed, which make it a popular choice for research and production environments.

Key Features:

- **Dynamic Computation Graphs**: PyTorch provides dynamic computational graphs, which allow users to make changes on-the-fly during model training.

- **Extensive Libraries**: It offers libraries such as TorchVision, TorchText, and TorchAudio, making it versatile for a wide range of tasks.

- **Integration with Python**: PyTorch integrates seamlessly with Python, which is a go-to language for cybersecurity AI applications.

- **Cybersecurity Use Cases**:

- o **Malware detection** through deep learning classification models.

- o **Intrusion detection** systems (IDS) leveraging AI models.

- o **Botnet identification** through traffic pattern analysis.

Hugging Face

Hugging Face is an open-source platform specializing in natural language processing (NLP), with tools that have a direct impact on cybersecurity, especially in detecting phishing attempts, social engineering attacks, and malicious email campaigns.

Key Features:

- **Transformer Models**: Hugging Face offers pre-trained transformer models, such as BERT, GPT, and T5, that can be fine-tuned for various NLP tasks.

- **Easy Model Deployment**: The Hugging Face Hub makes it easy to share and deploy models for use in cybersecurity.

- **Integration with PyTorch and TensorFlow**: Hugging Face supports both PyTorch and TensorFlow, giving developers flexibility in selecting the right framework.

- **Cybersecurity Use Cases**:

  - o **Phishing email detection** using NLP.

  - o **Malicious URL identification** through text classification.

  - o **Content filtering** in social engineering attacks.

12.2 AI-Powered Cybersecurity Platforms: IBM QRadar, Darktrace, and CrowdStrike

Several commercial platforms are incorporating generative AI into their cybersecurity offerings. These platforms provide sophisticated AI-powered tools that automate threat detection, incident response, and vulnerability management.

IBM QRadar

IBM QRadar is a Security Information and Event Management (SIEM) platform that leverages AI and machine learning to analyze security data in real-time. It integrates with other security tools and provides insights into potential threats.

Key Features:

- **Real-Time Analysis**: QRadar uses AI to analyze network traffic, logs, and vulnerabilities in real-time.

- **Automated Incident Response**: It can automatically generate alerts and respond to security incidents based on AI-powered threat intelligence.

- **Behavioral Analytics**: Uses AI to model normal user behavior and identify deviations that could indicate insider threats or compromised accounts.

- **Cybersecurity Use Cases**:

  o **Threat detection**: Detecting sophisticated attacks such as APTs and ransomware.

  o **Automated alerts**: Notifying security teams when generative AI identifies unusual patterns or behaviors.

  o **Incident response**: Generating playbooks for response based on detected anomalies.

Darktrace

Darktrace is an AI-driven cybersecurity platform that uses machine learning and unsupervised learning techniques to detect and respond to cyber threats autonomously. Its self-learning capabilities make it effective in identifying new and unknown threats.

Key Features:

- **Autonomous Response**: Darktrace uses its AI model, the "Antigena," to take immediate action against threats by isolating affected systems and stopping lateral movement.

- **Behavioral Analytics**: The platform models baseline user behaviors and network traffic to detect anomalies and intrusions.

- **Threat Visualizations**: Provides real-time visualizations of threats within an organization's network for easier analysis.

- **Cybersecurity Use Cases**:

  o **Real-time threat detection**: Identifying and mitigating novel or unknown threats.

  o **Ransomware prevention**: Using generative AI to stop ransomware attacks before they spread.

  o **Insider threat detection**: Analyzing deviations in employee behavior to detect potential insider threats.

CrowdStrike

CrowdStrike is a cloud-based endpoint protection platform that uses AI to detect, prevent, and respond to cyber threats across enterprise environments. Its AI engine, Falcon, continuously learns from new data to protect endpoints against a wide variety of threats.

Key Features:

- **AI-Driven Malware Detection**: CrowdStrike uses generative AI to analyze and predict new strains of malware in real-time.

- **Incident Response**: The platform helps security teams respond to incidents faster by providing AI-powered insights and recommendations.

- **Endpoint Visibility**: Provides real-time visibility into endpoint activities, helping teams quickly detect and mitigate attacks.

- **Cybersecurity Use Cases**:

    o **Advanced threat protection**: Using generative AI to detect previously unknown malware or zero-day exploits.

    o **Endpoint monitoring**: Real-time monitoring and alerting of suspicious activities across endpoints.

    o **Incident forensics**: Providing detailed data and analysis for incident investigation and remediation.

12.3 Security-Specific Generative AI Solutions

In addition to general-purpose AI platforms, several specialized solutions focus specifically on cybersecurity. These tools utilize generative AI techniques to detect, predict, and respond to cyber threats effectively.

Deep Instinct

Deep Instinct is a cybersecurity platform that applies deep learning to detect and prevent threats. Unlike traditional AI models, Deep Instinct's models are trained end-to-end to identify threats at the point of execution.

Key Features:

- **Zero-Day Threat Detection**: Deep Instinct uses generative AI models to detect previously unknown threats based on their behavior and characteristics.

- **Malware Prevention**: It predicts and prevents malware infections in real-time using deep learning.

- **Fast Execution**: Its AI models operate quickly, enabling real-time prevention without delays in system performance.

- **Cybersecurity Use Cases**:

    o **Zero-day threat detection**: Identifying and stopping previously unseen attacks.

    o **Real-time malware blocking**: Blocking malware before it can execute.

    o **Advanced persistent threat (APT) defense**: Detecting and mitigating long-term, stealthy attacks.

Vormetric Data Security Platform

Vormetric, acquired by Thales, provides generative AI-powered data protection, focusing on data privacy and compliance. It uses machine learning to detect anomalies in data access patterns, helping organizations prevent data breaches.

Key Features:

- **Data Access Control**: AI-driven analysis of who is accessing what data and why, helping to prevent unauthorized access.

- **Encryption and Tokenization**: Encrypts sensitive data while using AI to manage key access and monitor for any breaches.

- **Compliance Monitoring**: AI models help organizations maintain compliance with data protection laws like GDPR and CCPA.

- **Cybersecurity Use Cases**:

    o **Data leak prevention**: Detecting and preventing unauthorized data access and exfiltration.

    o **Insider threat detection**: Monitoring unusual access patterns that may indicate malicious or accidental data leaks.

o **Compliance auditing**: Using AI to ensure data security measures align with regulatory requirements.

12.4 Cloud-Based Generative AI Tools for Security Professionals

Cloud-based AI tools offer flexibility, scalability, and ease of deployment, making them ideal for organizations seeking to integrate generative AI into their cybersecurity efforts.

Amazon Web Services (AWS) AI Security Services

AWS provides a suite of AI and machine learning tools, such as Amazon GuardDuty and Amazon Macie, which use generative AI to help secure cloud environments.

- **Amazon GuardDuty**: Uses machine learning to identify and respond to suspicious activities in AWS environments.

- **Amazon Macie**: Detects sensitive data and uses AI to identify potential security risks such as inadvertent data exposure.

Microsoft Azure Security Center

Azure Security Center uses AI and machine learning to provide a unified security management system across cloud workloads. It provides threat detection and security posture management, powered by AI.

Key Features:

- **Security Posture Management**: Automatically detects vulnerabilities and security risks in real-time.

- **Advanced Threat Protection**: Uses AI to detect threats in cloud environments and provide actionable insights.

12.5 How to Choose the Right Generative AI Tools for Your Organization

Selecting the right generative AI tools is crucial for ensuring your cybersecurity measures are effective and scalable. Below are key considerations when evaluating and choosing the right AI tools for your organization.

1. Identify Your Organization's Needs

Understand your cybersecurity goals. Are you focusing on threat detection, vulnerability management, incident response, or endpoint protection? Different tools specialize in different areas.

2. Scalability and Performance

Ensure the tools you choose can handle the volume of data your organization processes. Generative AI models, especially those dealing with large datasets, should be scalable and perform well in real-time scenarios.

3. Integration with Existing Systems

Check whether the tools integrate seamlessly with your existing security infrastructure, such as SIEM platforms, endpoint protection solutions, and firewalls.

4. Cost and Licensing

Cost is always a factor in choosing AI tools. Evaluate both upfront costs and ongoing maintenance fees to ensure they align with your budget.

5. Vendor Support and Community

Opt for tools from vendors that provide strong customer support, regular updates, and community resources. Open-source tools with a large developer community can provide additional resources for troubleshooting.

Conclusion

Generative AI tools and frameworks have revolutionized the cybersecurity landscape, offering advanced detection, response, and prevention mechanisms. By utilizing open-source frameworks, AI-powered platforms, and cloud-based solutions, organizations can enhance their cybersecurity efforts, minimize risks, and ensure a more resilient defense against ever-evolving threats.

Chapter 13: Generative AI Models with Practical Implementation in Cybersecurity

Introduction

Generative AI refers to a subset of artificial intelligence techniques that enable systems to generate new data, such as images, text, or even security-related information, that mimics real-world data. In the realm of cybersecurity, Generative AI has emerged as a powerful tool to bolster defense mechanisms, automate complex tasks, and predict new threats. By leveraging advanced machine learning algorithms, these models can generate synthetic data, simulate cyberattacks, and assist in automating incident responses. This chapter will explore the practical implementation of Generative AI models in cybersecurity, including how they are used to protect networks, enhance threat intelligence, and improve operational efficiency.

13.1. Key Generative AI Models Used in Cybersecurity

13.1.1 Generative Adversarial Networks (GANs)

Generative Adversarial Networks (GANs) consist of two neural networks: the generator and the discriminator. The generator creates synthetic data, while the discriminator evaluates how real the data appears. These networks engage in a constant back-and-forth process, refining their abilities until the generator produces data that is indistinguishable from the original. GANs are widely used in cybersecurity to:

- **Generate synthetic malware samples** for training detection systems.

- **Simulate realistic attack patterns** to enhance defense mechanisms and test security systems.

- **Create realistic network traffic data** for security monitoring and intrusion detection systems (IDS).

Practical Example: Generating Synthetic Malware with GANs

To generate synthetic malware samples using a GAN, we can use the Python tensorflow and keras libraries for building the model. Below is an example of how to set up a basic GAN architecture for generating synthetic malware samples:

```python
import tensorflow as tf
from tensorflow.keras import layers, models

# Define the generator model
def build_generator():
    model = models.Sequential()
    model.add(layers.Dense(128, activation='relu', input_dim=100))
    model.add(layers.BatchNormalization(momentum=0.8))
    model.add(layers.Dense(256, activation='relu'))
    model.add(layers.BatchNormalization(momentum=0.8))
    model.add(layers.Dense(512, activation='relu'))
    model.add(layers.Dense(1024, activation='relu'))
    model.add(layers.Dense(784, activation='tanh'))
    return model
```

```
# Define the discriminator model
def build_discriminator():
    model = models.Sequential()
    model.add(layers.Dense(512, activation='relu', input_dim=784))
    model.add(layers.Dropout(0.3))
    model.add(layers.Dense(256, activation='relu'))
    model.add(layers.Dropout(0.3))
    model.add(layers.Dense(1, activation='sigmoid'))
    return model


# Compile and train the GAN
def train_gan(generator, discriminator, epochs=10000, batch_size=64):
    noise = tf.random.normal([batch_size, 100])  # Noise input for generator
    fake_images = generator(noise)  # Generate fake malware samples
    real_images = get_real_malware_samples(batch_size)   # Placeholder function to fetch real data


    # Training loop (simplified)
    for epoch in range(epochs):
        # Train the discriminator
        with tf.GradientTape() as tape:
            real_preds = discriminator(real_images)
            fake_preds = discriminator(fake_images)
            loss = tf.reduce_mean(real_preds) + tf.reduce_mean(fake_preds)
        grads = tape.gradient(loss, discriminator.trainable_variables)
        discriminator.optimizer.apply_gradients(zip(grads,
```

```
discriminator.trainable_variables))


    # Train the generator (via discriminator feedback)

    with tf.GradientTape() as tape:

        fake_images = generator(noise)

        fake_preds = discriminator(fake_images)

        g_loss = tf.reduce_mean(fake_preds)

        grads = tape.gradient(g_loss, generator.trainable_variables)

        generator.optimizer.apply_gradients(zip(grads, generator.trainable_variables))


# Initialize the GAN models

generator = build_generator()

discriminator = build_discriminator()


# Training the GAN

train_gan(generator, discriminator)
```

This code creates a simple GAN for generating synthetic malware samples. The key here is that GANs can generate synthetic data to train malware detection systems without relying on real-world malware samples.

13.1.2 Variational Autoencoders (VAEs)

Variational Autoencoders are deep learning models that compress data into a smaller representation and then reconstruct it. VAEs are beneficial in cybersecurity for anomaly detection because they can learn the normal behavior of a system and flag deviations as potential threats. Some practical applications include:

- **Anomaly detection in network traffic** by learning normal behavior and spotting any unusual activity.

- **Threat modeling and detection** by generating "what-if" scenarios to simulate attacks and vulnerabilities.

- **Fraud detection** in financial and identity systems by recognizing patterns that deviate from normal behavior.

Practical Example: Anomaly Detection with VAE

Below is a simple VAE model implemented using tensorflow and keras. The model can be trained on network traffic data to detect anomalies.

```python

import tensorflow as tf
from tensorflow.keras import layers, models


# Define the encoder model
def build_encoder():
    model = models.Sequential()
    model.add(layers.InputLayer(input_shape=(784,)))
    model.add(layers.Dense(128, activation='relu'))
    model.add(layers.Dense(64, activation='relu'))
    return model


# Define the decoder model
def build_decoder():
    model = models.Sequential()
    model.add(layers.Dense(64, activation='relu', input_dim=64))
    model.add(layers.Dense(128, activation='relu'))
```

```
      model.add(layers.Dense(784, activation='sigmoid'))

      return model


# Define the VAE model
def build_vae(encoder, decoder):
    inputs = layers.Input(shape=(784,))

    encoded = encoder(inputs)

    decoded = decoder(encoded)

    vae = models.Model(inputs, decoded)

    vae.compile(optimizer='adam', loss='binary_crossentropy')

    return vae


# Training the VAE
def train_vae(vae, data):
    vae.fit(data, data, epochs=50, batch_size=128)


# Initialize the encoder and decoder
encoder = build_encoder()
decoder = build_decoder()


# Initialize and train the VAE
vae = build_vae(encoder, decoder)
train_vae(vae, network_traffic_data)  # Replace with actual network traffic dataset
```

This simple VAE model can be trained on network traffic data to reconstruct normal traffic patterns and detect deviations, which could indicate potential threats.

13.1.3 Recurrent Neural Networks (RNNs)

RNNs are a class of neural networks where the output from previous steps is fed into the current step, making them particularly useful for sequential data, like time-series data or network logs. RNNs can be employed in cybersecurity to:

- **Detect threats in real-time** by analyzing patterns of activity over time, such as network traffic logs.

- **Simulate cyberattack sequences** to understand how attacks evolve over time and create predictive models for future threats.

- **Automate incident response** by generating appropriate actions or recommendations based on sequential events in security logs.

Practical Example: Detecting Anomalies in Network Traffic Using an RNN

```python

import tensorflow as tf

from tensorflow.keras import layers, models


# Define the RNN model

def build_rnn():

  model = models.Sequential()

  model.add(layers.LSTM(128, input_shape=(time_steps, features), return_sequences=True))

  model.add(layers.LSTM(64))

  model.add(layers.Dense(32, activation='relu'))

  model.add(layers.Dense(1, activation='sigmoid'))  # Output whether anomaly or not

  return model
```

```
# Training the RNN for anomaly detection

def train_rnn(model, data):

    model.compile(optimizer='adam', loss='binary_crossentropy', metrics=['accuracy'])

    model.fit(data, labels, epochs=10, batch_size=32)


# Initialize the RNN model

rnn = build_rnn()


# Train the model (using real or synthetic network traffic data)

train_rnn(rnn, network_traffic_data)
```

RNNs, particularly Long Short-Term Memory (LSTM) networks, are useful for detecting anomalies in sequential network data. This method can be used to identify threats such as DDoS attacks, data exfiltration, or unauthorized access.

13.1.4 Transformer Models

Transformers, like the GPT (Generative Pretrained Transformer) model, are designed to handle large datasets and understand complex relationships in the data. These models are ideal for handling large-scale cybersecurity tasks, such as:

- **Phishing detection** by analyzing textual data such as emails or websites and identifying patterns indicative of phishing.

- **Malware detection** by analyzing binary data and identifying code snippets associated with malicious activity.

- **Threat intelligence analysis** by processing large volumes of data and extracting actionable insights, including new attack vectors.

Practical Example: Phishing Detection Using Transformers

Phishing detection involves analyzing textual data from emails or websites to identify indicators of phishing attempts. A transformer model can be used to understand the context and identify malicious patterns in the text.

```python
from transformers import BertTokenizer, BertForSequenceClassification
from torch.utils.data import DataLoader, Dataset
import torch


# Example: Phishing detection using a BERT transformer model


# Sample phishing email data (texts) and labels (1 for phishing, 0 for legitimate)
emails = [
    "You have won a lottery, click this link to claim your prize!",
    "Important security update, click here to verify your account.",
    "Your invoice has been processed, download the attachment.",
    "Urgent! Your account has been suspended, click to resolve.",
    "Hey, let's meet up for lunch tomorrow."
]
labels = [1, 1, 0, 1, 0]  # Labels indicating phishing (1) or legitimate (0)


# Define a custom dataset class
```

```
class EmailDataset(Dataset):

    def __init__(self, emails, labels, tokenizer):

        self.emails = emails

        self.labels = labels

        self.tokenizer = tokenizer


    def __len__(self):

        return len(self.emails)


    def __getitem__(self, idx):

        email = self.emails[idx]

        label = self.labels[idx]

        encoding = self.tokenizer(email, padding=True, truncation=True,
        return_tensors="pt", max_length=512)

        return                                    encoding['input_ids'].squeeze(0),
        encoding['attention_mask'].squeeze(0), label


# Load pre-trained BERT tokenizer

tokenizer = BertTokenizer.from_pretrained('bert-base-uncased')


# Prepare the dataset

dataset = EmailDataset(emails, labels, tokenizer)

dataloader = DataLoader(dataset, batch_size=2)


# Load pre-trained BERT model
```

```
model    =    BertForSequenceClassification.from_pretrained('bert-base-uncased',
num_labels=2)


# Example: Predict if an email is phishing or legitimate

model.eval()

with torch.no_grad():

    for input_ids, attention_mask, label in dataloader:

        outputs = model(input_ids, attention_mask=attention_mask)

        logits = outputs.logits

        predictions = torch.argmax(logits, dim=1)

    print("Predictions:", predictions)
```

In this example, a pre-trained BERT model is fine-tuned to detect phishing emails by analyzing textual content. The model is trained to classify emails as phishing (label = 1) or legitimate (label = 0). Using the tokenizer, the emails are tokenized, and the model predicts whether an email is a phishing attempt.

13.2. Practical Implementation of Generative AI in Cybersecurity

13.2.1 Enhancing Threat Detection Systems

Generative AI models can significantly enhance traditional threat detection systems by generating synthetic attack data that helps train models to recognize emerging threats. For instance:

- **Simulating zero-day attacks**: GANs and VAEs can generate novel attack vectors that are not yet seen in the wild, allowing security systems to be trained to detect such attacks before they happen.

- **Synthetic attack generation**: Generative models can create simulated data, like malware signatures or network traffic, to train detection systems without relying on real-world attack data, which may be scarce.

Generative AI can simulate cyberattacks and generate synthetic attack data that helps train traditional detection systems. Below is an example of how to integrate synthetic data generation into a network traffic anomaly detection system.

```python

# Example: Training an anomaly detection system using synthetic data


import numpy as np
from sklearn.ensemble import IsolationForest


# Generate synthetic attack data (example)
synthetic_attack_data = np.random.normal(0, 1, (1000, 784))  # Simulated attack data
normal_traffic_data = np.random.normal(0, 1, (10000, 784))   # Simulated normal traffic


# Train an Isolation Forest on the generated synthetic attack data
model = IsolationForest()
model.fit(normal_traffic_data)


# Predict anomalies in the network traffic (both real and synthetic)
predictions = model.predict(synthetic_attack_data)
```

In this example, the IsolationForest algorithm is used to detect anomalies in both normal and synthetic network traffic data generated by the model.

13.2.2 Automated Incident Response

AI-powered cybersecurity systems can significantly reduce response time to security incidents by automating the decision-making process. Generative AI models can:

- **Generate appropriate responses** to detected threats based on historical data and pre-programmed rules.

- **Automate attack mitigation** by generating scripts to isolate infected systems or block malicious traffic in real-time.

- **Assist in recovery efforts** by generating backup protocols or recommendations to restore systems to a secure state.

Generative AI can help automate incident responses. For example, an AI model can analyze an attack scenario and generate an automated response (e.g., isolate infected machines, block malicious IPs). Below is a simple AI-driven script for automating the blocking of a malicious IP address based on detected attack traffic:

```python
import requests

# Example: Blocking a malicious IP address using an API call
def block_malicious_ip(ip_address):
    url = "https://your-firewall-api.com/block_ip"
    payload = {"ip": ip_address}
    response = requests.post(url, json=payload)
    if response.status_code == 200:
```

```
    print(f"Successfully blocked IP: {ip_address}")
  else:
    print("Failed to block IP")


# Example of detecting a malicious IP (simplified)
malicious_ip = "192.168.1.100"
block_malicious_ip(malicious_ip)
```

13.2.3 Enhancing Security Operations Centers (SOCs)

Generative AI models can enhance the efficiency of Security Operations Centers (SOCs) by automating routine tasks and focusing human efforts on more complex issues. Some key ways to integrate AI into SOCs include:

- **Threat hunting**: AI models can autonomously identify potential threats by analyzing large volumes of data and generating hypotheses for further investigation.

- **Alert triage**: Generative AI models can classify alerts and generate prioritized lists of incidents based on severity, reducing manual review time for analysts.

- **Incident simulation**: AI models can create simulations of cyberattacks to train SOC teams in recognizing and responding to emerging threats.

Practical Example: AI-Driven Threat Hunting

In threat hunting, AI models can automatically analyze massive datasets, detect potential indicators of compromise (IoCs), and generate hypotheses for further human investigation.

```
python
```

```
import tensorflow as tf

from tensorflow.keras import layers, models

import numpy as np


# Example: Threat hunting using an AI model trained on network logs

def build_threat_hunting_model():

    model = models.Sequential()

    model.add(layers.LSTM(128, input_shape=(100, 3)))   # Time series of
network events

    model.add(layers.Dense(64, activation='relu'))

    model.add(layers.Dense(1, activation='sigmoid'))  # Predict if an event is
malicious

    return model


# Simulate network log data (time series)

network_logs = np.random.rand(1000, 100, 3)  # Example data with 100 time
steps and 3 features

labels = np.random.randint(0, 2, 1000)  # Binary labels (0 for benign, 1 for
malicious)


# Train the threat hunting model

model = build_threat_hunting_model()

model.compile(optimizer='adam',                    loss='binary_crossentropy',
metrics=['accuracy'])

model.fit(network_logs, labels, epochs=10, batch_size=32)
```

```
# Example of predicting new network logs to detect potential threats

new_logs = np.random.rand(1, 100, 3)  # Simulated incoming log data

prediction = model.predict(new_logs)

if prediction > 0.5:

    print("Potential Threat Detected")

else:

    print("No Threat Detected")
```

In this example, a Long Short-Term Memory (LSTM) model is trained to detect potential threats based on network log data. The model can autonomously generate hypotheses about suspicious events, allowing SOC analysts to focus on high-priority threats.

13.2.4 Malware Analysis and Reverse Engineering

Generative AI can play a crucial role in malware analysis by generating synthetic malware samples for research and testing purposes. This helps security teams identify new types of malware and develop appropriate defenses. Generative AI applications in malware analysis include:

- **Automating malware reverse engineering** by generating code snippets and analyzing their behavior.

- **Training malware detection systems** with synthetic malware samples to improve detection rates.

- **Generating threat intelligence** by studying malware variants and developing countermeasures before the malware spreads.

Practical Example: Automating Malware Reverse Engineering

Generative AI can generate synthetic code snippets or exploit patterns to simulate malware behavior, assisting in reverse engineering and understanding malware's functionality.

```python
import random

# Example: Generating synthetic malware code snippets for analysis
def generate_synthetic_malware_code():
    malware_types = ['Trojan', 'Ransomware', 'Keylogger', 'Worm']
    code_snippets = {
        'Trojan': "import os\nos.system('rm -rf /')  # Deletes system files",
        'Ransomware': "import crypt\ncrypt.encrypt('user_files')  # Encrypts user files",
        'Keylogger': "import keyboard\nkeyboard.record()  # Records user keystrokes",
        'Worm': "import socket\nsocket.send('worm_payload')  # Propagates worm payload"
    }

    malware_type = random.choice(malware_types)
    return malware_type, code_snippets[malware_type]

# Generating a synthetic malware code snippet
malware_type, code_snippet = generate_synthetic_malware_code()
print(f"Generated Malware Type: {malware_type}\nCode Snippet:\n{code_snippet}")
```

In this example, generative AI is used to simulate different types of malware code snippets for analysis. This synthetic data helps security researchers reverse-engineer malware behaviors and develop appropriate countermeasures.

13.3. Case Studies and Real-World Applications

13.3.1 Case Study: GANs for Malware Detection

A large cybersecurity firm implemented GANs to enhance their malware detection system. By generating synthetic malware samples, the company was able to improve their detection system's ability to identify never-before-seen variants. The model also helped reduce false positives, making it more accurate in identifying actual threats.

13.3.2 Case Study: AI in Phishing Detection

Generative AI models, particularly transformer-based models, have been used to detect phishing emails with high accuracy. By training models to understand the nuanced language used in phishing attacks, AI systems can flag suspicious emails in real-time, helping organizations reduce the risk of successful phishing attempts.

13.3.3 Case Study: Automated Incident Response with RNNs

A financial institution utilized Recurrent Neural Networks (RNNs) to automate their incident response. The model analyzed sequences of security events and generated automated responses based on learned attack patterns. This significantly reduced response times, allowing the company to mitigate threats more efficiently.

13.4. Challenges and Limitations

13.4.1 Data Privacy Concerns

Generative AI models often require large datasets to be effective. The use of such models in cybersecurity may raise concerns regarding the privacy of sensitive data. It is essential to ensure that these models are trained in a manner that respects user privacy and complies with relevant regulations, such as GDPR.

13.4.2 Model Robustness

AI models can be susceptible to adversarial attacks, where malicious actors manipulate input data to deceive the model. For instance, a GAN-generated attack scenario might be exploited by an attacker to learn how to evade detection. Organizations must ensure that generative models are robust and resilient against such attacks.

13.4.3 High Computational Costs

Generative AI models, especially deep learning-based models, require significant computational resources to train and operate effectively. For many organizations, the cost of setting up and maintaining these systems may be prohibitive. This limitation can slow down the widespread adoption of generative AI in cybersecurity.

13.4.4 Ethical and Bias Concerns

Generative AI models are only as good as the data they are trained on. If biased or incomplete data is used, the models may produce inaccurate results, potentially leading to the misidentification of threats or generating ineffective countermeasures. Ensuring that AI models are ethically trained and free from biases is critical.

13.5. Future of Generative AI in Cybersecurity

The future of Generative AI in cybersecurity holds immense potential. As AI technology continues to evolve, we can expect:

- **More adaptive security solutions** that dynamically adjust to evolving threats using AI-generated insights.

- **Smarter malware defenses**, powered by AI models that can anticipate and counter new attack vectors before they happen.

- **Autonomous cybersecurity operations** with AI models that can not only detect and mitigate attacks but also predict and prevent them with minimal human intervention.

Generative AI will continue to transform the cybersecurity landscape, providing organizations with the tools to stay ahead of sophisticated threats. As the technology matures, the integration of Generative AI with traditional cybersecurity systems will be a key factor in achieving more proactive and resilient defense strategies.

Conclusion

Generative AI models present a unique opportunity to revolutionize cybersecurity by providing advanced tools for threat detection, incident response, and security automation. By leveraging GANs, VAEs, RNNs, and transformer-based models, organizations can create robust and adaptive security frameworks that can quickly detect and mitigate emerging threats. However, the challenges of data privacy, model robustness, and computational costs must be addressed to unlock the full potential of these technologies. As AI continues to evolve, its role in cybersecurity will only grow, offering more powerful and autonomous defenses against the ever-growing landscape of cyber threats.

Chapter 14: Future Trends in Generative AI for Cybersecurity

Introduction

As generative AI continues to evolve, its role in cybersecurity will expand and transform how organizations defend against threats, manage vulnerabilities, and ensure data privacy. This chapter explores key future trends that are shaping the integration of generative AI in cybersecurity, from quantum-safe cryptography to AI-driven defense for autonomous systems, synthetic data applications, and enhanced collaboration between humans and machines. It also delves into the challenges of preparing for AI-powered cyber threats in the future.

14.1 Generative AI for Quantum-Safe Cryptography

Quantum computing poses a significant threat to existing cryptographic systems, particularly those based on traditional algorithms such as RSA and ECC (Elliptic Curve Cryptography). Quantum computers have the potential to break these systems by leveraging their massive computational power to solve problems in a fraction of the time that classical computers would require. As quantum computing advances, there is an increasing need to develop **quantum-safe cryptography**, which is resistant to quantum-based attacks.

Generative AI's Role in Quantum-Safe Cryptography

Generative AI can play a pivotal role in creating new cryptographic algorithms designed to withstand the capabilities of quantum computing. These AI systems can generate innovative solutions by testing vast amounts of cryptographic permutations in real-time, simulating quantum attacks, and identifying potential vulnerabilities.

Key Functions:

- **Quantum Algorithm Development**: Generative AI can be trained to generate quantum-safe cryptographic algorithms by simulating quantum computing's impact on current cryptography schemes.

- **Cryptographic Key Generation**: AI can be used to design more complex and secure cryptographic keys that are resistant to quantum decryption methods.

- **Simulating Quantum Attacks**: AI-driven systems can simulate how quantum computers could break existing cryptographic systems, allowing researchers to design stronger algorithms that are more resilient.

Applications:

- **Post-Quantum Cryptography**: AI could assist in developing cryptographic systems that are not only resistant to quantum attacks but also scalable to accommodate future advancements in quantum computing.

- **Cryptanalysis**: Using generative AI to identify potential weaknesses in post-quantum cryptographic systems, ensuring they remain secure against emerging quantum technologies.

14.2 AI-Driven Defense for Autonomous Systems

As autonomous systems, such as self-driving cars, drones, and robotic devices, become more widespread, the cybersecurity challenges associated with them intensify. These systems operate in complex environments and often rely on real-time decision-making powered by AI algorithms. Cyber threats targeting autonomous systems could have catastrophic consequences, making AI-driven defense essential.

Generative AI for Autonomous Systems Defense

Generative AI can provide enhanced protection for autonomous systems by improving detection, prediction, and response capabilities in real-time. AI models can analyze massive datasets from sensors, cameras, and other IoT devices, generating threat models and defense strategies to protect autonomous systems from attacks.

Key Functions:

- **Real-time Anomaly Detection**: Generative AI can analyze sensor data from autonomous systems in real-time to detect anomalies or potential security breaches, ensuring quick intervention.

- **Adaptive Defense Mechanisms**: AI models can continuously evolve and adapt based on new attack vectors, learning from previous cyber incidents to improve system defenses over time.

- **Behavioral Modeling**: By modeling the typical behavior of autonomous systems, AI can recognize malicious actions that deviate from established patterns, triggering defensive measures.

Applications:

- **Self-Driving Cars**: Protecting self-driving vehicles from cyber-attacks that could alter navigation systems or steal sensitive data.

- **Drones and UAVs**: Safeguarding drones from hijacking or malicious control, ensuring they continue to operate safely in unpredictable environments.

- **Industrial Robots**: Protecting automated manufacturing systems from cyber interference that could lead to production halts or even physical damage.

14.3 Advances in Synthetic Data for Cybersecurity Applications

Data is central to machine learning and AI, but generating high-quality, labeled data for training AI models in cybersecurity can be challenging due to privacy concerns, data scarcity, or the need for labeled attack data. Synthetic data, generated by AI models, offers a solution by creating artificial datasets that mimic real-world data without compromising privacy.

Generative AI for Synthetic Data

Generative AI, particularly generative adversarial networks (GANs), can be used to create synthetic datasets that are highly realistic and suitable for training cybersecurity models. These datasets can simulate various attack scenarios, enabling AI models to be trained without requiring access to sensitive or proprietary data.

Key Functions:

- **Creating Realistic Attack Scenarios**: AI can generate synthetic data for a wide range of cyberattack simulations, including malware, phishing, and APTs, to train detection systems.

- **Data Augmentation**: Generative AI can enhance existing cybersecurity datasets by generating additional labeled data for rare or new attack patterns.

- **Privacy Preservation**: Synthetic data can be used to maintain privacy while still allowing organizations to train AI models on data that closely resembles real-world environments.

Applications:

- **Malware Detection**: Generating synthetic malware samples for training AI models without exposing actual harmful software.

- **Anomaly Detection**: Simulating network traffic data to help models recognize and classify anomalous behaviors or intrusion attempts.

- **Data Privacy**: Using synthetic data in compliance with data privacy regulations (GDPR, CCPA) for AI model training and testing.

14.4 AI-Enhanced Collaboration Between Humans and Machines

The future of cybersecurity lies in **human-AI collaboration**, where AI systems work alongside security professionals to provide enhanced decision-making, faster response times, and more accurate threat detection. Rather than replacing humans, AI tools will serve as force multipliers, augmenting human expertise and helping professionals make better-informed decisions.

Generative AI for Human-Machine Collaboration

Generative AI enhances collaboration by assisting cybersecurity experts in decision-making, automating routine tasks, and providing recommendations based on real-time data analysis. These systems can generate responses to cyber threats, offer remediation strategies, and even help predict the potential impact of security incidents.

Key Functions:

- **Automated Threat Intelligence**: Generative AI can generate summaries of threat intelligence reports, helping analysts quickly understand emerging threats and vulnerabilities.

- **Incident Response**: AI can propose remediation steps based on the nature of the attack, allowing security teams to act more decisively.

- **Enhanced Decision-Making**: By processing vast amounts of data, AI can provide security experts with insights and recommendations to improve decision-making and strategic planning.

Applications:

- **Security Operations Centers (SOCs)**: AI tools assist SOC analysts by automating alerts, categorizing incidents, and suggesting responses to threats.

- **AI-Driven Risk Assessments**: Generative AI can assist security teams in evaluating risk levels and prioritizing remediation actions based on potential impact.

- **Collaborative Security Automation**: AI and human teams working together to automate routine security tasks like patching vulnerabilities or monitoring network traffic.

14.5 Preparing for the Next Wave of AI-Powered Cyber Threats

As AI technologies evolve, they not only enhance cybersecurity but also introduce new types of cyber threats. The future will likely see increasingly sophisticated attacks that leverage AI to exploit vulnerabilities at scale, making it essential for organizations to prepare for AI-powered cyber threats.

AI-Powered Cyber Threats

AI-powered cyber threats include advanced malware that can adapt to defenses, AI-driven phishing attacks that use natural language processing (NLP) to craft convincing messages, and deepfakes used for social engineering or identity theft. These threats can evolve rapidly, making traditional defense mechanisms obsolete.

Key Threats:

- **AI-Powered Malware**: Malware that learns from its environment and adapts to evade detection by traditional antivirus tools.

- **Automated Phishing Attacks**: AI systems that generate highly personalized phishing emails and messages, making them more difficult for humans to recognize.

- **Deepfake Attacks**: Using deep learning to create convincing video or audio impersonations of trusted individuals for fraudulent purposes.

Preparing for AI-Powered Cyber Threats

Organizations must proactively prepare for these threats by adopting **AI-powered defenses** that can detect, mitigate, and respond to these new types of attacks. This includes implementing advanced threat detection systems, continuous monitoring, and incorporating AI into every aspect of cybersecurity strategy.

Key Strategies:

- **AI Threat Hunting**: Implementing AI-driven threat hunting to identify malicious activity before it escalates.

- **Adaptive Security**: Developing AI-powered defense systems that continuously learn from new attacks and adjust security protocols in real-time.

- **AI Security Training**: Ensuring that cybersecurity professionals are trained to understand AI-generated threats and how to combat them.

Conclusion

The future of cybersecurity will undoubtedly be shaped by the evolution of generative AI technologies. From quantum-safe cryptography to defense for autonomous systems and synthetic data generation, AI is enhancing every aspect of cybersecurity. However, as AI continues to grow in sophistication, so too will the complexity and scale of AI-powered threats. Preparing for these challenges requires a comprehensive strategy that includes AI-driven defense systems, collaborative human-AI efforts, and ongoing vigilance against new types of cyber threats. The next wave of cybersecurity will be defined by how well organizations adapt to the changing landscape and harness AI to stay one step ahead of cyber adversaries.

Chapter 15: Case Studies: Real-World Success Stories of Generative AI in Cybersecurity

Introduction

As generative AI technologies continue to evolve, their application in cybersecurity has led to significant advancements in threat detection, response, and prevention. In this chapter, we explore how organizations across various sectors are leveraging generative AI to combat cyber threats, prevent high-profile attacks, and enhance the capabilities of Security Operations Centers (SOCs). Additionally, we discuss key success stories and the lessons learned from real-world implementations of AI-driven security systems.

15.1 How Organizations Are Using Generative AI to Combat Cyber Threats

Organizations across industries are increasingly turning to generative AI for its ability to enhance security and adapt to the ever-changing landscape of cyber threats. By automating threat detection, accelerating incident response, and improving decision-making, generative AI is transforming the way organizations approach cybersecurity.

Case Study: Financial Services Sector – Detecting Fraudulent Transactions

A leading global bank implemented a generative AI solution to combat financial fraud. By leveraging machine learning and generative algorithms, the bank was able to model a wide range of normal transaction behaviors and generate synthetic examples of potential fraud.

These models were then used to train fraud detection systems capable of identifying unusual or suspicious activity in real-time.

Key Achievements:

- **Real-time Fraud Detection**: AI was able to detect and block fraudulent transactions as they occurred, reducing financial losses by 30%.

- **Enhanced Training Datasets**: By generating synthetic data of potential fraudulent transactions, the AI model was able to learn even from rare or previously unseen attack patterns.

- **Adaptive Learning**: The system continuously evolved and adapted to new fraud tactics, ensuring ongoing effectiveness.

Case Study: E-Commerce Industry – Preventing Account Takeovers

An e-commerce giant implemented generative AI to prevent account takeovers and credential stuffing attacks. The AI system analyzed user login patterns and generated profiles of legitimate behaviors, helping to distinguish between genuine users and malicious actors attempting to access customer accounts using stolen credentials.

Key Achievements:

- **Reduced Account Takeovers**: By detecting anomalies in login patterns, the AI system helped prevent over 90% of account takeover attempts.

- **Improved Customer Experience**: Customers experienced fewer false positives, with AI only flagging suspicious activities that truly posed a risk.

- **Real-time Adaptation**: The system quickly adjusted to new attack vectors, such as multi-layered credential stuffing attacks.

15.2 The Role of Generative AI in Preventing High-Profile Attacks

Generative AI is playing an increasingly vital role in preventing high-profile cyberattacks, which have the potential to cause significant damage to organizations' reputations, finances, and operations. Through predictive analytics and advanced threat modeling, AI is enabling companies to defend against even the most sophisticated attacks proactively.

Case Study: Government Agency – Preventing APT Attacks

A government agency responsible for national security integrated generative AI into its cybersecurity infrastructure to defend against advanced persistent threats (APTs). The AI system was trained to simulate attack patterns, generating realistic attack scenarios that mirrored the tactics, techniques, and procedures (TTPs) of known APT groups.

Key Achievements:

- **Early Detection of APTs**: The AI was able to identify suspicious behavior and potential APT activities months before traditional methods could detect them.

- **Threat Intelligence Generation**: By continuously generating new attack scenarios, the AI system contributed to an evolving database of threat intelligence that kept pace with emerging threat actors.

- **Proactive Defense Measures**: The AI helped the agency adopt a proactive defense strategy, where potential attacks were mitigated before they could escalate into full-fledged breaches.

Case Study: Healthcare Provider – Thwarting Ransomware Attacks

A major healthcare provider leveraged generative AI to defend against ransomware attacks targeting patient data. The AI system analyzed historical attack data, created models for identifying malicious encryption behaviors, and simulated ransomware attacks in a sandbox environment to test response protocols.

Key Achievements:

- **Real-Time Ransomware Detection**: AI generated synthetic ransomware behaviors that helped the system identify attacks as they unfolded, blocking encryption attempts before they could cause harm.

- **Minimized Disruption**: The AI system helped the healthcare provider avoid significant downtime and data loss, ensuring continued patient care and protecting sensitive medical records.

- **Automation of Incident Response**: The AI-driven response system allowed for rapid containment of the attack, triggering automated alerts and isolating infected systems without human intervention.

15.3 Success Stories from SOCs Leveraging Generative AI

Security Operations Centers (SOCs) are increasingly adopting generative AI to enhance their ability to monitor, detect, and respond to cyber threats. By automating threat intelligence collection, analysis, and incident response, SOCs can improve efficiency, reduce response times, and provide higher-quality security outcomes.

Case Study: Large Enterprise – AI-Enhanced Threat Detection

A large multinational enterprise with an extensive network of systems and data used generative AI to bolster its SOC operations. The AI solution was integrated into the SOC's existing infrastructure, using real-time data to generate threat models, identify anomalous behavior, and predict potential attack vectors.

Key Achievements:

- **Improved Threat Detection**: The AI system was able to detect previously undetected threats, such as zero-day vulnerabilities and subtle lateral movement within the network.

- **Faster Incident Response**: With AI-generated alerts and remediation steps, the SOC was able to reduce mean time to detection (MTTD) and mean time to resolution (MTTR) by over 40%.

- **Enhanced Collaboration**: SOC analysts could collaborate more effectively with the AI system, which presented threat data in a format that was easy to understand and act upon.

Case Study: Managed Security Service Provider (MSSP) – AI-Driven Automation

A leading MSSP integrated generative AI into its operations to provide enhanced cybersecurity services to clients across industries. By automating the analysis of vast amounts of security data, the AI system generated real-time alerts and responses, significantly reducing the workload for human analysts.

Key Achievements:

- **24/7 Threat Monitoring**: The AI-powered system provided continuous monitoring and analysis, ensuring that threats were detected and addressed in real-time, even outside of regular business hours.

- **Scalable Security**: By automating routine tasks such as alert triage and false positive filtering, the MSSP was able to scale its operations without having to hire additional staff.

- **Cost Efficiency**: Generative AI helped reduce operational costs while increasing the effectiveness of the MSSP's threat detection and response capabilities.

15.4 Lessons Learned from AI-Driven Security Implementations

While generative AI has shown tremendous potential in enhancing cybersecurity, its implementation also presents challenges. Organizations that have integrated AI into their cybersecurity operations have learned valuable lessons about the technology's strengths, limitations, and best practices.

Lesson 1: Balancing Automation with Human Expertise

While generative AI can automate many aspects of cybersecurity, human expertise remains crucial. AI should be viewed as a tool to augment human capabilities, not replace them. Organizations that succeed in integrating AI effectively combine AI-driven automation with skilled cybersecurity professionals who can make final decisions and provide contextual judgment.

Lesson 2: Continuous Training and Model Updates

Generative AI models require continuous training and updates to stay effective against evolving cyber threats. Successful implementations involve regular updates to the AI models, incorporating new threat intelligence, attack patterns, and system behavior. Without continuous learning, AI models can become obsolete and less capable of detecting emerging threats.

Lesson 3: Addressing Data Privacy and Ethical Concerns

The use of AI in cybersecurity raises important data privacy and ethical concerns. Organizations must ensure that their AI systems comply with data privacy regulations and that they do not inadvertently violate users' rights. Careful consideration must be given to how sensitive data is handled and processed by AI models, especially in sectors like healthcare, finance, and government.

Lesson 4: Managing False Positives and Alerts

One of the challenges of using AI in cybersecurity is managing false positives. AI systems can sometimes generate excessive alerts, leading to alert fatigue among analysts. Successful implementations involve fine-tuning AI systems to reduce false positives while maintaining a high level of detection accuracy. Collaboration between human analysts and AI tools is critical to achieving this balance.

Lesson 5: Ensuring Robustness Against Adversarial Attacks

AI systems themselves are vulnerable to adversarial attacks, where malicious actors manipulate the AI model to evade detection. Organizations must build resilience into their AI-driven security systems, ensuring that they are robust against attempts to deceive or manipulate them. Regular testing and validation of AI models are essential to maintaining security.

Conclusion

Generative AI is rapidly transforming the cybersecurity landscape, offering organizations a powerful tool to combat cyber threats, prevent high-profile attacks, and enhance the capabilities of SOCs. Through the exploration of real-world success stories, we see how AI is being successfully integrated into cybersecurity operations, providing improved threat detection, faster response times, and more efficient processes. However, the lessons learned from these implementations emphasize the need for continuous training, human oversight, and a balanced approach to leveraging AI in cybersecurity. As generative AI continues to evolve, its role in cybersecurity will only become more critical, driving innovation and providing organizations with the tools needed to stay ahead of emerging threats.

Chapter 16: Roadmap for Implementing Generative AI in Cybersecurity

Introduction

Implementing generative AI in cybersecurity is a transformative process that requires careful planning, execution, and continuous evaluation. As organizations face an increasing volume and sophistication of cyber threats, leveraging AI-driven solutions has become essential to enhancing cybersecurity posture. This chapter provides a detailed roadmap for successfully integrating generative AI into cybersecurity operations, guiding organizations through the process of assessing readiness, developing a strategy, training teams, scaling AI systems, and overcoming common challenges.

16.1 Assessing Organizational Readiness for Generative AI Integration

Before diving into the implementation of generative AI, it is crucial for organizations to assess their readiness. This involves evaluating both technological and organizational factors to determine whether the current infrastructure, processes, and culture are prepared for AI adoption.

Key Considerations for Readiness Assessment:

- **Current Cybersecurity Maturity**: Assess the existing cybersecurity posture and capabilities. Organizations with a mature cybersecurity infrastructure may find it easier to integrate AI solutions. However, those with limited security frameworks may need foundational improvements before implementing AI.

- **Data Quality and Availability**: Generative AI systems rely heavily on large datasets for training and functioning. Organizations should assess whether they have access to clean, structured, and relevant data. Without sufficient data, AI models may not perform as expected, leading to inaccurate predictions and detections.

- **Existing Tools and Infrastructure**: Evaluate the current security tools, systems, and infrastructure. AI integration requires compatibility with existing cybersecurity platforms, such as SIEM systems, endpoint protection, and network monitoring tools. A gap in integration capabilities could delay or complicate the implementation.

- **Organizational Culture**: The readiness of the workforce to embrace AI-driven solutions is crucial. Organizational culture should be supportive of innovation, data-driven decision-making, and change management. This also includes leadership buy-in and investment in AI.

- **Regulatory and Compliance Frameworks**: Understanding the regulatory landscape is essential. Organizations must ensure that the use of generative AI complies with data protection laws (e.g., GDPR, HIPAA) and industry-specific regulations. Non-compliance could lead to legal and reputational risks.

16.2 Building a Strategy for AI-Powered Security Operations

Once organizational readiness is assessed, the next step is to build a strategic plan for implementing AI-powered security operations. A clear strategy ensures that AI is aligned with the overall goals of the cybersecurity team and the broader business objectives.

Strategic Planning Steps:

- **Define AI Objectives**: Establish clear objectives for AI integration, such as improving threat detection, automating incident response, enhancing vulnerability management, or streamlining security monitoring. These goals will help prioritize use cases and measure success.

- **Select AI Technologies**: Based on the organization's needs, choose the appropriate generative AI technologies. Consider open-source platforms, such as TensorFlow and PyTorch, or commercial solutions tailored for security, such as IBM QRadar, Darktrace, or CrowdStrike. Evaluate these technologies for their scalability, security features, and ease of integration with existing systems.

- **Threat Modeling and Use Cases**: Identify and prioritize key use cases where generative AI can have the most significant impact. These could include anomaly detection, predictive analytics, data exfiltration prevention, or phishing attack detection. Customizing AI models for specific threat scenarios enhances effectiveness.

- **Resource Allocation and Budgeting**: Allocate necessary resources, both in terms of finances and personnel, to implement the AI strategy. This includes investing in hardware for AI processing, such as GPUs, and hiring or training data scientists, AI engineers, and cybersecurity experts.

- **Timeline and Milestones**: Develop a realistic timeline with achievable milestones for the implementation process. This helps track progress, manage expectations, and ensure that the deployment stays on schedule.

16.3 Training Teams and Aligning Processes

AI-driven cybersecurity solutions require collaboration between multiple teams, including cybersecurity professionals, data scientists, and IT infrastructure staff. A comprehensive training plan ensures that teams understand how to effectively use and manage AI tools, as well as how AI fits into the organization's broader cybersecurity strategy.

Key Training Considerations:

- **AI Fundamentals for Cybersecurity Teams**: Provide foundational AI training for security teams to help them understand the core concepts behind generative AI, including machine learning, neural networks, and natural language processing. This knowledge empowers analysts to better interpret AI-generated insights and make informed decisions.

- **AI-Driven Tool Usage**: Training should cover how to use specific AI-powered cybersecurity tools, including how to monitor AI-generated alerts, investigate anomalies, and interpret results. Practical, hands-on labs can help staff build confidence in using AI-powered security platforms.

- **Collaboration Between AI and Security Teams**: Encourage communication between AI engineers and security professionals. Data scientists and AI engineers should work closely with cybersecurity experts to fine-tune models, ensure that AI-generated alerts align with real-world security needs, and continuously improve the system.

- **Process Alignment**: Align the use of AI with existing cybersecurity processes, such as incident response, threat hunting, and vulnerability management. Generative AI should complement and enhance these processes rather than disrupt them. Define clear workflows for when and how AI models should be incorporated into security operations.

- **Security Awareness Training**: While the primary focus is on technical training, it's also essential to provide security awareness training to ensure that employees understand the role of AI in cybersecurity and how it contributes to the overall security ecosystem.

16.4 Continuous Improvement and Scaling Generative AI Systems

AI adoption is not a one-time event but an ongoing process that requires continuous improvement. Once generative AI systems are deployed, it is essential to monitor their performance, refine models, and scale solutions to meet growing demands and new threats.

Continuous Improvement Strategies:

- **Feedback Loops for Model Refinement**: Establish feedback loops where AI models are continually updated based on new data, emerging threats, and feedback from security analysts. Regular model retraining ensures that the AI system adapts to changing threat landscapes and enhances its accuracy over time.

- **Performance Monitoring**: Regularly monitor AI system performance, such as detection accuracy, false positives, and response times. Establish KPIs to measure the effectiveness of AI-driven solutions and adjust strategies if needed.

- **Scaling AI Systems**: As the organization's cybersecurity needs grow, AI solutions must scale accordingly. This includes upgrading hardware for increased processing power, expanding AI models to cover new use cases, and incorporating AI tools into additional parts of the organization's security architecture (e.g., cloud environments, IoT networks).

- **Integration with Emerging Technologies**: To stay ahead of evolving threats, consider integrating generative AI with other emerging technologies, such as quantum-safe cryptography, blockchain for security, and autonomous systems. Combining AI with these technologies creates a more robust defense mechanism.

- **Cross-Department Collaboration**: Scaling AI systems requires coordination with other departments, including IT, legal, and compliance teams. These departments should be involved in the scaling process to ensure that new AI solutions meet regulatory and compliance requirements.

16.5 Overcoming Challenges in AI Adoption

Despite its potential, adopting generative AI in cybersecurity presents several challenges. Understanding these challenges and having strategies in place to overcome them is crucial to successful implementation.

Common Challenges and Solutions:

- **Data Privacy and Security Concerns**: One of the main challenges of AI adoption is ensuring that sensitive data used to train AI models is protected. Implementing robust data encryption, access controls, and compliance with privacy regulations (e.g., GDPR, HIPAA) can mitigate these concerns.

- **Model Bias and Accuracy**: AI models can sometimes produce biased results if they are trained on biased datasets. To address this, ensure that the data used to train AI models is diverse and representative of the actual threat landscape. Regular audits and testing of AI models can help identify and correct any bias.

- **Resistance to Change**: Employees may be resistant to AI adoption, fearing that AI will replace their jobs or disrupt their workflows. To overcome this, focus on the augmentation of human expertise rather than replacement. Engage employees early in the process, involve them in the design and implementation stages, and emphasize the benefits of AI in enhancing job performance.

- **Integration Complexity**: Integrating generative AI with existing cybersecurity infrastructure can be complex. To minimize disruption, take a phased approach, starting with pilot projects that integrate AI into specific areas of the organization's cybersecurity operations. This allows for testing, troubleshooting, and optimization before a full-scale rollout.

- **Cost of Implementation**: The initial cost of AI implementation, including software, hardware, and training, can be significant. However, organizations should view this as an investment in long-term security. To justify the cost, focus on the return on investment (ROI) that generative AI provides, such as reduced response times, better threat detection, and lower operational costs.

Conclusion

Implementing generative AI in cybersecurity is a strategic and multifaceted process that involves assessing readiness, building a robust strategy, training teams, and scaling solutions. While the benefits of AI-powered security operations are clear, overcoming challenges such as data privacy concerns, model accuracy, and integration complexity is essential for successful adoption. By following a detailed roadmap and continuously refining AI systems, organizations can harness the power of generative AI to enhance their cybersecurity defenses and stay ahead of emerging threats.

Appendices

A. Glossary of Terms

Access Control: The practice of managing and restricting access to systems, data, and resources within an organization. It ensures that only authorized users or systems can access sensitive information.

AI (Artificial Intelligence): The simulation of human intelligence processes by machines, particularly computer systems. AI involves learning, reasoning, and self-correction to perform tasks that typically require human intelligence.

AI-Driven Threat Modeling: The process of using AI to simulate and predict potential attack scenarios based on known vulnerabilities, threat actors, and attack vectors. Threat modeling helps organizations proactively identify risks and improve their security posture.

AI Model Training: The process of teaching an AI model to make predictions or decisions based on data. During training, the model learns from a dataset to recognize patterns and generate accurate outputs.

AI-Powered Phishing Detection: The use of AI algorithms to detect and block phishing attempts by analyzing email content, sender behavior, and communication patterns. AI helps identify phishing attempts more accurately by learning from historical data.

AI-Powered Security Platforms: Integrated cybersecurity platforms that use AI algorithms to detect, analyze, and respond to cyber threats in real-time. These platforms often incorporate machine learning, behavior analytics, and threat intelligence to provide advanced defense mechanisms.

Anomaly Detection: A technique used to identify unusual patterns or behaviors in data that deviate from the norm, potentially indicating a security breach or system malfunction. AI can improve anomaly detection by analyzing large datasets for subtle irregularities.

API Security: The practice of securing application programming interfaces (APIs) to prevent unauthorized access and ensure the confidentiality and integrity of data transmitted through APIs. AI can help detect abnormal API calls that may indicate malicious activity.

Autonomous Systems: Systems that operate independently and can make decisions without human intervention. In cybersecurity, autonomous systems can help identify and respond to threats in real-time.

Behavioral Biometrics: A security measure that analyzes patterns in human behavior, such as typing speed or mouse movements, to authenticate users. Generative AI can enhance this by learning and recognizing individual behavior patterns.

Blockchain: A decentralized, distributed ledger technology that securely records transactions across multiple computers. In cybersecurity, blockchain can be used to create secure systems for managing data, identity, and access.

Blockchain Security: Security measures applied to blockchain systems to protect against threats such as double-spending, fraudulent transactions, and unauthorized access to smart contracts. Generative AI can enhance blockchain security by analyzing transaction patterns and identifying anomalies.

Cloud-Native Security: Security solutions that are specifically designed for cloud environments. These solutions integrate security practices directly into cloud-native architectures and can leverage AI for real-time monitoring and response.

Cloud-Native Security: Security practices and tools designed to operate natively in cloud environments. AI is increasingly integrated into cloud-native security solutions to offer automated threat detection and real-time remediation.

Cloud Security: The practice of protecting data, applications, and services that are hosted on cloud platforms. Cloud security strategies involve encryption, access control, threat detection, and compliance with regulations. AI plays a growing role in automating and enhancing cloud security measures.

Compliance: Adherence to laws, regulations, and industry standards governing how data is handled, protected, and stored. In cybersecurity, compliance ensures that organizations meet the required security measures to protect data and systems.

Continuous Monitoring: The ongoing process of observing and analyzing systems and networks in real-time to detect potential threats. AI-powered tools provide real-time insights and alerts, significantly improving threat detection.

Cryptographic Hashing: A process of converting input data into a fixed-size string of characters, typically used in securing data. It plays an important role in data integrity verification and is an essential concept in cybersecurity, particularly in ensuring data has not been altered.

Cyber Resilience: The ability of an organization to recover and maintain operations after a cyber attack or security breach. Generative AI can improve cyber resilience by enabling faster detection, response, and recovery.

Cyber Threat Hunting: The proactive search for signs of malicious activity or potential threats within a network. AI can assist in automating threat hunting tasks by analyzing large datasets and identifying patterns indicative of cyberattacks.

Cybersecurity: The practice of protecting systems, networks, and data from digital attacks, unauthorized access, or damage. Cybersecurity encompasses various strategies and technologies to defend against cyber threats.

Data Exfiltration: The unauthorized transfer of data from a system to an external location. It often occurs during cyberattacks and can lead to the loss of sensitive information.

Data Loss Prevention (DLP): A strategy to prevent unauthorized access to, leakage, or loss of sensitive data. AI can help DLP systems detect and block unauthorized attempts to transfer or share data.

Data Privacy: The protection of personal and sensitive information from unauthorized access, use, or disclosure. Generative AI systems must comply with data privacy regulations to prevent misuse of data.

Deep Learning: A subset of machine learning that uses neural networks with many layers to analyze and process complex data. Deep learning algorithms are often used in generative AI to produce high-quality outputs such as text and images.

Deception Technology: Cybersecurity measures that involve setting up traps, decoys, or fake resources to deceive attackers into revealing their presence. AI can enhance deception technologies by adapting decoys to real-time threats.

Digital Footprint: The record of a person's or organization's activities and interactions on the internet, including websites visited, social media posts, and online transactions. Generative AI can be used to analyze and secure digital footprints from cyber threats.

Endpoint Detection and Response (EDR): Security solutions that focus on detecting and responding to threats at the device level, such as laptops or smartphones. AI enhances EDR by enabling rapid detection of malicious activities and automated remediation.

Endpoint Protection: A cybersecurity strategy that focuses on securing individual devices (endpoints) within a network, such as laptops, smartphones, and servers. AI is increasingly used in endpoint protection to detect malware, ransomware, and other threats.

Ethical Hacking: The practice of testing computer systems, networks, or applications for security vulnerabilities by performing authorized attacks. Ethical hackers help identify weaknesses before malicious actors can exploit them.

Edge Security: Protecting the network and data at the edge of a network, typically on IoT devices and remote locations, rather than relying solely on central systems. AI helps secure edge devices by providing real-time analysis and detection of threats.

Fuzzy Logic: A form of logic that handles imprecise or vague information, often used in machine learning and AI for decision-making in uncertain environments. Fuzzy logic helps AI systems make informed decisions based on incomplete or ambiguous data.

Generative AI: A class of AI models that generate new content, including text, images, audio, and other types of data, based on patterns learned from large datasets. These models can create content that mimics human creativity and intelligence.

Global Threat Intelligence: The gathering, analysis, and dissemination of information about cyber threats from a global perspective. AI tools can sift through vast amounts of global threat data to detect emerging trends and potential vulnerabilities.

Incident Detection and Mitigation: The process of identifying security incidents and taking actions to mitigate their impact. AI can enhance this process by detecting threats more accurately and automating responses.

Incident Response: The process of managing and responding to cybersecurity incidents, such as data breaches or cyberattacks. AI can assist in automating and accelerating incident response workflows.

Incident Response Automation: The use of AI and machine learning to automate the process of detecting, analyzing, and responding to cybersecurity incidents, reducing response time and improving the efficiency of security teams.

Intrusion Detection System (IDS): A system that monitors network traffic for signs of potential security threats or attacks. AI-based IDS systems can improve detection rates by analyzing patterns in network traffic and identifying anomalies.

Machine Learning (ML): A type of AI that enables systems to learn from data and improve their performance over time without being explicitly programmed. ML is used in cybersecurity for tasks like anomaly detection and threat prediction.

Machine Learning Operations (MLOps): The practice of managing and deploying machine learning models into production environments. MLOps combines machine learning development with DevOps practices to ensure models are continuously updated and monitored.

Malware Analysis: The process of examining and understanding malicious software (malware) to identify its behavior, origin, and impact. AI systems can assist in automating malware analysis and detection by learning from past attacks.

Multi-Factor Authentication (MFA): A security process that requires users to present multiple forms of verification (e.g., password, biometrics, or a hardware token) to access a system. AI-driven MFA can dynamically adjust authentication factors based on the perceived risk.

Network Traffic Analysis: The process of monitoring and analyzing the data transmitted over a network to detect potential security threats or unusual behavior. AI can enhance network traffic analysis by identifying patterns and anomalies in real-time.

Penetration Testing: A simulated cyber attack on a computer system or network to identify vulnerabilities and weaknesses. It is typically performed by ethical hackers (also known as "white-hat hackers") to improve security.

Phishing Attacks: A form of cyberattack where attackers impersonate legitimate entities to trick individuals into revealing sensitive information, such as passwords or financial details. AI is used to detect phishing attempts by analyzing communication patterns and content.

Phishing Simulation: The practice of simulating phishing attacks to test the readiness of an organization's employees in identifying and responding to phishing attempts. Generative AI can create more realistic phishing simulations based on real-world attack tactics.

Privacy-Enhancing Computation: Techniques used to protect data privacy while still allowing for data processing and analysis. AI models can be designed to use privacy-preserving methods like differential privacy to prevent data leaks during processing.

Quantum-Safe Cryptography: Cryptographic algorithms that are designed to be secure against potential future attacks from quantum computers, which may be able to break current encryption methods.

Red Teaming: The practice of using simulated attacks to test and evaluate the security of a system or organization. Red teams often mimic adversarial tactics to uncover weaknesses in defense mechanisms.

Ransomware Detection: The process of identifying ransomware attacks, which involve malicious software that locks or encrypts data until a ransom is paid. AI can help detect ransomware by analyzing abnormal file behavior and network traffic.

Secure Access Service Edge (SASE): A cybersecurity framework that combines network security functions with wide-area networking (WAN) capabilities to provide secure access to applications from any location. AI is often used in SASE platforms for real-time threat detection and policy enforcement.

Security Information and Event Management (SIEM): A software solution that aggregates and analyzes security data from various sources within an organization's IT infrastructure to detect, monitor, and respond to potential security incidents.

Security Operations Center (SOC): A centralized team responsible for monitoring and responding to security incidents across an organization's network. AI tools are increasingly being integrated into SOCs to automate threat detection and response.

Threat Intelligence: The process of collecting and analyzing data related to potential or existing cyber threats. Threat intelligence is often used to enhance cybersecurity defenses and provide insights into attack techniques.

Threat Intelligence Platform (TIP): A software solution that aggregates and analyzes threat intelligence data from multiple sources, providing actionable insights for security teams. AI-powered TIPs can help organizations proactively defend against emerging threats.

User and Entity Behavior Analytics (UEBA): A security approach that uses AI and machine learning to analyze the behavior of users and entities within a network. UEBA can detect abnormal behaviors that might indicate insider threats or cyberattacks.

Vulnerability Management: The process of identifying, assessing, and addressing security vulnerabilities within an organization's IT infrastructure. Vulnerability management tools help prioritize and mitigate risks before they can be exploited.

Zero-Day Vulnerability: A security flaw in software or hardware that is unknown to the vendor and has no available patch. AI can assist in detecting zero-day vulnerabilities by analyzing patterns of malicious activity and identifying previously unknown threats.

Zero Trust Security: A security model that assumes no entity, inside or outside the organization, is trustworthy by default. Every user and device must be continuously authenticated and authorized before accessing resources.

B. FAQs

General Understanding of Generative AI in Cybersecurity

1. What is Generative AI in cybersecurity?

Generative AI refers to the use of AI models that can generate new data, such as synthetic network traffic or malicious payloads, for enhancing cybersecurity operations like threat detection, vulnerability testing, and incident response.

2. How does Generative AI enhance cybersecurity?

It helps in detecting unknown threats, generating realistic attack scenarios for red teaming, identifying patterns in vast datasets, and automating responses to incidents.

3. What are the key differences between traditional AI and Generative AI in cybersecurity?

Traditional AI focuses on recognizing patterns or making decisions based on existing data, while generative AI creates new data or scenarios that simulate real-world conditions or cyberattacks.

4. What is a GAN (Generative Adversarial Network)?

A GAN is a type of generative AI model that uses two neural networks— a generator and a discriminator—to create data that closely resembles real-world data, useful in cybersecurity for generating malicious traffic or synthetic attack scenarios.

5. Can Generative AI be used for malware detection?

Yes, Generative AI can help by generating synthetic malware samples for training detection models, improving the recognition of previously unseen threats.

6. How does Generative AI improve threat detection systems?

It creates realistic attack scenarios, aiding in training detection models, refining anomaly detection capabilities, and improving false positive rates.

7. What role does Generative AI play in phishing attack prevention?

By simulating phishing scenarios, generative AI can train security systems to recognize various forms of phishing attacks and better detect suspicious behavior.

8. Can Generative AI help in penetration testing?

Yes, it can simulate cyberattacks, allowing security teams to better understand vulnerabilities, test defenses, and improve overall security posture.

9. Is Generative AI useful in network traffic analysis?

Yes, it can generate synthetic network traffic for testing and anomaly detection, helping cybersecurity tools detect abnormal traffic patterns indicative of cyberattacks.

10. How is Generative AI used for anomaly detection?

By analyzing large datasets, generative AI models can identify unusual patterns or behaviors, helping detect potential threats like insider threats or malicious activities.

Technical Applications of Generative AI in Cybersecurity

11. How does Generative AI help in automating incident response?

It can automate responses based on the type of attack, generating appropriate countermeasures, such as blocking suspicious IPs, mitigating DDoS attacks, or alerting security teams in real-time.

12. Can Generative AI create realistic cyberattack simulations?

Yes, generative AI can simulate various types of cyberattacks, such as ransomware, SQL injections, or data exfiltration, allowing organizations to test their defenses.

13. How does Generative AI assist in vulnerability scanning?

It can simulate attack scenarios to identify vulnerabilities that may not be detected by traditional scanning methods, improving the security scanning process.

14. What is synthetic data, and how does it relate to Generative AI in cybersecurity?

Synthetic data refers to artificially generated datasets that mimic real-world data. Generative AI creates these datasets to train and validate security models without exposing real, sensitive information.

15. Can Generative AI assist in detecting insider threats?

Yes, it can analyze user behavior, generate baseline patterns, and identify deviations from these patterns, helping detect potential insider threats.

16. How does Generative AI contribute to automated malware analysis?

Generative AI can create malware samples to test the effectiveness of malware detection tools, improving their accuracy in identifying and neutralizing new malware types.

17. What role does Generative AI play in enhancing security event management?

It helps generate new security events based on historical data to improve event correlation and help security operations teams prioritize and investigate incidents.

18. How does Generative AI assist in simulating advanced persistent threats (APTs)?

It can model the behavior of APTs, simulate their tactics, techniques, and procedures (TTPs), and help organizations build defenses against these sophisticated attacks.

19. Can Generative AI improve intrusion detection systems (IDS)?

Yes, by generating attack traffic, generative AI can help improve IDS models to detect even the most advanced and novel attacks.

20. How does Generative AI help with secure software development?

Generative AI can identify vulnerabilities in code and suggest patches by simulating various attack vectors, improving software security during development.

Ethical and Regulatory Considerations

21. Are there ethical concerns with using Generative AI in cybersecurity?

Yes, ethical concerns include the potential for creating deepfake attacks, the misuse of AI in offensive hacking, and the lack of transparency in AI decision-making processes.

22. Can Generative AI be misused by cybercriminals?

Yes, malicious actors could use Generative AI to create convincing phishing emails, malware, or simulate fake cybersecurity defenses to deceive organizations.

23. What are the privacy implications of using Generative AI in cybersecurity?

There may be concerns regarding data privacy if sensitive personal information is used to train AI models, or if generative models are used to create fake data that could impact privacy.

24. How does Generative AI handle data privacy issues in cybersecurity?

Responsible AI models are designed to adhere to privacy regulations like GDPR, ensuring that the use of data in training and threat detection complies with legal standards.

25. What regulations govern the use of AI in cybersecurity?

Key regulations include the EU's GDPR, the US's CCPA, and industry-specific standards like HIPAA and PCI DSS, which address data privacy and security practices.

26. Is AI-based cybersecurity subject to audits?

Yes, AI systems in cybersecurity are often subject to audits to ensure compliance with security policies, ethical guidelines, and legal regulations.

27. How do regulatory frameworks adapt to the rise of Generative AI in cybersecurity?

Regulatory frameworks must evolve to address the challenges posed by AI, ensuring that AI technologies are used responsibly, securely, and transparently.

28. What is the role of transparency in the ethical use of Generative AI in cybersecurity?

Transparency is critical for ensuring that AI systems' decision-making processes are explainable and auditable, minimizing risks and preventing misuse.

29. How can we ensure Generative AI systems are fair in cybersecurity?

By ensuring that AI models are trained on diverse datasets and regularly evaluated to minimize bias, ensuring fair and equitable security outcomes.

30. What are the risks of relying too heavily on Generative AI in cybersecurity operations?

Over-reliance on AI can lead to vulnerabilities if the models become too rigid or fail to adapt to evolving threat landscapes, and human oversight is necessary.

Training and Implementing Generative AI in Cybersecurity

31. What are the training requirements for implementing

Generative AI in cybersecurity?

Professionals need expertise in machine learning, cybersecurity concepts, data science, and AI ethics to successfully implement generative AI in security operations.

32. How do organizations implement Generative AI in their cybersecurity strategy?

Implementation involves integrating AI-powered tools with existing security systems, training models using historical security data, and continuously refining the models for optimal performance.

33. Do security teams need specialized knowledge to work with Generative AI?

Yes, teams should have knowledge of AI/ML algorithms, threat modeling, and the cybersecurity landscape to effectively leverage Generative AI in their security operations.

34. How can Generative AI be scaled for enterprise-level cybersecurity?

By ensuring that AI models are cloud-based and can process large volumes of data, enterprises can scale AI systems to monitor extensive network traffic, endpoint activity, and security incidents.

35. What are the common challenges in adopting Generative AI for cybersecurity?

Challenges include data quality issues, high computational costs, ensuring AI models are trained with representative data, and integrating AI seamlessly with legacy security systems.

36. How do AI models need to be trained for cybersecurity use cases?

AI models must be trained on a diverse dataset that includes examples of normal and malicious behavior to learn to differentiate between them and generate accurate predictions.

37. What tools are commonly used to integrate Generative AI into cybersecurity?

Popular tools include TensorFlow, PyTorch, Keras, and platforms like IBM QRadar, Darktrace, and CrowdStrike for implementing AI-driven cybersecurity solutions.

38. Is Generative AI effective for proactive cybersecurity measures?

Yes, by simulating attacks and generating synthetic data, Generative AI helps organizations proactively identify vulnerabilities and strengthen defenses before real-world attacks occur.

39. How can Generative AI help in improving SIEM (Security Information and Event Management) systems?

Generative AI can create realistic event scenarios, helping SIEM systems enhance their ability to correlate and identify suspicious activities in real-time.

40. Can Generative AI be used in endpoint protection systems?

Yes, AI models can identify patterns of malicious activity and generate alerts for unusual behavior on endpoints, improving the detection of sophisticated threats.

Emerging Trends and Future of Generative AI in Cybersecurity

41. What are the future trends for Generative AI in cybersecurity?

Trends include better integration of AI with automated security systems, real-time threat intelligence, and AI models that can predict new attack strategies before they happen.

42. How is Generative AI used in cyber threat intelligence?

Generative AI models analyze past attack data and create predictive models for new threats, improving threat intelligence and response time.

43. Will Generative AI replace traditional cybersecurity tools?

Generative AI will complement traditional tools by enhancing threat detection and incident response, but it is unlikely to fully replace existing cybersecurity practices.

44. What are the most significant limitations of using Generative AI in cybersecurity?

Limitations include the need for high-quality data, computational resources, model interpretability, and the potential for adversarial AI attacks that can deceive models.

45. How does Generative AI address zero-day vulnerabilities?

By simulating attack scenarios and identifying vulnerabilities before they are exploited, Generative AI helps discover and patch zero-day vulnerabilities.

46. What are the implications of Generative AI on cybersecurity job roles?

AI will enhance job roles by automating routine tasks, but it will also require cybersecurity professionals to adapt by acquiring skills in AI, machine learning, and data analysis.

47. How can organizations protect themselves from AI-driven cyberattacks?

Organizations should employ AI-powered defense systems, regularly update AI models, and combine traditional defenses with new AI capabilities to create a comprehensive security strategy.

48. How will Generative AI influence the next generation of cybersecurity products?

It will lead to more adaptive, self-learning security products capable of predicting and responding to cyber threats with minimal human intervention.

49. What is the long-term impact of Generative AI on the cybersecurity industry?

The long-term impact includes more efficient and automated security operations, more accurate threat detection, and improved defenses against evolving attack methods.

50. What are the best practices for using Generative AI responsibly in cybersecurity?

Best practices include maintaining transparency, ensuring the models are unbiased, securing AI systems from misuse, and ensuring human oversight in decision-making.

AI Integration with Existing Security Infrastructure

51. How can Generative AI be integrated into existing cybersecurity infrastructure?

Generative AI can be integrated into legacy systems by using AI-driven modules that complement existing security technologies, such as firewalls, IDS/IPS systems, and SIEM platforms.

52. What are the best practices for deploying AI-powered cybersecurity solutions?

Best practices include ensuring that AI models are regularly trained on fresh data, using AI in conjunction with human expertise, maintaining strict data privacy controls, and conducting regular performance assessments.

53. Can Generative AI be integrated with existing Security Information and Event Management (SIEM) systems?

Yes, Generative AI can integrate with SIEM systems to enhance threat detection by generating synthetic data to improve event correlation and pattern recognition, leading to more accurate alerts.

54. How do AI models work with existing endpoint protection systems?

AI models can work with endpoint protection tools by analyzing endpoint behaviors, detecting deviations from normal patterns, and generating alerts for potential threats like malware or unauthorized access.

55. Can Generative AI enhance the effectiveness of firewalls?

Yes, by generating real-time attack scenarios and traffic patterns, AI can enhance firewall configurations, making them more adaptive to evolving threats and capable of blocking novel attack vectors.

AI for Cybersecurity Automation

56. How does Generative AI contribute to cybersecurity automation?

Generative AI automates tasks such as threat detection, incident response, and malware analysis by generating appropriate actions based on identified threats, reducing the manual workload for security teams.

57. Can Generative AI automate patch management?

Yes, Generative AI can automate the identification of vulnerabilities, prioritize them, and generate suitable patching strategies, helping reduce the time required to patch systems.

58. What is the role of AI in automating vulnerability management?

AI models can automatically scan for vulnerabilities, simulate attack scenarios, and generate vulnerability reports for immediate remediation, accelerating the overall vulnerability management process.

59. How does AI-powered automation improve response times during cyberattacks?

AI-driven automation allows for faster detection and response by reducing manual intervention, enabling security systems to respond to incidents in real-time and mitigate attacks before they escalate.

60. What are the challenges of automating cybersecurity with AI?

Challenges include ensuring AI models are trained with accurate and up-to-date data, avoiding false positives, ensuring human oversight, and addressing potential limitations in AI models' ability to adapt to new attack techniques.

AI for Predictive Security and Risk Assessment

61. How does Generative AI help with predictive cybersecurity?

Generative AI uses historical attack data to build models that predict future cyber threats, enabling organizations to take proactive measures before attacks occur.

62. Can Generative AI be used for threat forecasting?

Yes, by analyzing past cyberattack data and identifying trends, Generative AI can forecast potential future threats, helping organizations prepare for emerging attack vectors.

63. How can AI assist in risk assessment and management?

AI models can assess the risk of various security incidents by analyzing the likelihood of attacks the potential impact on assets and generating risk mitigation strategies tailored to the organization.

64. Can AI predict the next wave of cyber threats?

Yes, by recognizing attack patterns and using predictive modeling, AI can anticipate emerging cyber threats, enabling proactive defense strategies.

65. What role does Generative AI play in identifying high-risk vulnerabilities?

AI can simulate attacks and test various vulnerabilities, identifying those most likely to be exploited and generating risk profiles to prioritize remediation efforts.

AI and Cybersecurity Threat Intelligence

66. How does Generative AI enhance threat intelligence?

Generative AI generates synthetic data to train threat intelligence systems, enhances the identification of attack trends, and creates predictive models to recognize and mitigate new threats.

67. Can Generative AI help in the creation of threat intelligence feeds?

Yes, Generative AI can analyze vast amounts of data from different sources to identify potential threats and create real-time threat intelligence feeds for security teams.

68. What is the role of Generative AI in gathering cyber threat intelligence?

Generative AI helps automate the collection and analysis of threat intelligence from multiple sources, including dark web monitoring, malware analysis, and social media platforms, to stay ahead of potential attacks.

69. How does Generative AI assist in malware analysis for threat intelligence?

Generative AI models can generate and analyze new forms of malware, identifying their behavior and generating signatures that can be shared with threat intelligence platforms.

70. What are the benefits of using Generative AI in cyber threat intelligence sharing?

AI models can automatically analyze and classify threats, create threat reports, and share relevant intelligence, improving collaboration and ensuring that organizations have up-to-date information on emerging threats.

AI in Cybersecurity Workforce and Skills Development

71. How can Generative AI assist in cybersecurity training?

AI can create realistic attack simulations, which can be used to train cybersecurity professionals in threat detection, incident response, and vulnerability management.

72. What impact will Generative AI have on cybersecurity job roles?

While it will automate routine tasks, Generative AI will create new opportunities for cybersecurity professionals skilled in AI, data science, and machine learning, requiring them to manage and interpret AI-generated insights.

73. How can Generative AI help improve cybersecurity awareness among employees?

AI-powered simulations and training tools can expose employees to realistic cyberattack scenarios, helping them recognize phishing emails, social engineering tactics, and other common threats.

74. Will Generative AI replace cybersecurity professionals?

No, Generative AI will complement cybersecurity professionals by automating repetitive tasks and providing advanced threat detection capabilities, but human expertise is still crucial for strategic decision-making and oversight.

75. How does AI-based training compare to traditional training methods in cybersecurity?

AI-based training offers more interactive, real-world scenarios that evolve with the latest threats, providing more practical and adaptive learning experiences compared to traditional methods.

AI and Cybersecurity Incident Management

76. How does Generative AI improve incident response?

Generative AI helps by providing real-time, AI-driven suggestions for mitigating cyberattacks, automating the containment of threats, and assisting in root cause analysis.

77. Can Generative AI predict the effectiveness of incident response measures?

Yes, Generative AI can simulate incident response measures and predict their effectiveness in containing and mitigating various types of cyberattacks.

78. How does AI help in forensic analysis during a cybersecurity incident?

AI can generate forensic insights from log data, network traffic, and security alerts, helping investigators identify the source, method, and impact of the attack.

79. Can Generative AI assist in incident triage and prioritization?

Yes, AI models can analyze incoming security incidents and automatically prioritize them based on severity, impact, and attack type, streamlining incident response efforts.

80. What is the role of AI in improving the post-incident analysis phase?

AI can analyze the data collected during an incident, identify patterns, and suggest improvements for security measures to prevent future incidents.

Security Risks and Challenges Associated with Generative AI

81. What are the security risks associated with Generative AI?

Risks include adversarial attacks where malicious actors could manipulate AI systems, the generation of misleading or harmful synthetic data, and the potential for model biases that could be exploited.

82. How do adversarial attacks affect Generative AI models in cybersecurity?

Adversarial attacks can deceive AI models by presenting data in a way that causes the AI to make incorrect predictions, potentially undermining security defenses.

83. Can Generative AI be tricked into creating dangerous malware?

If not properly monitored, Generative AI models could be exploited to create malware that appears benign but is capable of evading detection by conventional defenses.

84. How can organizations defend against adversarial attacks on Generative AI models?

Techniques such as adversarial training, robustness testing, and continual model evaluation can help defend AI models from manipulation and ensure they remain effective against real-world attacks.

85. What are the limitations of using Generative AI in cybersecurity?

Limitations include high computational costs, dependency on large datasets for training, the need for continuous monitoring, and potential vulnerability to adversarial attacks.

Future Directions and Emerging Trends

86. What emerging trends are shaping the future of Generative AI in cybersecurity?

Emerging trends include the integration of AI with zero-trust architectures, AI for autonomous response systems, and AI-driven threat intelligence sharing platforms.

87. Will Generative AI evolve to defend against cyberattacks autonomously?

Yes, Generative AI will likely evolve to autonomously respond to certain types of attacks by generating countermeasures and deploying them in real-time, minimizing human intervention.

88. How will Generative AI contribute to the development of quantum-safe cryptography?

Generative AI can simulate quantum computing scenarios and help in designing cryptographic algorithms that are resilient to the capabilities of quantum computers.

89. What role will Generative AI play in securing the Internet of Things (IoT)?

AI will help secure IoT devices by generating and analyzing traffic patterns, detecting anomalies, and ensuring that IoT ecosystems remain resilient against attacks.

90. What are the next big challenges for Generative AI in cybersecurity?

Future challenges include improving the transparency and explainability of AI models, protecting AI systems from adversarial manipulation, and addressing ethical concerns related to AI's role in security operations.

Long-Term Impacts of Generative AI on the Cybersecurity Industry

91. What is the long-term impact of Generative AI on the cybersecurity industry?

Generative AI will drive more proactive, adaptive, and efficient cybersecurity practices, reducing the time and effort needed for manual intervention while providing stronger defenses against emerging threats.

92. Will Generative AI create new job opportunities in cybersecurity?

Yes, the adoption of Generative AI will create new opportunities for cybersecurity professionals skilled in AI, machine learning, and cybersecurity to develop, manage, and optimize AI-driven security solutions.

93. How will Generative AI transform the role of Chief Information Security Officers (CISOs)?

CISOs will rely on AI-driven insights to make strategic decisions, focusing more on overseeing AI implementation and ensuring security operations align with organizational goals.

94. Will Generative AI lead to an arms race in cybersecurity?

As AI is increasingly used by both attackers and defenders, an arms race is likely, with cybersecurity professionals continually evolving their AI models to stay ahead of attackers.

95. How can Generative AI be used for ethical decision-making in cybersecurity?

AI systems can be trained to adhere to ethical guidelines, helping organizations make decisions that prioritize privacy, fairness, and transparency in their cybersecurity policies.

Conclusion

96. How should organizations begin their journey of integrating Generative AI in cybersecurity?

Organizations should start by assessing their cybersecurity needs, setting clear goals, selecting the right AI tools, and investing in the right skill sets for their cybersecurity teams.

97. What are the most promising areas for Generative AI applications in cybersecurity?

Promising areas include threat intelligence, incident response, autonomous defense systems, vulnerability management, and predictive security analytics.

98. How can organizations assess the effectiveness of Generative AI in their cybersecurity operations?

Organizations can assess effectiveness by continuously monitoring AI system performance, comparing it against traditional methods, and measuring improvements in incident detection, response times, and threat mitigation.

99. What is the future of human and AI collaboration in cybersecurity?

The future involves a collaborative approach where AI handles repetitive tasks and identifies threats, while humans oversee the decision-making process and manage strategic defense operations.

100. What steps should cybersecurity professionals take to prepare for the rise of Generative AI in the industry?

Cybersecurity professionals should stay informed about AI advancements, acquire skills in machine learning, and develop expertise in AI ethics and security to remain valuable assets in the evolving cybersecurity landscape.

C. Additional Resources for Learning Generative AI and Cybersecurity

1. Online Courses and Platforms

- **Coursera**

  - *Generative AI for Cybersecurity* – Courses offered by leading universities and organizations like Stanford, MIT, and IBM on applying AI to cybersecurity problems.

  - *AI For Everyone* – A non-technical introduction to AI, perfect for understanding foundational concepts.

  - *Deep Learning Specialization* – Offered by Andrew Ng, covering deep learning techniques crucial for understanding generative models.

- **edX**

  - *Artificial Intelligence in Cybersecurity* – An online course from the University of Maryland that explores the intersection of AI and security.

  - *Introduction to AI for Security* – A course that provides practical skills for integrating AI models into security operations.

- **Udacity**

  - *AI for Cybersecurity Nanodegree* – Focuses on using AI to automate the detection, analysis, and response to cyber threats.

  - *Data Science and Machine Learning for Cybersecurity* – A nanodegree program that teaches the use of machine learning in cyber defense.

- **Pluralsight**

- ○ *AI & Machine Learning in Cybersecurity* – A comprehensive series of courses exploring AI applications in detecting threats, vulnerabilities, and automating security processes.

- **MIT OpenCourseWare**

  - ○ *Artificial Intelligence: A Modern Approach* – Based on Stuart Russell and Peter Norvig's widely respected textbook, this course covers core AI concepts, which form the foundation for understanding generative AI in cybersecurity.

2. Books

- **"Artificial Intelligence for Cybersecurity: A Hands-on Approach" by S. K. Das and S. Rajasekaran**

  - ○ A practical guide to understanding AI and machine learning techniques that are transforming cybersecurity practices.

- **"Machine Learning for Cybersecurity: A Practical Guide" by Kennesaw State University**

  - ○ This book provides an in-depth look at how machine learning models are applied to detect, classify, and respond to security incidents.

- **"Generative Deep Learning: Teaching Machines to Paint, Write, Compose, and Play" by David Foster**

  - ○ While not cybersecurity-focused, this book provides a solid understanding of generative models like GANs and their potential applications across domains, including cybersecurity.

- **"Cybersecurity and Cyberwar: What Everyone Needs to Know" by P.W. Singer and Allan Friedman** o   A comprehensive guide that covers the current landscape of cybersecurity and emerging threats, setting the stage for the integration of AI into security strategies.

3. Research Papers and Journals

- **IEEE Xplore Digital Library**

    o   Search for research papers on AI applications in cybersecurity, such as *"Machine Learning for Cybersecurity: A Survey"* and *"AI for Intrusion Detection Systems."*

- **ACM Digital Library**

    o   Articles like *"Generative Adversarial Networks for Security Applications"* provide insights into how generative models are utilized in various cybersecurity applications.

- **Google Scholar**

    o   Use Google Scholar to explore papers on *"AI in Threat Detection"* or *"Generative Models for Malware Analysis"*.

4. Websites and Blogs

- **AI in Cybersecurity Blog by IBM Security**

    o   *https://www.ibm.com/security/artificial-intelligence*

    o   A dedicated blog exploring the role of AI in securing cloud, IoT, and enterprise environments.

- **Dark Reading**

    o   *https://www.darkreading.com/*

    o   A leading cybersecurity news site with resources and articles on the use of AI in threat detection, penetration testing, and automation.

- **Security Weekly**

- ○ *https://www.securityweekly.com/*
- ○ A podcast and blog that discusses various AI and machine learning trends within the context of cybersecurity.

- **Krebs on Security**

  - ○ *https://krebsonsecurity.com/*
  - ○ A highly respected blog that frequently discusses advanced cybersecurity topics, including how generative AI could influence the future of threat detection.

- **The AI Alignment Blog**

  - ○ *https://www.alignmentforum.org/*
  - ○ A technical blog that explores AI safety concerns, which include potential malicious uses of AI in cybersecurity.

5. Communities and Forums

- **Reddit**

  - ○ *r/cybersecurity* – A community where professionals discuss the latest security trends, including AI applications in cybersecurity.
  - ○ *r/MachineLearning* – While focused on machine learning, this subreddit often features discussions on generative AI techniques for use in security operations.

- **Stack Overflow**

  - ○ Participate in threads discussing AI-based security technologies, where professionals share code snippets, best practices, and solutions for integrating AI into security systems.

- **AI Alignment Forum**

- *https://www.alignmentforum.org/*

- A platform for researchers and engineers focused on AI ethics, which includes discussions on AI's role in cybersecurity.

- **LinkedIn Groups**

  - *AI in Cybersecurity* – Join LinkedIn groups where cybersecurity experts discuss AI's evolving role in threat detection, prevention, and defense strategies.

6. Webinars and Conferences

- **Black Hat USA**

  - One of the most prominent cybersecurity conferences that features cutting-edge research on AI-powered security solutions. Many sessions are focused on using AI to prevent cyberattacks.

- **DEF CON**

  - The world's largest hacker conference, with presentations on how AI and machine learning can be applied to both offensive and defensive cybersecurity strategies.

- **RSA Conference**

  - *https://www.rsaconference.com/*

  - RSA features sessions and discussions on AI in cybersecurity, including real-world case studies and best practices.

- **Cybersecurity and AI Webinars by SANS Institute**

  - SANS offers various free and paid webinars on integrating AI into security programs and how it can be leveraged in threat intelligence, monitoring, and response.

7. AI Cybersecurity Tools and Frameworks

- **TensorFlow:**

    o *https://www.tensorflow.org/*

    o An open-source machine learning framework that can be used to create AI models for cybersecurity applications, including intrusion detection and malware analysis.

- **PyTorch:**

    o *https://pytorch.org/*

    o A deep learning framework that is widely used for generative models and can be applied in cybersecurity contexts like anomaly detection.

- **Hugging Face:**

    o *https://huggingface.co/*

    o A repository for pre-trained machine learning models, including models that can be used in cybersecurity for natural language processing and attack detection.

- **Darktrace:**

    o *https://www.darktrace.com/*

    o An AI-powered cybersecurity company that uses machine learning to detect and respond to cyber threats in real-time, a leading example of AI-based security.

- **CrowdStrike:**

    o *https://www.crowdstrike.com/*

    o A cybersecurity company using AI and machine learning to detect and respond to cyberattacks, including those involving generative AI for adversary behavior prediction.

8. Certification Programs

- **Certified Information Systems Security Professional (CISSP)**

  o One of the most recognized certifications in the cybersecurity industry, now including an emphasis on AI and machine learning applications for security.

- **Certified Ethical Hacker (CEH)**

  o A globally recognized certification for ethical hackers that covers AI-powered tools and techniques used in penetration testing.

- **CompTIA Security+**

  o A foundational certification in cybersecurity, now incorporating advanced concepts around AI and machine learning in security contexts.

- **Certified AI Practitioner (CAIP)**

  o A certification focused on applying AI to practical scenarios, including cybersecurity, network defense, and threat detection.

D. AI Cybersecurity Certifications and Frameworks

1. AI Cybersecurity Certifications

- **Certified Information Systems Security Professional (CISSP)**

  - **Overview:** One of the most prestigious certifications in the cybersecurity domain, CISSP now includes emerging trends, such as AI and machine learning, and their impact on cybersecurity.

  - **Focus Areas:**

    - AI and machine learning in threat intelligence.

    - AI-driven security analytics and incident response.

    - Ethical considerations for AI in cybersecurity.

  - **Certification Body:** (ISC)²

  - **More Info:** *https://www.isc2.org/*

- **Certified Ethical Hacker (CEH)**

  - **Overview:** This certification focuses on penetration testing and ethical hacking. As AI tools evolve, CEH incorporates AI-powered penetration testing tools and techniques, helping cybersecurity professionals understand the latest advancements in AI for offensive security.

  - **Focus Areas:**

    - Use of AI in vulnerability scanning.

    - Leveraging machine learning to understand attack patterns.

- Penetration testing with AI-based automation tools.

  o **Certification Body:** EC-Council

  o **More Info:** *https://www.eccouncil.org/*

- **Certified AI Practitioner (CAIP)**

  o **Overview:** CAIP focuses on integrating AI in cybersecurity processes, specifically emphasizing security automation and using AI for real-time threat detection and mitigation.

  o **Focus Areas:**

    - AI tools in cybersecurity.

    - Automating security workflows with machine learning.

    - Ethical AI use in defense.

  o **Certification Body:** CertNexus

  o **More Info:** *https://www.certnexus.com/*

- **CompTIA Security+**

  o **Overview:** A foundational cybersecurity certification that includes topics like AI and machine learning as they relate to securing networks, systems, and devices.

  o **Focus Areas:**

    - Cybersecurity fundamentals and integrating AI-driven security tools.

    - Managing identity and access management (IAM) with AI.

- Risk management in an AI-driven threat landscape.

  o **Certification Body:** CompTIA

  o **More Info:** *https://www.comptia.org/*

- **GIAC Cyber Threat Intelligence (GCTI)**

  o **Overview:** This certification focuses on threat intelligence and the use of AI to analyze and mitigate cyber threats. It provides knowledge on how AI can assist in identifying threat actors and automating threat intelligence tasks.

  o **Focus Areas:**

    - Machine learning in cyber threat intelligence.

    - Analyzing data for actionable insights using AI.

    - Using AI for automated threat identification and response.

  o **Certification Body:** Global Information Assurance Certification (GIAC)

  o **More Info:** *https://www.giac.org/*

- **AWS Certified Security - Specialty**

  o **Overview:** This certification focuses on cloud security, including the use of AI-powered security tools within AWS environments. It provides professionals with knowledge on using AWS AI services for security purposes.

  o **Focus Areas:**

    - Cloud security best practices using AI.

    - Automated threat detection using AWS services.

- Managing data privacy and compliance with AI in cloud environments.

- o **Certification Body:** Amazon Web Services (AWS)

- o **More Info:** *https://aws.amazon.com/certification/*

- **Microsoft Certified: Azure Security Engineer Associate**

  - o **Overview:** This certification includes AI-driven solutions in the Azure ecosystem, focusing on cloud security and incorporating machine learning techniques to secure environments.

  - o **Focus Areas:**

    - Protecting cloud workloads using AI.

    - Implementing threat detection using Azure AI tools.

    - Security monitoring and incident response using machine learning.

  - o **Certification Body:** Microsoft

  - o **More Info:** *https://learn.microsoft.com/en-us/certifications/*

- **Certified Information Security Manager (CISM)**

  - o **Overview:** CISM focuses on managing and governing information security. With the rise of AI, this certification now includes how AI can be utilized for risk management, threat detection, and securing corporate data.

  - o **Focus Areas:**

    - AI-powered security governance.

    - Risk management using AI and machine learning tools.

- Information security program management with AI.

  o **Certification Body:** ISACA

  o **More Info:** *https://www.isaca.org/*

2. AI Cybersecurity Frameworks

Frameworks help organizations develop and implement effective AI-driven cybersecurity strategies. These frameworks provide guidelines and best practices for leveraging AI and machine learning technologies to enhance security posture.

- **NIST Cybersecurity Framework (CSF)**

  o **Overview:** The NIST CSF offers a comprehensive guide for improving the cybersecurity practices of organizations, including the integration of AI technologies to better detect and mitigate cyber threats.

  o **AI Relevance:**

    - Integrating AI-driven anomaly detection into the Identify, Protect, Detect, Respond, and Recover phases of cybersecurity operations.

    - Using machine learning models for predictive threat analysis and risk management.

  o **More Info:** *https://www.nist.gov/cyberframework*

- **MITRE ATT&CK Framework**

  o **Overview:** A knowledge base used by cybersecurity professionals to identify adversary tactics and techniques. The framework is increasingly incorporating AI-driven methods for threat detection and analysis.

  o **AI Relevance:**

- Automating threat detection using machine learning.

- Integrating AI for real-time response to adversary behaviors.

- Generating predictive threat models using AI techniques.

  o **More Info:** *https://attack.mitre.org/*

- **ISO/IEC 27001:2013 (Information Security Management)**

  o **Overview:** An international standard for managing information security risks. With AI gaining prominence, the standard encourages the use of AI to enhance threat detection, response, and monitoring.

  o **AI Relevance:**

    - AI-based risk management strategies.

    - Enhancing security controls with machine learning.

    - Improving security monitoring using AI technologies.

  o **More Info:** *https://www.iso.org/isoiec-27001-information-security.html*

- **AI Risk Management Framework (AI RMF)**

  o **Overview:** Developed by NIST, the AI RMF provides organizations with a comprehensive framework for managing risks associated with AI technologies, including their use in cybersecurity.

  o **AI Relevance:**

- Identifying and mitigating risks of AI misuse in cybersecurity.

- Establishing responsible AI practices and ensuring transparency.

- Enhancing cybersecurity efforts through AI-powered risk assessment.

  o **More Info:** *https://www.nist.gov/ai-risk-management-framework*

- **Cybersecurity Capability Maturity Model (C2M2)**

  o **Overview:** C2M2 provides a framework for organizations to assess and improve their cybersecurity capabilities. AI and machine learning are used to enhance capabilities in detecting, responding to, and preventing cyber threats.

  o **AI Relevance:**

    - Maturing cybersecurity capabilities through AI-driven automation and analytics.

    - Using machine learning to optimize detection and response.

    - Improving cybersecurity resilience by incorporating AI technologies.

  o **More Info:** *https://www.energy.gov/cybersecurity-capability-maturity-model-c2m2*

3. AI Cybersecurity Tools and Solutions

Several tools and platforms provide AI-powered cybersecurity solutions, including generative AI-based systems for threat detection and mitigation.

- **Darktrace**

- o **Overview:** An AI-powered cybersecurity platform that uses machine learning and AI to detect and respond to cyber threats autonomously.

- o **AI Relevance:**

  - Real-time threat detection powered by unsupervised machine learning algorithms.

  - AI models that evolve and adapt to new and emerging threats.

- o **More Info:** *https://www.darktrace.com/*

- **CrowdStrike**

  - o **Overview:** A leader in endpoint protection, CrowdStrike leverages AI and machine learning to detect, investigate, and respond to security incidents.

  - o **AI Relevance:**

    - AI-powered threat detection and incident response automation.

    - Machine learning algorithms for predictive threat analysis.

  - o **More Info:** *https://www.crowdstrike.com/*

- **IBM QRadar**

  - o **Overview:** A SIEM solution that integrates AI and machine learning for advanced threat detection and incident response.

  - o **AI Relevance:**

    - AI-driven correlation of security events to detect sophisticated cyber threats.

- Real-time monitoring and predictive analytics using AI.

o **More Info:** *https://www.ibm.com/security/qradar*

E. References

Books and Articles

1. **"Artificial Intelligence: A Guide for Thinking Humans"** by Melanie Mitchell

   o A comprehensive introduction to the concepts of AI and its applications, including its use in cybersecurity.

   o *Publisher: Farrar, Straus and Giroux, 2019.*

   o ISBN: 978-0374257835

2. **"AI Superpowers: China, Silicon Valley, and the New World Order"** by Kai-Fu Lee

   o Discusses the global implications of AI technologies and their potential for transforming various sectors, including cybersecurity.

   o *Publisher: Houghton Mifflin Harcourt, 2018.*

   o ISBN: 978-1328518480

3. **"Machine Learning for Cybersecurity"** by Josh Lospinoso

   o Focuses on machine learning algorithms used in cybersecurity for threat detection, data classification, and incident response.

   o *Publisher: Wiley, 2020.*

   o ISBN: 978-1119633611

4. **"The Fourth Industrial Revolution"** by Klaus Schwab

   o Covers the impact of emerging technologies like AI on industries, including cybersecurity.

   o *Publisher: Portfolio, 2016.*

   o   ISBN: 978-0241300754

5. **"AI in Cybersecurity"** by Lesley A. Shillington

   o   This book provides an in-depth analysis of AI and its role in securing digital systems, networks, and data.

   o   *Publisher: Springer, 2021.*

   o   ISBN: 978-3030504541

6. **"Generative Deep Learning: Teaching Machines to Paint, Write, Compose, and Play"** by David Foster

   o   Explains how generative AI models work, with examples of their potential use in cybersecurity.

   o   *Publisher: O'Reilly Media, 2021.*

   o   ISBN: 978-1098115280

7. **"Cybersecurity and Cyberwar: What Everyone Needs to Know"** by P.W. Singer and Allan Friedman

   o   Provides an overview of modern cybersecurity challenges, including the role of AI in tackling these issues.

   o   *Publisher: Oxford University Press, 2014.*

   o   ISBN: 978-0199918119

Websites and Online Resources

1. **National Institute of Standards and Technology (NIST)**

   o   NIST provides guidelines and frameworks for integrating AI into cybersecurity strategies. Their publications like the NIST Cybersecurity Framework (CSF) and AI Risk Management Framework are essential reading.

   o   *Website:* https://www.nist.gov

2. **MITRE ATT&CK Framework**

   o MITRE ATT&CK is a knowledge base that helps organizations understand adversary tactics and techniques. The integration of AI-driven methods into the framework is an important trend.

   o *Website:* https://attack.mitre.org

3. **Darktrace: AI Cybersecurity Solutions**

   o Darktrace's AI platform uses machine learning for autonomous threat detection and response, providing real-world use cases of generative AI in cybersecurity.

   o *Website:* https://www.darktrace.com

4. **CrowdStrike: AI and Endpoint Protection**

   o CrowdStrike's AI-driven cybersecurity solutions highlight how AI models can protect against advanced threats and malware.

   o *Website:* https://www.crowdstrike.com

5. **IBM QRadar: AI-Driven Security Intelligence**

   o QRadar's integration of AI and machine learning in security operations to detect and respond to threats in real-time is a key resource for AI cybersecurity professionals.

   o *Website:* https://www.ibm.com/security/qradar

6. **The European Union Agency for Cybersecurity (ENISA)**

   o ENISA publishes reports and guidelines on integrating AI into cybersecurity policies, focusing on AI risks and opportunities in cybersecurity operations.

   o *Website:* https://www.enisa.europa.eu

7. **AI for Cybersecurity at NIST**

   o NIST has a dedicated section on AI and cybersecurity, exploring frameworks, standards, and best practices for AI in securing digital environments.

   o *Website:* https://www.nist.gov/news-events/ai-cybersecurity

Research Papers and Journals

1. **"AI in Cybersecurity: A Survey"** by V. K. Khanna, S. P. Sharma, and N. S. Prabhu

   o This research paper explores the various applications of AI in cybersecurity, from anomaly detection to automated incident response.

   o *Journal: Future Generation Computer Systems, 2021.*

2. **"A Survey on the Role of Artificial Intelligence in Cybersecurity"** by S. A. Rehman, M. M. B. Khan, and M. S. N. Z. Shah

   o Offers a comprehensive overview of how AI technologies are transforming cybersecurity practices, including the use of AI in attack detection and response.

   o *Journal: Cybersecurity, 2020.*

3. **"Deep Learning for Cybersecurity: A Review"** by N. K. Shukla, S. Kumar, and S. Agarwal

   o A detailed examination of how deep learning algorithms are used to enhance cybersecurity operations.

   o *Journal: IEEE Access, 2021.*

4. **"The Ethics of AI in Cybersecurity"** by L. H. McAfee and T. S. Wilson

o This paper delves into the ethical concerns around using AI in cybersecurity, discussing transparency, accountability, and potential biases in AI models.

o *Journal: AI & Ethics, 2022.*

5. **"Generative Adversarial Networks for Cybersecurity"** by M. P. M. H. van Eerten and A. L. Y. Mulder

o Discusses the potential of generative adversarial networks (GANs) in creating synthetic data for cybersecurity applications.

o *Journal: Journal of Cybersecurity, 2021.*

Government and Industry Reports

1. **The Global AI Strategy Report** (AI Global)

o A report on global AI policies and strategies, including AI's role in cybersecurity and defense applications.

o *Link:* https://www.ai.global

2. **Artificial Intelligence in Cybersecurity: Market Research Report** by MarketsandMarkets

o A detailed market research report on AI applications in cybersecurity, including insights into the growth and adoption of AI-powered cybersecurity tools.

o *Link:* https://www.marketsandmarkets.com

3. **AI and Cybersecurity: Opportunities and Risks** by the European Commission

o A European Commission report exploring the benefits and risks associated with the use of AI in cybersecurity.

o *Link:* https://ec.europa.eu/digital-strategy

4. **AI Cybersecurity: The State of the Art in 2021** by IBM Security

   o   IBM's annual report on the state of AI in cybersecurity, highlighting the current trends, challenges, and opportunities in AI-powered security.

   o   *Link:* https://www.ibm.com/security